CREATIVE
COMMUNICATION

Victor Annigian

R & E Publishers ❖ Saratoga, California

R & E Publishers
P.O. Box 2008, Saratoga, CA 95070
Tel: (408) 866-6303   Fax: (408) 866-0825

Book Design by Diane Parker

Cover by Kaye Quinn

Library of Congress Card Catalog Number: 92-50173

ISBN 0-88247-932-6

Acknowledgments

FIRST, I must give my mother, Azniv or Anna, credit for bringing me to this world and helping raise me following her suffering through the Armenian holocaust. Toiling as an immigrant to pay off debts incurred to travel to America by ship that took more than a month, on limited income, and without welfare, she survived years of struggle to the age of 96 and living as this book is published. Even though she had no schooling, her faith in me and my education gave me the determination and strength to graduate New York's City College.

SECOND, as an American citizen of Armenian parents, I seek, but cannot find any Christian ethnic peoples who have endured crushing massacres and barbaric cruelties, such as perpetrated by Turkey and moslem majorities in Asia Minor. How the world has changed since Christian missionaries rounded up Armenian orphans in Turkey, even though American public opinion was dominated by a few Senators with isolationist views in the early 1920's. We've sent American boys to die in Viet Nam and Korea in our opposition to Communist China and Russia. On the other hand, we've poured billions in economic and military aid to Turkey, proof that lobbies have a big hand in running our State Department and other branches of our Government.

THIRD, if it were not for the G.I. Bill and my luck to survive two tours of duty, for a total of 6 1/2 years in the Air Force, this book would not have been possible. Although I washed out of pilot training, I reenlisted and rose from private to captain during World War II, when we had much more morality and honesty in the Defense Department. In 1953, when it was evident that incompetence and negligence caused B-36 aircraft accidents in which many of my fellow officers lost their lives, I resigned my commission.

FOURTH, through the G. I. Bill, I was able to study playwriting and production, film, radio, and television writing, and music professionally. These disciplines provided the foundation, coupled with my experience as a technical writer and editor, to undertake the challenging task of writing a manual on communication skills. We all communicate, but do we ever examine carefully the skills we take for granted? Our whole educational system depends on our ability to develop disciplines as tools to advance professionally to rewarding careers, such as law, medicine, engineering, and politics. I must acknowledge the wonderful high school education I received at Townsend Harris, the 3-year high school for "bright" students accepted for college preparation by competitive examination.

Now known as New York City University, which has since expanded its curricula and facilities to include graduate schools, New York's City College stands out as a rewarding investment by the citizens of New York City. The relaxation of standards for admission and completion existing before the 1950's reflects the general downturn in the character and quality of life in America. In the 1990's, we are paying the price for negligence, incompetence, corruption, and fraud, which seem to have become a way of life in Government, in all its branches and at all levels.

With the national and international problems starving for solutions, the future of America, as a symbol of prestige, respect, pride, and integrity, but also the world are at stake. We have a civilization that churns with discontent and suffering. Neither books nor rhetoric are going stem the chaotic tides that can overwhelm us and turn things around. Rather, we need a firm determination by leaders, hopefully altruistic and considerate, to do something about deteriorating relations, conditions, and attitudes about fellow humans on earth. We need positive communication —not religious prejudices, ethnic violence, and nationalistic greed—to put this world back on a harmonious track of peace and good will.

Contents

LIST OF FIGURES

Preface

Dr. Robert M. Solow, a professor at the Massachusetts Institute of Technology, won the 1987 Nobel prize in Economics for his pioneering work, showing how technological change affects long-term economic growth. His mathematical model of the economy demonstrated, in explicit terms, that technology is the driving force of economic development; that technology is far more important than capital investment and labor supply in generating growth. What is not surprising is that Solow's work has been responsible for spurring industrial countries, like Japan and Germany, to allocate more resources to higher education and research.

Continued lag in literacy on a national scale and continued neglect of applied research, that enhances the productivity of the economy, will only deepen the three crises that threaten our economic existence: the national debt, the balance of trade, and the budget deficit. You have a right to ask: what has creative communication to do with the nation's economy? It's a proper question, because the relationship is not direct or obvious. We all know you can't live on credit forever. There is no bliss in ignorance and there is no comfort in neglect. The stakes are high and the price is higher as time moves inexorably on. Improved skills in communication can raise the level of education, the quality of life, and the creative productivity of a nation.

Creative communication emphasizes the quality of expression, the quality of thinking, and the quality of productivity; not the quantity of speech, emotional reactions, and the quantity of junk Americans accept. We must stop this obsession with violence, alcohol, drugs, and the primitive drumbeat served as music flavored with visual cacophony. It may be too late. We may soon reach a point of no return, ending up in hock as servants or lackeys of foreign powers. The psychological misery that looms in the horizon is a frightening possibility. The surgery necessary to save the patient will be painful, but the alternative can be worse.

We must rise to the occasion as if we are at war against poverty, ignorance, and weakness. We must, as masters of our destiny, set new goals, rearrange our priorities, and put our shrinking resources in the right places.

We are not only a relatively illiterate society when compared with some of the major powers of the world, but we are also losing our ability to communicate because we have virtually lost contact with our fellow Americans. Our illiteracy and loss of contact can be attributed to our educational system, our automobiles, and the electronic media, namely television. The networks of the television industry have already laid claim as responsible agents of peoples' "right to know." In the process, they pose as authorities of the English language while they exact a high toll in time for advertising and "entertainment." We have a global network of transmissions covering information, various types of gossip, sex, violence, and insipid comedy masquerading as humor.

With the help of the auto, which has raised radio from its doldrums, we have isolated ourselves from contact. Our schools are too weak and undisciplined to impose rigorous and enlightening educational curricula. We are conditioned to violence, subjected to partisan rhetoric, and brainwashed by deceptive messages. By the year 2000, we will not only be broke, but we will be fat, dumb, and miserable. We may even be dominated by one of the less desirable cultures that inhabit this planet and could take control of the economy.

Most of us think we know how to communicate effectively in most situations because of our apparent fluency with language. Recent research points to the fact that many subtleties associated with communicating thoughts and emotions are overlooked. We take many communication skills for granted and don't do enough in our schools or personal training programs to improve them.

During a survey of literature on communication and contact with potential readers, it was found that the exchange of messages can be a creative process. It was also found that there was a need for something more than "effective communication" and "communication in business." Not only have many aspects of business communication been neglected, but the average individual often overlooks hidden potentials of the intellect and emotions. The communication process has become a pattern: instinctive and reactive, rather than creative.

Although there's an attempt to be comprehensive, skills involved in print and electronic media have been deliberately avoided. News reporting, advertising, and commercial television were considered specialized skills, beyond the scope of this book. Creative communication, designed for broad appeal, can be considered useful for the student, the businessman, the professional, and the executive. It has an important message in terms of developing an awareness, presenting methods for improving skills, and suggesting approaches to various forms of communication.

To communicate creatively, one must concentrate, i.e., free the mind and senses from distortions, whether it's noise, an attention getter, or something that occupies one of the senses. Emotional involvement has the effect of energizing the brain or motivating it for action, however the thinking processes and creative activity tend to suffer. Just as one cannot watch television and listen to another at the same time, so one cannot generate an idea or respond productively when concentration is diminished. Whether one is thinking, listening, writing, observing, or reading, one cannot overlook the importance of concentrating on the issue, question, or situation involved at that moment.

We are all creative. Both the left and right side of our brain work together to develop intelligence, recognize patterns, form associations, and understand relationships. When we communicate creatively, we are expressing our knowledge, experience, culture, and hereditary characteristics in a positive or productive manner. The act of creative communication may involve a combination of memory, analysis, imagination, selection, organization, synthesis, and elimination.

Instead of responses based on conditioning or reflex reactions, we can respond with balance, consideration, empathy, persuasion, humor, or logic. In any event, we have the control and the ability to decide what to say, how to say it, when, and to whom. We can listen more carefully, think more accurately, act more flexibly, or even choose to remain silent. In either case, we can communicate creatively because we can overcome whatever fundamental conditioning to which we have been exposed. We can free our brain to think about the inputs our receptors have provided and generate the responses our senses can put out, whether it's in the form of silence, gesture, action, speech, or writing.

Foreword

Destiny must have led to the publishing of this book, since the elective courses I selected as a student of the College of the City of New York appeared to set the tone of my varied career over the next 50 years. During the depression, I majored in economics as preparation to find a job upon graduation. My interest in communication skills appeared to germinate and bear fruit as a result of courses I took: narration, public speaking, psychology, Shakespeare, history of education, and art.

The ideas developed for this book grew naturally out of my background, experience in sales, professional training, exposure to the aerospace industry as technical writer/editor, and active membership in Toastmaster clubs. Speaking semantically, I've become familiar with the maps and territories that embrace the various skills associated with human communication. It is through direct contact with fellow citizens that communication can best produce creative exchanges of views to stimulate ideas, help resolve problems, and produce useful results.

Unfortunately, much of our society is personally isolated, depending on autos for travel, radio and print media for information; and, television for entertainment or release from boredom. In the process we've lost personal contact with each other and opportunities to exchange views. Much of what we get from mass media are forms of gossip and some propaganda, rather than experiences and mutual support from our fellow neighbors, even strangers.

How can we find out what is really going on if we don't maintain many contacts with fellow citizens? It's easy to become believers and followers of demagogues who exploit our minds through our ears, using rhetoric and the conscious use of language to deceive, confuse, and achieve. When government, industry, and the legal system use language to mislead you, it's time to wake up and learn what is going on every day of our lives.

Whether it's real estate, autos, law, or medicine, it's easy to pay a high price for ignorance and negligence by not asking the right questions. The rhetoric in our legal system and government flourish without equal. Many things are kept secret and the most frequent is "national security," a buzzword often used to gouge the taxpayer for expensive and unnecessary defense systems.

Why is it that General Motors takes 5.2 years to go from design to finished product, whereas Chrysler and most Japanese companies can do the same in 3.6 years? As reported in the <u>Los Angeles Times</u>, it may have something to do with with communication and the help of computers. When you operate a large organization, like General Motors, which is buffered with 14 layers of management, communication is virtually impossible. We can bash Japan for high tariffs and limitations to imports by use of quotas, but not for their efficiency and responsible management which does not reward incompetence at upper levels at the expense of labor.

With poor management, which is highly rewarded in private industry, and politicized management in the Executive branch of our government, American taxpayers are footing big bills for incompetence, neglect, and corruption. We have become a democracy of rhetoric, vague platforms, unnecessary investigations for "reform," and oversight by Congress, which appears to coddle and cater to various departments of the Federal government.

When funds for educational standards and upgrading are diverted for defense and bailouts of savings and loans through a questionable Resolution Trust Corporation, a Republican Party agency, the misplaced priorities are obvious. They smack of a dictatorship by the military-industrial complex on the one hand and wholesale fraud on the other. Both appear to operate as sacred cows milked only for the benefit of the Republican Party and conservative Democrats, otherwise identified as "boll weevils."

About the Author

Victor Annigian grew up in Bronx and Manhattan, New York City, graduated from Townsend Harris High School and the College of the City of New York, where he received his Bachelor of Arts degree. Although his major was in economics, his formal education featured a broad liberal education with an emphasis on languages. To obtain his degree, he strived through five years of Latin and five of a second language, French. During his senior year, he supplemented his formal training with courses in narration, public speaking, art, psychology, and history of education.

After a four-year stint in the United States Air Force, in which he rose from private to captain, he studied playwriting and theater production at the American Theater Wing's School for Professional Training; writing for film, radio, and television at New York's Dramatic Workshop; graphic arts and design at the Art Students' League. As a consequence of his background in violin and piano, he entered Juilliard Institute of Music, majoring in piano and composition. Unfortunately, this stage in his career was cut short after one semester of study when he was recalled to active duty in the Air Force as a reserve officer.

After serving another two and a half years, he resigned his commission in 1953, having taught electronic fundamentals and flown reconnaissance missions in B-36 lead combat crews. During the next year, enrolled in School of Music at the University of Southern California, he also attended John Balderston's course in playwriting and Dr. Frank Baxter's famous course in Shakespeare.

His technical training in the Air Force provided the basic skills which enabled him to work as a technical writer and editor for aerospace companies, including Litton, McDonnell-Douglas, and the Jet Propulsion Laboratory. He has also had experience selling real estate, appraising real property, advertising, publications, management, and merchandising consulting.

The ideas Victor Annigian developed for *Creative Communication* grew naturally out of his background, formal training, exposure to a variety of aerospace publications, and six years of active membership in Toastmaster clubs. Speaking semantically, he knows the maps and territories that comprise the various disciplines embracing human communication. He strongly believes that it is through direct contact with fellow human beings that communication can best produce creative exchanges of views to stimulate ideas, help resolve problems, and produce useful results.

Introduction

The notion of creative communication came about a score of years ago as an outgrowth of interest in creativity and intelligence. Although it was apparent that heredity, formal education, environment, and experiences establish our patterns or habits of communication, there was also evidence about how much we must consider the brain, the nervous system, the emotions, and the body. These are major factors to consider in the quality and control of communication skills, not just our speech organs, eyes, and ears.

Creative communication can be explained as a system of skills that can convey messages to persuade, inspire, inform, entertain, or a combination of these purposes. The messages may be delivered through speech, writing, or other graphic media, and are characterized by impact, achievement of purpose, and ability to evoke response. The creative aspect is also involved when receiving and interpreting messages. Consequently, creativity adds another dimension to the process and message used. When communicating creatively, for example, a speaker takes into account the audience, the occasion, and the purpose.

Creative communication is not just a manner of speaking and writing creatively, but also of listening, observing, thinking, and reading. Everyone has the potential to communicate creatively and many people exercise creative communication without being aware of it. On the other hand, when we react emotionally or communicate out of habit, we deny ourselves opportunities to make the best of situations that turn up. Excellence in creative communication involves a blend of related skills brought about by a genuine desire to improve, practicing the skills, and using them with precision.

Training your memory is an important aspect of creative communication. Einstein's ability to observe and remember facts and phenomena about the universe, combined with his training as a mathematician to manipulate formulas creatively, were major factors in his discovery of the theory of relativity. A partial list of potential accomplishments, typical outgrowths of proficiency in creative communication, are listed.

Exchange views effectively
Transmit useful messages
Initiate positive action
Elicit facts to achieve a goal
Control situations
Discuss issues effectively
Deal with facts logically
Influence attitudes
Motivate for learning
Achieve goals
Develop understanding
Initiate positive action
Expand creativity and innovation
Respond to needs and desires
Generate positive results
Solve problems
Resolve conflicts
Accomplish purposes
Evoke intended responses
Expand interests and intelligence
Increase sales
Promote business growth
Raise levels of competence
Improve abilities to communicate
Raise thinking abilities
Generate enthusiasm
Improve the quality of life
Exercise leadership

THE CREATIVE PERSON

You have some kind of a vision in which you project yourself in the future as someone more than a hack. A hack comes from the word hackney, a horse of a breed developed in England—generally suited for routine riding or driving. This has become a slang word for a political hireling, one who hires himself out to do routine writing, or a taxicab. If that's what you want, the life and income of a hack, there are many jobs open.

A creative person, on the other hand, is a person who has the ability to make new combinations of social worth. He can be an artist, an inventor, a programmer, a problem solver, in other words, a Renaissance man. To put it in simpler terms, as a person who moves around, looks, sees, and feels; who absorbs life, taking what is going on around him; he finds a way to make changes by expressing something that he has within himself. He has diverse interests and knows how to handle adversity or failure. He thinks with a purpose. Once he has a good idea, he explores it, develops it, tests it, and makes it work for him and for his environment. He does not selfishly keep it to himself. Like a speaker, he analyzes his audience so that he can give them an original message they want to hear and they can understand. He is blessed with altruism, not selfishness and greed. The creative person responds to needs that are external and have been defined. He is motivated to find a need and to fill it . . . something productive for society, industry, and the world.

When you are interested in something, motivation should not be a problem. Once you are aware of the benefits or rewards that result from the goals or prizes that are not far off in the future, your desire comes from within. In creative communication, the combination of learning and practice cannot fail. I define practice as a form of dynamic discipline. You set a goal, establish a flexible schedule to reach that goal; and, to give it some urgency to motivate you, you set a deadline. That's how newspapers are put out day after day. That's how people make money. They set goals and deadlines. Why not set them for yourself so that you can move ahead and make money?

In creative communication, you look into yourself and ask what you feel intuitively, try to produce what you feel is true, and don't let anything discourage you. You've got to be honest with yourself. I've asked myself and others: Do I really want to sell? Do you think you'd like to live the life of a salesman? If you want to be a writer, are you willing to lock yourself in a room and produce on a typewriter or a word processor? Do you really want to be an actor or a doctor? Do you know what is involved in effort vs. benefits? Ask yourself some hard questions.

No matter what your interests are, creative communication cannot fail to move you forward, make you a better person, or add to your productivity, whether it's in terms of money or achievements, and often both. While we're at it, let's bear in mind that the great achievers and the creative communicators usually have healthy bodies, clear memories, good reflexes, and alert minds. They thrive on nutrition, weight control, exercise, mental activity, and a balanced program of activities and interests.

THREE IMPORTANT WORDS

One can achieve recognition or success in various fields by developing communication skills channeled in specific directions. There are three important words to define. Communication, message, and context are essential to understand if we decide to improve skills and develop the ability to communicate creatively.

The word *communication* is derived from the Latin "communi-care," which means, "to share." Sharing should be interpreted as the exchange of information (or messages) with objectivity, positive attitudes, and responses with empathy. In a recent survey, two out of three parents agreed that they had problems communicating with children about drugs, alcohol, sex, crime, and money. Instead of exchanging messages for mutual understanding, parents and children confused the process. Instead of sharing with empathy, there was an adversary relationship characterized by emotional outbursts and loud personal attacks. Not only was communication absent, but breakdowns were typical.

A *message* is information sent out in some form: spoken, written, pictorial, or symbolic. It generally has a purpose and can be prepared carefully for an audience (receiver) in suitable language. If the sender fails to prepare the message adequately; i.e., adapt it for the receiver's understanding, the response cannot return as intended. When preparing a written or spoken message, you must also consider the receiver's capacity to understand and attitude or willingness to accept. In addition, any signals or gestures we send with our messages must not distort, but rather reinforce our purpose.

Context relates to the subject discussed or the environment that establishes the specific meaning of a word to make sense for its use in a situation. Context is derived from Latin (contexere) meaning to join together or weave. When you know the time, place, circumstance, and purpose of an event; i.e., the context, you can have a clear notion of its meaning. For example, a ring can be a wedding band, a boxing arena, a part that encircles a piston, an inner circle of people, or a group of atoms bound together in a circle. We are not clear about the meaning of a word until it has been defined or introduced in relation to the subject matter presented. It's common for one, when asked what a word means to ask how it is used in a sentence.

If someone tells you of an accident, it can be about a vehicle in traffic, a fall, a cut, something major, or minor. If the context is not immediately established, we can be surprised, disturbed, or disappointed, depending on what really happened. Since contexts determine meanings, one cannot be oblivious to quotations or passages that can be distorted because they were incomplete and taken out of context. It is common to make subjective interpretations of words depending on our knowledge and experience. We learn through verbal, physical, and social contact. Meanings come to us not so much from dictionaries, as they do from the physical world, where we can be precise, objective, and specific.

GAPS, BARRIERS, AND BREAKDOWNS

A *gap* implies lack of communication, an opening, as if no connections or lines existed. A *barrier* implies the presence of an obstacle or a refusal to exchange views. As such, barriers block effective communication. A *breakdown* suggests a collapse of existing communication between parties, or failures of the communication dialogue. Gaps exist in many situations involving families, company personnel, government offices, and between officials of government and citizens they are elected to serve.

Gaps are inherent in a political system of different parties and persons who are not members of special interest groups. We can't really know what's going on when we rely on secondary sources of information and media, which edit events before passing them on to the general public. In a society that contains many segments, most of us have a little direct contact, for example, with agencies that manage our economy, welfare, and defense.

As creatures of conditioning or habit, the public accepts the gaps that exist by assuming we have sufficient communication for various situations. When you think a gap exists, there's nothing wrong with asking questions or making inquiries. Find out why a gap exists between you and another person or group. Many situations require frequent exchange and feedback, even within families who apparently live close physically.

When people know there's opposition to an idea and do nothing about it, imaginary barriers become real. If a person is unavailable for comment or answers to questions, one can reasonably assume an artificial barrier has been erected. Indifference or a conflict of attitudes to the point of flat refusal to communicate or discuss issues can also be considered barriers.

One of the biggest mistakes some people make is to state opinions as if they were facts. Here is where the training of attorneys and established arbitration procedures are useful. The parties can introduce evidence and elicit testimony from experts to put the negotiations on a solid footing. Extraneous issues and disruptive tactics must be avoided. Even too much information, like too much paperwork, can become artificial barriers that distract and confuse those who are working to resolve issues.

According to F. J. Roethlisberger, "The biggest block to personal communication is man's inability to listen intelligently, understandingly, and skillfully to another person. This deficiency in the modern world is widespread and appalling. In our universities, as well as elsewhere, too little is being done about it."

Dr. Stephan A. Seymour, author of "How To Improve Your Thinking To Solve Your Problems," stated, "The greatest cause of emotional problems in our country is broken-down communication...The result is emotional and thinking confusion."

HOW THE COMMUNICATION PROCESS WORKS

We know communication involves the exchange of information, ideas, and feelings between persons. In this exchange, the process consists of a speaker, a message, and a listener. In the ideal situation, the speaker conveys meaning accurately without disturbance as the message travels through the noise of the real world. On the other hand, the listener interprets the message accurately and understands exactly what the speaker meant. A model of the communication process is illustrated in Figure 1.

When the exchange of messages exists in a face-to-face situation, such as a conversation, both parties have opportunities to send and receive feedback signals. When the speaker is sensitive to the reactions of the listener, feedback can be used to adjust the content and treatment of the messages.

When Party A wants to ask a question or make a statement, he or she formulates the message from a storehouse in memory and routes it through an emotional filter. The spoken words then travel through the noise (or environment) of the real world to the listener. The ears act as conduits to transmit the message through the listener's emotions to the storehouse of messages, which are used to interpret and respond.

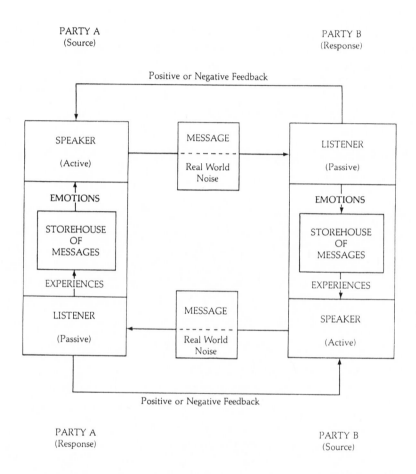

Figure 1. A Model of the Communication Process

Party B's response may be shrouded in an emotional color which not only determines its content and quality, but also provides positive or negative feedback to Party A. From Party B's storehouse of messages may come a statement (answer) or another question, possibly for clarification. Party A becomes the listener, who accepts the response through the noise of the real world. Before and after response, Party B is in a position to receive a positive or negative feedback signal that accompanied the original question or statement.

This complex exchange of messages and feedback signals are typical of most conversations between two parties. The messages and responses may also be accompanied by gestures which can reinforce or dilute the impact of the messages. In your next conversation, think about this dynamic process in which the many things that are transpiring are taken for granted. Note the gestures and the feelings that accompany the meanings in the messages when one party is speaking. Note also the silent and verbal responses made by the listener. Do we have an objective exchange of information for the mutual benefit of both parties? Is the conversation polite and devoid of genuine feeling?

A public speaker interprets applause as positive feedback to continue a speech along existing lines. If "boos" are heard or boredom is painted on the faces on an audience, these are signals to make adjustments. Competent speakers analyze the audiences in advance to forestall the potentials for negative feedback. The communicator (sender) is responsible for the content and purpose of a message; and, ensures that the receivers understand most of it, if not all.

The more that is known about the audience and the subject, the easier it is for the speaker to communicate creatively. The more the audience knows in advance, the greater the receptivity and range of messages that can be understood. Communication is a collaborative effort in which each party makes contributions for better understanding. Whereas the audience must be alert and receptive, the speaker must be clear and persuasive.

We are dealing constantly with human beings in a dynamic environment. To keep this in mind, think of this acronym, PEMBEC: a human being is a Physical, Emotional, Mental, Biological, Electrical, and Chemical entity who moves and breathes, externally and internally, with an identity, an ego, and someone with whom we must deal. Creative communication prepares you for operating and surviving in the real world teeming with people of various persuasions .

PASSIVE AND ACTIVE SKILLS

As shown in Figure 2, the communications skills have been arranged in an arbitrary fashion as active and passive groups, with thinking and feeling in the middle. The diagram indicates how the skills can relate to each other, since our sense organs, the nervous system, the intellect, emotions, and body operate as a system with inputs and outputs, like a computer. Action represents things we do physically through deliberate acts, movements, and gestures. Special skills refer to specialized or sophisticated abilities, such as sports, painting, performing arts, etc.

Observing—With the help of the brain and previous knowledge, based on training and experience, the eyes provide tools for perception. Perceptions of reality are influenced by the quality of your vision, lighting conditions, and mental associations. Subject to errors or distortions, the ability to observe depends on total awareness, attention to details, and attitudes. As one observes, the eyes also register what's in back of the mind of the observer. In other words, what one sees depends as much on the observer as it does on the object observed.

Listening—We listen with our ears, eyes, and brain. The listening process can be affected by where we are and how we feel at the time. Many of us pay attention only to what we want to hear. When listening with attention, our needs and motives are at work. On the other hand, when the tone, volume, or the character of the speaker sounds unpleasant, we feel justified in setting up a barrier.

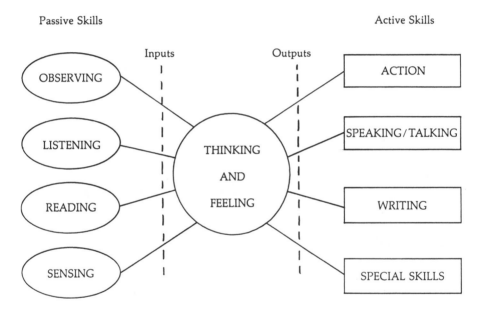

Figure 2. Passive and Active Groups of Communication Skills

During a conversation, one often has difficulty responding before the speaker has finished talking. It takes discipline to concentrate the listening process on something significant. One may listen for prejudices, attitudes, and motives, as revealed by the words, gestures, and intentions of the speaker. When the terms used sound vague or abstract, interest can flag.

Reading—We read for information, enlightenment, and enjoyment. The process becomes creative when the mind is stimulated for ideas, especially those that fuel interest for goals. During this activity, one can visualize what to expect or look at a subject from a new point of view. When there is a strong motivation to acquire facts, one tends to read faster and comprehend more. Considering the volumes of reading material available, an efficient selection method is necessary to make best use of the time available for reading. Since approximately two hours of an executive's day is spent reading, it follows that speed reading and the buildup of a vocabulary are prime investments.

Sensing—The ability to sense goes beyond sight, sound, taste, smell, and touch. There are also the capacities for sensing love, sex, indifference, and other complex conditions. Much depends on training, awareness, and for some, telepathy, or the sixth sense. The quality of sensory stimuli and perceptions vary with people in degree and impact on their psyches.

When sensory stimulations reach our brains, the sensations are subject to reactions, depending on interpretations, memories, and effects on our imaginations. The smell of garlic repels some person, whereas others may think of its beneficial attributes. Since sensing is inherent in the communication process, one must take into account possible prejudice, subjective judgements, and errors in interpretation.

Thinking — Through the senses and organs, the brain can be considered a complete processing system to store, control, and manipulate visual, symbolic, and verbal data. This complex package houses one of the most remarkable creations of all nature. Yet, during emotional upheavals and the infiltration of alcohol or drugs in its system, thought processes break down. An angry or drunk person can have the orderly flow of thoughts blocked or replaced by emotional reactions.

Creative thinking involves in mind under control so that logic or productive reasoning can take place. The nonrational thinker can be confused by emotions, fuzzy information, or unrelated assumptions. For example, previous experiences can take over as prejudices applied to an issue. Objectivity and reason cannot come about to solve problems or resolve differences if a person has already made up his or her mind. The creative thought processes are greatly enhanced through the study of mathematics, memory training, and improving one's vocabulary.

Action—This skill refers to the act of executing a decision, use of gestures, and deliberate physical movements. Actions definitely reveal what a person thinks at the time. Observing how one does something and the attitude indicated are also indicative of thoughts in a situation. At the same time, one can also consider the motive for an action taken.

If possible, one can consider the effects or implications of an action so that the outcome can be productive rather than wasteful. There are also situations in which timing is important to put the right emphasis on an act or deed. An act of kindness or courtesy can accomplish (communicate) more than writings or speeches. In many situations, a decision to take action should be planned carefully. The consequence of some actions cannot always be anticipated and occasionally, situations change to dilute the best of intentions.

Speaking/Talking—The average executive spends around one third of a day talking, often on the telephone and occasionally before large groups. The amount of talking that goes on in our society is staggering. Consider the routine activities of educators, salesmen, actors, politicians, attorneys, and those who transact business. Speech reveals personality through its content and quality, however, much of it is not creative.

In conversations, many opportunities exist for feedback and exchange of useful ideas. Candor and a natural manner are as important in formal speaking situations as they are in conversations. One can generally approach a speaking situation by first asking whether one has something to say. One can then concentrate on how to phrase ideas for meanings intended and for clarity of expression. No communication can be as effective as face-to-face talk. The combined skills of talking and listening, often taken for granted, are excellent opportunities for creative communication during conversations.

Writing—This skill, a powerful means of creative communication, is difficult to master because it flows in one direction with no opportunities for feedback. As such, it must not only be unmistakable, but also offer the readers rewards in the form of entertainment, information, enlightenment, or guidance. The excesses of government in the form of paperwork are staggering and wasteful writing by bureaucrats. Any efforts to condense or reduce the quantity of print would be a major advancement in civilization.

The writer's major task is that of conveying meaning through a selection and arrangement of words so that the readers can recreate the intended meanings. The certainty for complete understanding is not always there because the writer's words may not mean exactly the same to the readers. The use of simple words, where possible, and natural expressions are essential. The material should also be organized with a purpose for readers, in clear language for impact.

Special Skills — These apply to professional skills and arts that generally require a combination of education or training and practice. For example, a pianist begins training with supervised instruction at an early age, developing the artistic skills through hours and hours of practice. Professional golfers who learn the game at an early age have distinct advantages over those who take up the game later, especially without supervised training, practice, and experience in competition. Most special skills are characterized by genuine desire, extensive practice, and experience under simulated or actual conditions of performance. Special skills can be very creative because of the vast storehouse of experience organized in memory and the cumulative effect of varied training.

Many skills learned in high school or college are taken for granted during the formative years, however their neglect or acceptance are evident in the quality of the future careers and lives. The years spent in schools may appear long for some, but the rewards are rich and compounded. The satisfactions that result from scholastic achievements and professional careers are so much greater than those that spring from ordinary pursuits. For example, most winners of Nobel prizes have advanced degrees.

APPRAISE YOUR ABILITIES

We are in communication constantly: with ourselves, with others, and with a wide range of media in a dynamic environment. Since the mind provides the basis of all communication, it is the alert and active person who can improve skills, as well as develop new ones and apply skills creatively. This implies interest in meeting new people, effort in learning, exposure to varieties of experience, and practice. The old cliche about curiosity killing the cat is nonsense. Curiosity can provide information about what's going on around you, survival, and advancement in this competitive world.

Our complex society and changing environment more than suggests one do some searching and reporting for information at first hand, rather than depending on second hand sources. Rather than induce psychological paralysis by being glued to a television tube, one can visit libraries, museums, and centers of learning. One can find out much of what is going on by meeting people at meetings and special events. Travel provides an excellent source of accurate and significant information.

The simple questionnaire, figure 3, is a generalized checklist designed to help appraise your attitudes and abilities or skills in communication. Each of the 25 statements can be treated as a question. The answers can be "YES" for a score of 4 points each; "SOMETIMES" for 2 points; and, "NO" for 0 or no points.

APPRAISAL QUESTIONNAIRE

☐   1. Generally see the complete picture of a situation.

☐   2. Understand everything told about a situation.

☐   3. Know usually what is going on in immediate area.

☐   4. Specify main parts of a message when speaking.

☐   5. Have little difficulty being understood.

☐   6. Watch for misunderstanding using feedback signals.

☐   7. Encourage questions of listeners and repeat remarks.

☐   8. Qualify statements and use statistics to be exact.

☐   9. Also see gray shades, not just blacks and whites.

☐ 10. Think of others, using "You" and "We," not "I."

☐ 11. Keep up to date on meanings and changes of words.

☐ 12. Put self in speaker's position to see his viewpoint.

☐ 13. Recognize facts, inferences, and value judgments.

☐ 14. Never use words that hurt listener's self-respect.

☐ 15. Try to tell the whole story without self-defense.

☐ 16. Qualify statements and rarely generalize.

☐ 17. Think carefully before answering quickly.

☐ 18. Have strong feelings about some things in life.

☐ 19. Failure is something I recognize and can overcome.

☐ 20. Show enthusiasm and confidence, as necessary.

☐ 21. Recognize differences among instincts and emotions.

☐ 22. Resolve conflicts with objective review of facts.

☐ 23. Can be objective with loss of feelings on an issue.

☐ 24. Know differences between actual meanings and contexts.

☐ 25. Can visualize, sketch, and describe most things.

To score, multiply: TOTALS

        YES by 4 _____

SOMETIMES by 2 _____

        NO by 0 _____

Add total points and
enter in score.

SCORE _____

Figure 3. Self-Appraisal of Communication Skills.

A perfect score (100) would be unusual. A score of less than 50 shows a need to improve most skills and attitudes about communication. If we think of weaknesses as habits that can be changed by forming new habits with practice, we can really improve communication skills and concentrate on creative communication. No one can force changes in attitudes or desires to improve skills. Motivation must come from within. Ask yourself: What do I want to do? What must I work on ? What's in it for me? Am I willing to devote effort over a period of time?

Whether you are making personal decisions or managerial ones, start by being discriminating about what you observe, hear, and read. Consider the sources and accuracy of the information you receive. Can you separate or identify facts, assumptions, and inferences?

A fact is something known with certainty and capable of being verified. If one says it's ten o'clock in the morning and the time is verified by several clocks or watches that appear to be set accurately, the statement can be accepted as a fact. In many cases, facts can be verified by calendars, recordings, authoritative references, and credible testimony.

During court trials, the acceptance of facts from testimony depends primarily on the credibility or honesty of witnesses. If a jury feels that a witness is incompetent, the statements made can be contested or disregarded as inaccurate. Facts can also be brought out through circumstantial evidence, from which a judge or jury might raise questions as to validity. During the House hearings to impeach former President Nixon, one Representative supported the value of circumstantial evidence by referring to a weather occurrence. He stated that if the ground was clear at night and covered with snow the next morning, one could reasonably state that it had snowed during the night.

Testimony that a witness saw a person shoot another could be accepted as a fact if we believe the witness is honest and was present on that occasion. Finding a 30-caliber gun on the defendant's person during the scene of a crime, supported by ballistics test found on the victim and evidence that the gun was fired, would be another example of circumstantial evidence that produced facts about a case.

Assumptions, on the other hand, relate to inferences. An assumption is the acceptance of a statement as true without the need for proof. However, an inference is a conclusion based on evidence or proof based on facts. When an inference proceeds in a logical manner, the propositions for the inference must be true and properly stated. Therefore, an inference can be a judgment that begins with propositions.

Most problems in the thinking phase of communication are based on false assumptions or propositions that are false or not stated properly. Among some of the common faults are: making inferences (or conclusions) not based on facts; confusing facts with inferences; considering inferences only; and, reaching conclusions without valid proof. Many people treat experiences as evidence for another situation; or, confuse facts with feelings about a situation.

FIVE ESSENTIAL ELEMENTS

We complete this section with five essential elements necessary for creative communication. All five elements begin with the important third letter of the alphabet: C. They are contact, control, creative response, competence, and conditioning. Find ways to remind yourself or remember to put these five elements to work.

1. Make *contact* with people: directly in person, by telephone, by letter, or any other medium, such as television, radio, or printed media. Find out what is going on in your immediate environment and beyond. Otherwise, you may be living in an imaginary vacuum, a dream world of memories, fantasies, or possibly misinformation. It is direct experience through personal contact that provides the most accurate and reliable data.

2. Exercise *control*: which begins with yourself, including your emotions and faculties. Try to control your body, gestures, and thoughts. Think of your senses as useful input and output devices for all kinds of information: visual, verbal, and

sensual. Think of your brain as a giant processor with memory, both of which work best when active in a relaxed mode. There's nothing wrong with slowing down operations, like your driving, to get from one point to another under some kind of relaxed discipline. Self-control precedes leadership and the control of communications, which is often the control of your environment, including others. If you cannot control your environment, you may decide to move on. Not anyone can take on city hall and not everyone is going to win the top prize. Out of 13 candidates for President, 12 will lose the race. That does not make them losers, who may want to win other races or seek other goals. Confrontations can result in two losers.

3. Generate *creative response*: which comes from clear thinking about facts. Can we underestimate the Japanese any longer? Many of these economic wizards have adopted IBM's famous motto: THINK. They think, work, research, develop, improve, test, and advertise. They generate creative responses to the needs of the markets in more areas than we realize. You have a better chance of generating creative responses if you think positively. Slow down a bit and think in terms of priorities, needs, and productivity. You'll learn a lot more if you listen and observe. You'll come up with more ideas, because you'll add to your own storehouse of information. Don't exclude reading, even if you have to reserve some time for it every day, including newspapers, magazines, and books. Out of more contact and control come the potentials for creative responses to situations, to needs, and to desires.

4. Develop *competence*: through education, training, and practice. As you improve your communication skills, you become a more effective personality. In the process you can do a better job of adjusting to and taking advantage of your environment. By setting goals, preparing schedules to reach them, and getting professional help, you cannot fail to achieve competence in most endeavors. The sooner you start, the sooner you'll develop competence. For some this may require a crash course in literacy. At the same time, make sure you're

on the right track; not only in the right pew, but also in the right church. It's easy to take off on tangents and lose the focus on the central need or issue. Ask yourself: is this what I really want and need? If so, what must I do to get there? You may want to make a survey or do your own investigating.

5. Get in *condition*: so that you stay in shape. It's like warming up for a big game. Even when you have all these skills, such as speaking, listening, writing, and observing, you need to practice. Music is a good example: without practice and exercises, the pianist experiences stiffness, and with pro-longed layoff, he or she can let slip away real investments in time, effort, and money. Keep selling; take courses; practice the game, whether it's tennis or golf; speaking or writing. Don't fall back into a position or state of inactivity. At the same time, don't force yourself if you don't feel up to it at the time. You may be a victim of stress or jet lag. Find out what ails you. Whether it's the body or mind, activity, exercise, and stimuli are essential to keep you in condition. If you need rest, then give your body and mind a chance to recover. Avoid artificial stimulants, including alcohol, tobacco, and drugs. Think in terms of moving around, getting fresh air, making new acquaintances, and adjusting to real changes. It's easy to get out of touch with reality when your imagination can take off towards lands of fantasy. It's easy to lose your positive mental attitudes, objectivity, and concentration on your goals.

In summary, there's no magic formula to put these elements quickly under your belt. For example, it takes four years of elective and required courses to get a degree from an accredited college. Taking crap courses or easy ones to achieve high grades does not contribute to learning, which takes effort. At the same time, let's understand that a degree conferred on the graduate is no guarantee for high earnings or achievements, but rather an opener of doors for thinking and starting life in the tough world where we have much to learn and work at.

In closing, if you can plan your weeks in terms of exercise, nutrition, and creative communication; if you put to work the five elements of creative communication: *contact, control, creative response, competence,* and *conditioning,* you can't fail to make progress in the goals you set for yourself. Tell yourself you're going to stay healthy as you keep busy mentally and active physically.

With all these elements in mind, we still have problems in communication among citizens who represent various ethnic groups. Unfortunately, we have preconceptions about those who appear different than us, from white, black, Hispanic, Asian, European, to others who live in the big cities. Why do we foster attitudes that are tentative and negative? No race is perfect and few are willing to accept the differences rather than seek the things that make us similar. If we cannot change the human environment, why make it worse through favoritism, arson, looting, and assaults on innocent citizens?

It's relations and relationships that can contribute to the quality of our lives in a world that's becoming more populated, more polluted, and more difficult to enjoy in harmony. Resorting to flights to the suburbs because of rioting and fear will not solve the problems of unrest in the major cities. The causes of social unrest must be faced and reduced by peaceful means, through attention, communication, and action by all responsible parties, especially the Federal government.

On the other hand, we cannot have a legal system, law enforcement, and other branches of local government shirk their responsibilities through self-interest and neglect. Nor can a political party politicize, through favoritism and false rhetoric, the resources of this country in terms of misplaced and inhuman priorities. As John Milton wrote in Paradise Lost, we "Can make a heaven of hell, a hell of heaven."

Do we condition ourselves, or let others condition us through religion to take off in different directions and destroy the unity of a nation? The big question becomes: how do we communicate positively? Why not think about our feelings to connect us and reduce the thoughts and judgments that divide us? When Moses lost his temper and struck a rock, God banned him from Israel.

We are all conditioned by our upbringing, environment, education, philosophies, what we fear, and what motivates us. We know how much our minds and emotions affect our bodies, not simply to control, change, and develop skills. As communicators through speech, gesture, action, and writing, how productive our we in terms of maintaining a peaceful society dedicated to the common good? Do we think first before we speak and act, or do we fly off the handle emotionally?

In spite of poor or corrupt leadership, we cannot destroy our infrastructure; nor can we commit violence against our neighbors. We cannot run away from our weaknesses nor continue to neglect an environment, like a helpless child who needs attention. Much of our stress comes from how we react to the external world and fellow human beings. How we react often depends on how we perceive ourselves in relation to the world around us. What we read in the newspapers and see on television only fuel the fires of a perceived conflict that has been blown out of proportion.

We communicate better when we're happy. One of the major factors that contribute to this feeling of well being is changing our perceptions of isolation. The automobile and television have not helped. We have encouraged cynicism, hostility, and the concept that we are something special. If we succumb to stress by avoiding our personal management of its causes, we contribute to misery. When we react negatively to our environments at work, at play, and social contacts, we are really avoiding the individual responsibility of creative communication. As Rodney King, the victim of a senseless beating, asked, "why can't we get along?" We are intimately connected together on this shrinking planet. We've got to get along in peace and harmony. In the final analysis, isn't that what creative communication is all about?

America can be proud of its technical achievements, such as putting men on the moon, inventing the laser, and developing the microchip. On the other hand, the disgraceful conduct by some members of our executive and legislative branches during the past 15 years have changed attitudes of its citizens. We have many examples of the abuse of power through the misuse of rhetoric.

For example, the conscious use of language as a tool for those in power to achieve nefarious ends at taxpayers' expense, represents a form of cruelty against Americans.

Since politics thrives on communication, mostly one-way, those in positions of responsibility and power should relate rhetoric to reality, rather than fantasy, confusion, and doublespeak. An uneducated population without the skills to communicate will not only be ignorant of what is going on, but cannot exercise the teamwork necessary to change the chaotic status quo. Teamwork is a form of synergism in which the sum of a team's effort produce greater results than individuals without organization and leadership.

If crime pays for those associated with the savings and loan scandals involving billions of dollars and a Justice Department does little more than drag its feet in enforcing many other forms of white collar fraud, the damage to the nation will take a bigger toll than the Los Angeles riot of 1992. In many situations, what we call a healing process or communicating with gangs and the frustrated citizenry won't help much. Fear and flight to suburbs won't help solve some of the major problems.

Whenever possible, we must, for the common good, engage in:

CONTACT—when possible, directly with people

CONTROL—ourselves, our speech, and our actions

CREATIVE RESPONSE—productive in a positive direction

COMPETENCE—through education and training

CONDITIONING—activity and practice to stay in shape

Thinking and Communication

Although we sometimes communicate automatically, most of the skills associated with communication are controlled by our thoughts and feelings. Like a sophisticated data processor, the mind processes inputs, uses its memory, a storehouse of messages, and generates outputs. We know that a data processor must be programmed and stored to manipulate bits of information, whereas the brain is self-programmed. The human processor involves the nervous system, the senses, and the forebrain in which billions of cells are available for operations.

You're stuck with your brain. You can neglect or protect it; develop or ignore it; take it for granted or appreciate it; and, nourish or abuse it. It is difficult to comprehend the actual complexity, capacity, and various capabilities of the human brain. It controls bodily functions, mental processes, conversions of sounds, perceptions, and other sensations, storing them in meaningful patterns in its varied memory.

When we experience mental images, our brain cells and our body muscles are active. According to psychologists, our muscles not only respond to neural stimulations from the brain, but also control and regulate many of the brain's functions. In an experiment in the late 1940's, George Humphrey of Oxford University showed how the muscles were acting when the subject was merely *thinking* of doing something. It was concluded that thought never wholly frees itself from action.

From this experiment we know that we can often communicate our thoughts to others by telltale signs, such as body movements, changes in the eyes, and other signals. We exert control of muscle action through the interrelationships in our brain, which receives impulses from the external environment, and the interconnected nerve fibers which carry messages from one nerve cell to another.

We can therefore think of the brain and nervous system as a huge switchboard, with calls coming in through our senses, connections being made, and then messages being directed to our muscles for control of various parts and organs of the body. We have controls of our motor skills for fine movement, as well as, for large movements and inhibitions. We can now understand relationships between muscular tension and mental activity.

A LOOK AT THE BRAIN

The brain weighs about three pounds in a package as big as a grapefruit. This magnificent electrochemical communications processor and network uses about 25 watts of power and can store over 10 billion items of information: visual, verbal, numeric, symbolic, moving imagery, sound, sensual, touch, and taste. To operate efficiently, this remarkable instrument needs oxygen, blood supply, rest, and nourishment.

To preserve, help maintain the brain in good working order, for some we must remind that the influences of excesses of alcohol, tobacco, and drugs cannot be overlooked. The brain thrives on fresh air, normal temperatures, such as comfortable atmospheric conditions, as well as, relative calm or nonviolent environments.

We can think of the brain as operating in various modes and constantly processing inputs in the normal mode. It is usually ready to switch its routine to one of many special modes, depending on orders from the emotions or higher priority commands. Through the nervous system, the brain processes information from all parts of the body. Nerve cells or neurons can be considered a complex communication network through which impulses carry various types of messages traveling at high speeds.

According to Karl S. Lashley, . . . "all the cells of the cerebro-spinal area are being continually bombarded by nerve impulses from various sources and are firing regularly, probably even during sleep." In other words, the brain is a busy communication network, always active in some processing operation, and yet available to accept a new stimulus or input that can influence operations of the whole system. From studies about the brain and nervous system, we have learned the following:

1) Change takes time, because habitual nerve cell patterns are not easily rearranged.

2) Fast thinking can be considered more as reacting or solving simple problems. Creative thinking and solving complex problems take much more time.

3) Learning and understanding from others also takes time. If we stop and think about what others say or what we read, we have a better chance of "internalizing" the message.

4) Those who take time to doubt or question by weighing messages carefully, demonstrate the ability to discriminate, because they don't "follow the crowd," or are not easily persuaded.

Since the brain depends on external stimulation to function properly, a changeless environment would effectively be an isolation ward or a dark closet. In such a place, the brain would lose its dynamic characteristics and ability to think normally. The brain would lose its ability to recall, compute, decide, evaluate, and to discriminate or compare. When the brain is alerted to changes in its environment, the arriving data influences the attention the brain pays. If we are listening, the brain dampens the information entering the eyes and other senses, or recruits the other organs to support the hearing operation. Effectively, the brain's feedback system reduces the efficiency of the senses not involved in the primary data entry system. This sensory gating provides for handling possible distractions. However, any unusual sound or event can alert the brain so that we can shift our activity of primary attention to the direction of the new source. For example, when we hear a siren or see an accident, we stop what we're doing (for the siren) and slow down (when driving) at the scene.

In some environments, especially where there are no stimuli, it takes a certain amount of curiosity to get the will and the human processor to act on inputs or respond to the real world. People who travel, read extensively, and investigate through various forms of contact are in excellent positions to accumulate useful knowledge, enrich their lives, exercise judgements, develop ideas, and train themselves to communicate creatively. It boils down to matters of searching, questioning, controlling, and responding to changing environments in a dynamic world.

The body and its integrated processing and control system operate as a chemical and electrical mechanism to regulate, initiate, and respond to the environment. Consciously, subconsciously, and instinctively, various sections of the brain provide the directives in response to drives and external stimuli. These directives have their source in the glands and organs, such as the eyes, the skin, and the ears. The effect of shock, fear, love, and anger represent conditions under which directives are instituted.

Thoughts and emotions normally maintain an equilibrium in the brain. When the thinking part of the brain, the cerebral cortex, has difficulty communicating effectively with the emotional part of the brain, or when the priorities between messages from the emotional part conflict with the messages from the frontal cortex, stress and loss of control can result. Before the emotions are passed to the cortex, they are processed and external stimuli can motivate or discourage the individual. Goals and expectations effectively motivate a person, whereas failures can dampen how we process information. Without goals, lives can settle down into routines, without excitement or enjoyment that can result from achievements. When we are faced with anxieties and various kinds of stress, effectively we have built buffers between the external events and our responses to them.

When our internal systems do not communicate effectively, often because we are confused or loaded down in efforts to combat stress and its causes, we are distracted. Concentration on intellectual or creative activities become difficult or impossible. The most magnificent and potentially the most efficient processors in the world, our brains, or thinking machines, go down. The functions of processing, association, and decision-making break down. We can get emotionally charged, irrational, or respond angrily to problems or confrontations.

The brain cells constantly communicate with each other through neurotransmitters; i.e., chemical links. As a result of overloading the switchboard or network of neurotransmitters, we can become confused. Stimulated through the eyes and ears, external events reach the brain and get it to work, setting the responses in motion. The cerebral cortex of the brain uses memory, organizing, perceptions, and intellectual thoughts in the form of words and symbols to perform rational processing. On the other hand, the hypothalmic area activates many instinctive drives, such as hunger, sex, pleasure, and sleep. On orders from the brain, in a kind of executive routine, it gets many things done in the body. These operations are carried out through the neural connections of the autonomic nervous system, which regulates the involuntary organs of the body, including the breathing, the liver, the kidneys, etc.

The slightest chemical changes caused by emotions, stress, and responses to environmental pressures can distract the brain, including change of behavior patterns. Information passes from neuron to neuron through electrochemical interconnections. When stress occurs the communication links are disturbed. The brain releases chemical inhibitors to block chemical transmissions. This temporary and sometimes permanent loss of communication can explain such problems as, inability to remember or concentrate, to overlook, and to act or think irrationally.

In today's fast-paced and stressful environment one cannot neglect health and lead a balanced life that incorporates work, play, love, rest, and exercise that is practice in the form of fun for the mind and body. The ability to manage stress and to relax often depends on the individual's ability to communicate creatively with various facets of living in a complex society. In the process, one can search and find a quality of life that features peace, productivity, and enjoyment.

RELATIONSHIPS OF BODY AND MIND

We can see, feel, measure, and weigh the physical body, whereas the invisible mind controls itself, thoughts, feelings, and impulses. Everything we do consciously stems from the brain and nervous system, without which the mind cannot function. The body, in turn, influences the brain. A healthy body is reflected by a positive attitude and emotional control, emphasizing the complete and intimate relationship between the body and mind. This relationship must be recognized so that all aspects of communication can be understood, managed, and utilized effectively.

An important mental experience are sensations, which result from perceptions. The sensation in our experience with apples comes from our perceptions of size, color, weight, texture, and smell. Thoughts, which we can define as visual, verbal, symbolic, and moving images, do not by themselves control most of our lives and our communications. Instincts, reflexes, and habits also play major roles. In addition, we have more subtle and complicated attributes, such as emotions, complexes, and the ability to process thoughts.

Habits refer to bodily and mental processes that are learned. Implied is the notion of repetition, according to the same pattern or customary ways. Habit also implies that we do things automatically; that is, go through a process or movements with very little or no thought. Although most of the learning and formation of our habits take place during childhood and youth, they continue throughout our lives.

Reflexes, on the other hand, are inherited. They are present at birth. A child will swallow liquids placed in its mouth. Whereas reflexes are actions carried out as responses of a primitive type for survival and protection, sophisticated habits, such as speaking and writing, must be learned. Instincts explain primary types of activity performed spontaneously, referring to an innate drive and the appropriate activity to satisfy that drive. On the other hand, emotions supply the energy which makes the mind work, struggle, and achieve.

Emotion also provides the energy to survive when the mind recognizes a situation. Fear, for example, protects a person from a threat or apparent danger. Anger provides the energy to fight in the face of a conflict. Love provides energy to protect the loved one and sex functions for procreation. The emotions of fear, anger, love, and sex are accompanied by physiological changes in the body. Because they are a complicated set of complexes, managing the emotions include problems of handling the energies associated with them.

A complex is an idea or a group of ideas emotionally bound together strongly, and the ideas cover a variety of subjects. The complex generally leads to emotional rather than logical thinking, and often appeals to the emotions prevail over logic or reason. The three great complexes, which dominate thinking and determine the actions of the majority of adults are the ego, sex, and herd. Associated with each of the three complexes are instincts and emotions. Whenever these complexes are out of balance, or excessive in asserting its rights over the others, they create serious conflicts, especially indecision.

INSTINCTS	EMOTIONS
Ego Complex	
Self-assertion—Self-display	Elation—positive self-feeling, pride, superiority, mastery, domination
Acquisition—hoarding, property	Feeling of ownership—possession, protection
Nutritional—food seeking	Appetite—craving, gusto
Pugnacity—combat, aggressive	Anger—rage, fury, annoyance, displeasure, irritation
Construction	Feeling of creativeness—making, productivity
Curiosity—inquiry, discovery, investigation	Wonder—feeling mystery, strangeness or unknown
Play—laughter	Amusement—jollity, carelessness, relaxation
Self-abasement—submission	Depression—subjection, inferiority, devotion, humility
Flight—self-preservation, avoidance, danger instinct	Fear—terror, fright, alarm, trepidation
Repulsion—repugnance	Disgust—loathing, nausea, etc.
Sex Complex	
Sex-mating, reproduction, pairing	Love—jealousy, coyness
Parental—protective	Tender emotion—tenderness love
Herd Complex	
Gregarious	Feeling of loneliness—isolation, nostalgia
Suggestion—imitation	Sympathy
Appeal	Distress — attachment, helplessness, trust
Family-ethnic group-workshop	Loyalty—patriotism—religion
Inquisitive—inadequacy	Curiosity—inferiority

The Ego, Sex, and Herd Complexes Identified as Instincts and Emotions

According to Freud, the personality is constructed of three systems: the id, the ego, and the superego. These psychological forces interact with each other dynamically to produce an individual's resultant behavior. The id, the original source of psychic energy or libido, takes the form of conscious instincts that drive the person. These instincts are concerned with survival (life hunger, thirst, sex) or aggression (primitive, demands for gratification, or pleasure). To deal with the realities of the external world, the id impulses must be directed consciously by the ego, the second system of forces.

The ego is involved in the cognitive processes of perceiving, thinking, planning, and deciding in the individual's specific environment. This can all be lumped as the acquisition of knowledge for adaptation to the immediate world in the person's life. Since we have a society which has established rules and values for its members, the superego system evolves in the person. The superego acts to restrain or inhibit the basic impulses, especially sex and aggression. Eventually, the superego becomes the individual's conscience and moral sense or guide.

Since the id, ego, and superego are often in conflict, the struggles among these systems or forces can produce anxieties. In the process, the individual develops characteristic mechanisms to reduce the anxieties. When there are threats to our self-esteem, when we feel guilty, and when we fear punishment, we develop internal communication lines and messages. Examples of complexes that produce positive results are religion, politics, patriotism, and pride. They generate warmth, enthusiasm, and constructive energy. Bad complexes have the effect of producing bias, prejudice, and maladjustment. The three complexes have been grouped in terms of instincts and emotions.

LOGIC AND OBJECTIVITY

Logic is concerned with establishing general truths and abstractions (separation of inherent qualities) by using an orderly system of thinking. Untrained and uncontrolled thinking usually runs into contradictions, because the individual's imagination and internal communication has difficulties handling statements and conclusions. On the other hand, the logician asks questions about premises or statements or assumptions; i.e., statements accepted as true without proof. In the process, he checks the validity or truth of each premise. Statements are put to tests. When the premises are proved correct, the logician will try to reformulate the theory or proposition.

Although formal logic is useful, we can always apply common sense to problems of communication. The combination of logic and common sense are necessary, especially when we use words as tools of communication. Disagreements often resolved when the parties clarify meanings or understand what they are discussing. Mistakes in defining or isolating an issue are easy to make. As long as we are reminded of the concepts behind the words we use and how they are used in our reasoning, words serve us as convenient symbols. One can often ask: does this word I use mean the same thing to the other party?

We must also watch for shifts in meanings behind our terms, when causes can be confused for effects, when we jump to unsupported conclusions, and substituting inferences not based on facts for those that are. It is not necessary to examine all statements under the sharp scrutiny of formal logic. In most situations the following suggestions may be practical:

1) Use common sense to be aware of logical principles

2) Check reasoning behind statements of ours and those of others

3) Examine in detail a set of causes, observations, or clues

4) Reduce an argument to a conclusion from valid premises

5) Avoid all-inclusive premises—positive or negative.

An important logical relationship is called analogy. The relationship need not resemble reality, but show similarities in principle, such as a curve, a diagram, or a geographic map. One thing can symbolize another if both have the same logical form. By analogy we realize the common logical form in things and ideas. The thinking process is a set of ideas in which there is sequence, arrangement, and connection. Thinking requires a definite pattern composed of ideas related to each other, and arranged according to some scale of importance or priority. A simple sentence requires arranging words into relations and operations. The talent for discovering analogies, or logical relationships in various forms, is called logical intuition.

To make sense out of the masses of facts, ideas, and details that surround us, we must establish some common denominators or broad principles so that we can communicate with one another. We have the sense to simplify and abstract. Various elements of a common logical form compose a set, which we call by one general name. This set should not create the picture of any specific element in our mind, because we are consciously abstracting the logical form all elements in the set have in common. We form a mental image by generalization from particulars, or develop concepts. When we find applications for concepts, we are interpreting, the reverse of abstraction.

Abstract concepts are communicated to us by language or formal training. We learn an algebraic formula by seeing some examples and observing what they have in common. The ability to abstract makes it possible to discover new relationships, which can also be discovered by interpretation. The inventor and designer are concerned with interpretation, however the abstract work is performed so that physically interpretable forms can be found. The inventor's abstract form is his calculation, based on a concept; his development from concept to physical existence is his interpretation of the form.

Language is not only a medium for expressing thought, it is also an instrument of human reason. At the same time, there is no question that mathematics is the most universally understood language in the world, even though there is some variation in mathematical signs. Signs are arbitrary marks with fixed interpretations. A spoken word is a phonetic sign; written or printed words are visual signs. Pictures and symbols are also visual signs. A sign is useful only as long as all who deal with it understand clearly what the sign stands for. When you consider the symbols and logical systems involved, mathematics appears to be an elaborate system of knowledge.

Scientists often deal with probabilities based on statistics and verifiable data. They work with experiments, tests, plots, and relationships reduced to significant numbers which yield this data. Montaigne's famous question, "What do I know7" has its scientific parallel: "How do I know?" Listed separately are a series of suggestions which are intended to promote objectivity, intellectual clarity, and straight thinking.

Suggestions for Objectivity, Clarity, and Straight Thinking

a. Survey the facts of a territory (verbal map) scientifically. Observe, develop a theory, and verify by experiment.

b. Be absolutely certain about something and see all points of view before judging, claiming knowledge, deciding, or taking action.

c. Be open-minded and receptive. Distinguish between facts and fiction; objectivity and bias. Try to see the whole problem, even if you tend to believe what you have heard or read about.

d. Think in terms of degrees, shades, and accuracies, rather than absolute, superlative, all inclusive, or bi-valued verbal maps.

e. Exclude personal interests and experiences when justifying or rationalizing our decisions. Verbal concepts that are resolved as conclusions are not to be treated in the same class as observations that can be verified.

f. Assign index numbers to items to remind yourself of differences or variations; think in terms of facts, not words.

g. Accept changes resulting from differences in time place, situation, and persons. Change your mind when you have collected facts needed to convince yourself and others.

h. Question all generalizations, statistics, and one-sided views. Put ideas to tests. Ask questions. Prove a proposition under actual or simulated conditions.

i. Use all sense and faculties to learn who, what, when, where, why, and how. Try to see more clearly, think more maturely, read more critically, listen more discriminately, write more accurately, speak more distinctly, and act decisively.

j. Make decisions based on realities, facts, and alternatives. Think in terms of cost trade-offs and have the courage to trust to reason.

k. Define clearly and accurately the task you undertake or problem you attempt to solve. Write it down for examination.

l. Control ego, emotions, and complexes. As you simplify and clarify ideas, preserve content, purpose, and impact.

There can be no greater discipline for objectivity in thought than the application of the scientific method. Even after observations, hypotheses, and verification by experiments or tests, there is an additional task. The scientist must record and communicate his findings. His language must be clear enough for others to repeat the process of arriving at the same conclusions or interpreting findings. Clarity is the difficult key that opens doors of communication of knowledge, whether you report a discovery, relay a message, interpret a process, or speculate on a new problem.

When one thinks objectively and applies the scientific method, three major benefits are realized. First, one tends to approach the problem or subject from a detached point of view and confines efforts to the specified task at hand. Second, one tends to arrive at answers and decisions for action on a rational basis. Third, accuracy, clarity, and reliability tend to become the natural outgrowth of the logic applied.

Achievements and correct decisions are inevitable when the emotions are used to charge the battery of reason and efforts to move forward in a clearly defined direction. The scientist practices objectivity as a natural function of his disciplined training. His method can be summarized as follows:

1. Collect facts, classify, and correlate;

2. Define problem and break it down into specific questions;

3. Make intelligent guesses (ideas) to answer questions; consider theories that explain facts; and,

4. Devise experiments to test the likeliest theories that relate to the most crucial questions.

All thinking, learning, and problem solving result from perceptual processes and motivation. When we think about something, we start a stream of changing perceptions about the issue at hand. The stream will have "breaks" or "discontinuities." We may even go through a silent period, which is usually the case when thinking about complex problems. In some cases the stream is interrupted until the issue is resolved

While thinking, we work with memory images and created images, which can be visual, auditory, symbolic, or verbal. The biggest task the clear thinker has is to isolate the rational from the emotional process. If the emotions are guided to provide energy and motivation for objectivity and reason, clear thinking to the logical conclusion proceeds naturally to the decision or answer.

Any program to help think clearly begins with self-analysis in which one emphasizes objectivity rather than an experience or emotional bias. Since society can breed prejudice, one must examine opinions, the reliability of facts at hand, and the credibility of the evidence offered. For example, we can see and remember things that are influenced by what we add to the situation. One can always ask if what one observes is distorted by memory, attitude, or imagination. Strong convictions about people, places and things should be checked out by a review of the facts and authoritative references. It can be surprising how the opinions and convictions of others differ from yours.

Semanticists often ask the question: What is going on? This can be done by investigating various aspects of a situation so that you'll be better informed in the event that you talk, write, or work on it. Time can distort images and pictures in the mind can fade like old newsprint. If a matter is important, go back and refresh your recollection of the overall picture and the details. It will have the effect of sharpening your memory of a scene.

If you use words with care, being specific enough so that the meanings you intend match the meanings as understood by others, your listeners or readers. Abstract words have the effect of generalities and the characteristic of raising a host of unintended meanings and responses. Words like "liberty, freedom, truth, peace, democracy, and crime," may sound appealing for the context intended, however, they are too abstract to generate anything of significance to listeners.

To clarify points, there's nothing wrong with asking questions that are clear and specific. When you realize how you think and how others differ in their approach to an issue or situation, you'll be able to exercise more control in your communication skills. In addition, you'll find it easier to understand how others think. Oliver Wendell Holmes said significantly, "General propositions do not decide concrete cases." Some people use one instance or experience as a general rule to fit all similar situations.

We think because we must—much more often than because we want to. The inertia of the mind exists in many forms; such as, procrastination, negligence, laziness, and dislike to face an issue or a conflict. If you consider something important, direct the information available and use your abilities to resolve a situation, develop an idea, or solve a problem. Put your ideas, facts, and conclusions through tests. Ask whether it's an illusion, a coincidence, or an error. The only way to get rid of bad brakes is to have them fixed so that it can be a relief from stress, which comes from worrying about it.

ASPECTS OF INTELLIGENCE

Intelligence is difficult to define, however, we do know that many mental operations are involved; namely, comprehension (understanding through knowledge and learning), creativity (invention or innovation), goal-seeking (operation in a direction to a worthwhile conclusion), and evaluation (judging ideas to accept or reject them).

Most of the ingenious devices in use today, such as computers, airplanes, space vehicles, and color television, were invented by human beings who had the intelligence to visualize concepts and interpret them into useful arrangements. An important characteristic of intelligence is the ability to recognize significant relationships, establish basic principles, and develop some order out of apparent chaos. An intelligent person generally undertakes, with concentration and objectivity, activities that are:

A. Difficult
B. Complex
C. Abstract in quality (possess selectable features)
D. Economical (cost, size, weight, efficient)
E. Goal-seeking
F. Socially redeeming in values
G. Original

Naturally, such activities require time, motivation, and personal sacrifice. Most persons of high level intelligence are capable of abstract thinking, in which a mental concept is separated; i.e., considered apart from the total picture or from particular instances. There are many mental and physical operations associated with intelligence, including imagination, memory, association, selection, arithmetic, and sequencing. An intelligent person's abilities can include:

1. Recognition of significant relationships
2. Manipulation of variables and constants
3. Understanding shades of meaning
4. Visual perception of size, quantity, form, color, and texture
5. Abstraction, or separate in thought or consider a thing inde-pendently in its association; selection of qualities
6. Reason in two and three-dimensional figures
7. Directing attention in discerning relations

Directing attention to an operation and discriminating selectively can be called attentional processing. The mechanic who listens to engine sounds to analyze problems and the architect who remodels a house to enlarge, replace, and redesign various features are examples of selective attention.

One develops intelligence by working through details of analyzing relations, which in turn, results from a series of observations, interpretations of data, comparisons, and organizations. An athlete's coordinated moves are visible. The whole sequence of intelligence operations is invisible. Those who think, read, and verbalize aloud permit better understanding of learning problems or errors in judgment, reason, and processes.

Not measured in standard aptitude, intelligence, and scholastic tests are culture, motivation, and will power. What is generally measured by tests are:

Vocabulary—definitions, comparisons, contrasts, relationships

Arithmetic—reasoning, computation, proportion, logic

Interpretation—proverbs, stories, descriptions, explanations

Grammar—sentence completion, syntax, punctuation, modifiers

Problem Solving—physical, numerical, ingenuity

Memory/Comprehension—repeat a passage that is read aloud, summarize ideas, rephrase

Orientation—directions, rotations

Visual—figural identification, form selection

The intelligent person tends to be thorough in search, careful in selection, and accurate. The internal thinking process relies on feedback and checks for errors. It reflects about a problem, situation, and tentative solutions. Self-criticism or disbelief is also a common characteristic of the intelligent. Mental sets or frames of reference are developed as signals for interpretation of new data. The mental pattern of perceptual orientation becomes almost automatic. The memory becomes active and new frames of reference are developed. Thinking goes on while something else is performed.

All these processes are the products of a consciously or subconsciously motivated person. It takes persistent and directed thinking to grasp and solve a difficult question. It is neither automatic with the person of high intelligence, nor impossible for the one of low level intelligence. It was recently proven that the brain cells of persons with less intelligence work harder than those of the persons of higher intelligence. Learning takes effort and remembering becomes easier if one relaxes and does not force recall. It's mostly a matter of association; and, training the memory helps the processes involved in learning, thinking, and solving.

Your eyes register what's back of your mind and what you see depends as much on you as the object of your vision. For a fleeting moment, your mind meets facts and immediately proceeds to make them over in your own image. The basis of all concepts is the sense of sameness. A concept is the product of hindsight, of focusing on something you didn't pay attention to originally. Real thinkers can detach their ideas from their work, forgetting about themselves in thinking. Their minds range over a wide area of possible patterns. Often one must forget what he or she happens to wish before becoming susceptible to what the situation itself requires.

Thinking involves the scanning and manipulation of information stored in the memories. Einstein's brain was able to scan quickly one group of brain cells after another, better and faster than the ordinary brain. When remembering, patterns of nerve cells (neurons) are activated electrically. Your brain registers experience differently from everybody else's, and everybody has only his or her own experience and development to think with. Learning how to translate helps thinking because you use two sets of nerve patterns instead of one. Abstract ideas are the patterns two or more ideas have in common. They come forward whenever someone realizes that similarity.

Creative Listening

If we listen more than twice as much time as we read, why not do something about improving our abilities to listen actively, mentally, and with skill? Whether it's to a boss, an employee, a friend, or a commentator, no day goes by in business or socially without the need to listen. Our different relationships with the persons to whom we listen makes it a challenge to do it creatively. If the creative person can be considered as one who aspires to achieve or innovate, the creative listener knows how to maintain a receptive attitude. In addition, the creative listener knows when to listen actively, how to remember the essentials of a message, when and how to ask questions.

Like reading or writing, there are listening situations that represent one-way communication; that is, without opportunities for feedback or response. This limitation makes it more important to listen carefully and analytically. As a creative listener, one adapts a listening technique to the confronting situation or context. It takes the awareness of an attentive ear and an open mind poised to accept a variety of information. In mastering listening techniques, one can develop an attitude that involves flexibility and control.

In this era of advanced technology, we listen through the telephone receiver, to radio, and the audio that accompanies television and motion pictures. The complex mental and physical process of listening is supported by visual and other sensory cues. In other words, we don't listen with our ears alone. On occasion, our emotions are involved in the listening process. If we listen ineffectively, it may be due to habits, attitudes, and prejudgments, all of which can influence the clarity and objectivity of the message.

Since listening is a slower and more difficult process than thinking, it is possible to lose some of the ideas that we accept into our storehouse of memory. Extraneous thoughts of our own can impede the ability to concentrate on the messages. Listening can become difficult if we think about what we are going to say next or in response.

Listening to words, inflections, meanings, and tones of voice amounts to much more than listening to the abstract language of music. Although we use our ears to listen, it is our mind that registers and accepts the impact and the meaning of the messages. When the listener has a purpose or motive, attention becomes concentrated. Just as advance knowledge of the speaker, subject, and purpose helps the listening process for the audience.

An effective and organized speaker makes it easier for listeners when important points are emphasized and repeated. When listening to a theatrical performance, it is the identification with the characters and involvement of the audience that enhances listening. Music and song provide gratification through the images and meanings that listeners interpret.

The emotional and physical benefits produced by music stem from its rhythmic beats and variations in dynamics and tempo. The effect of music on our emotions cannot be overestimated, such as producing excitement or soothing effects. Unfortunately, much of our music is so loud and repetitious, that in addition to slowly degenerating our hearing mechanisms, it also affects our ability to learn and remember. The effect of hearing loss on the ability to converse is an unfortunate byproduct of our noisy environment and loud percussive beat of rock "music."

ACTIVE LISTENING

Creative listening is limited when listening ability is taken for granted and process is treated in a passive manner. The ability to listen actively takes effort, practice, and discipline. When people are mentally preoccupied, they stare and inhibit the listening process. However, listening is not easy. Even when listening carefully, most people remember about half of what others say. Becoming an active listener takes improvement through practice and programming of listening habits.

The listening process directs sounds to the center of hearing on the side of the brain, where it is perceived and related to previous sounds. It also directs the sounds to the autonomic nervous system, affecting responses or reactions in the form of stepped up heart rate, blood pressure, and release of hormones.

Like a high-speed transmission, the electrical responses to sounds, such as explosions, the click of a switch, or the ring of a bell, the brain tries to identify its character and source. In a split second, the listener can be startled, warned, or reminded of something that transpired, so that a corresponding response or action can be initiated. This mental interpretation, generally taken for granted, varies with individuals, depending on experience or familiarity with the sound.

The pleasing sounds of music not only affect mood, but also the atmosphere in a gathering of people. Depending on the character of the music, strangers are slow to interact or can be gregarious and more cheerful. The use of upbeat songs or music, generally in the major mode, are often used at meetings and conferences to stimulate a friendly mood by the attendees.

Some people cannot start a morning without the catalyst of light or cheerful music. Music can change your mood, however, it can also interfere with concentration on tasks, such as reading, locating a point on a map, or writing. In work areas, music is often subdued to limit interference with difficult operations.

Psychologists, psychiatrists, attorneys, and sales persons are generally trained to listen actively to their clients. Skilled and active listeners can sense when they are being brain-washed or conditioned for eventual exploitation by some cults. An active listener uses his or her sharpened skills for learning, negotiating, and solving problems. Listening often offers opportunities to ask questions that reading and observing do not.

Before the advent of writing and the printed word, speech and listening to it were the most common forms of communication. Speech was probably preceded by hand signals and gestures. A child learns to speak by imitating speech sounds heard from its mother. After a while the sounds take on meaning and the talking makes sense. Active listening to the radio, as against watching television, provides exercise of the imagination by interpreting words to stimulate mental images.

As patient and understanding listeners, we can often provide answers to the problems of others. Parents and children can improve relationships by reducing the chances of misunderstanding through active listening to what they have to say. Like adults, children want attention, which often means somebody to listen to them and satisfy their sense of self-esteem or understanding of the world or events as they see them. One can become an active listener and a more creative one, by observing the 17 suggestions listed.

1) Listen to the complete story or explanation by another. This can help avoid arguments, misunderstandings, and loss of mutual respect.

2) If you're there to listen, give the speaker your full attention. Listen with concentrated effort.

3) If you agree with the speaker, do it without interrupting; i.e., by nodding.

4) Avoid interrupting by timing questions at the proper moment, when there's a pause or anticipation for one.

5) Anger or sympathy can affect listening as emotional responses that stem from related experiences. One can guard against the use of such emotional filters.

6) Gestures or facial signals while listening should be positive and negative ones avoided, if possible.

7) If you disagree with a statement, as a matter of fact, make certain you are correct before contradicting the speaker.

8) Problems may not be solved by listening, but the listener can find out more about what is going on by sharing some experiences of the speaker.

9) Assume the speaker will have something important or of interest to say.

10) Keep an open mind. Treat the speech objectively and consider it as a constructive presentation.

11) Avoid mental distractions or emotional reactions to the point of shutting off your mind to points being offered by the speaker.

12) Control tendencies to be distracted by the speaker's accent, manner, or dress. Concentrate on the ideas, as presented.

13) Search for meaning and ideas, especially the main points. Listen for the facts presented to support main points.

14) Take notes, using a form of shorthand, outlining ideas and making note of key words. If the speech or message is very important, use a tape recorder to review the whole speech at a convenient time.

15) If certain words disturb you, check the context in which they are used.

16) Listen with your eyes as well as your brain. Treat your ears as conduits or phone lines to your storehouse of information.

17) Be patient with the speaker, and resist premature evaluation of the speech.

ANALYTICAL LISTENING

The analytical listener tries to understand the significant issue in the same context as the speaker. This is a form of empathy, the active entry into the speaker's situation by using imagination. This frame of reference, different from yours, is figuratively standing in the shoes of the speaker. The analytical listener anticipates subjects, summarizes ideas, and questions statements made with an objective attitude. The purpose of the analysis is not to disagree, but to come up with a sort of balance sheet of pros and cons, or various sides of an issue.

Analytical listening, an aspect of creative listening, starts with motivation or the desire to listen for substance. One cannot expect to listen well if concentration is reserved only for those things we like to hear, such as flattery and favorable generalities. One must temporarily set aside judgments so that one can be fair with oneself and as one can be with others. The more you care about what the speaker says (involvement), the more effort you can exert in the form of attention. This attention serves to stimulate the speaker in the form of feedback.

Also taking part in the complex skill of human speech are the eyes, gestures, the pauses, and the unique characteristics of the speaker. For example, the speaker is often remembered by the sound and quality of the voice. Speakers can vary emphasis and meaning through inflections, dynamics, and eye contact. The nonverbal communication through the eyes, gestures, and modes of expression can reinforce, soften, or contradict the verbal messages. A simple sentence can be stated in scores of different ways, depending on context and purpose. When we are really interested in what the speaker has to say, we listen with our eyes, attitudes, and brains, not just with our ears.

When listening analytically, one can search for ideas through the process of anticipating and evaluating. Would you reject or modify the statements made? Do the supporting materials presented by the speaker relate clearly and directly to the ideas? Finally, in summarizing, did you find the ideas presented worthwhile? Stated another way, the listener asks what the speaker tried to say, how it was said, and what was the value of the speech or presentation.

Good listening habits and attitudes restrain the mind from wandering. At the same time, the ability to listen analytically reinforces the ability to recall. If the speaker is worth listening to, then he or she is worth listening to creatively and analytically. Keep your ears open for new and original ideas. To ensure recall, take notes and review important points as a summary. To improve the ability to listen creatively, think analytically and in terms of the essential points the speaker made.

As in other skills, listening requires attention and isolation from distractions, especially freedom from noise. Because speech and sound have a continuity that is time oriented, it is easy to miss something. Because of this feature, occasionally what is lost cannot be recovered or recreated. Whereas one can go over something read, one may lose a word or phrase when listening to a speech or an announcement. Like many other disciplines, the investments in time and effort eventually pay off in a sharpened sense of hearing, a discriminating ear, and the ability to listen to what is going on in the world around you.

Creative Conversing

Creative conversing can be defined as the process by which two or more persons communicate verbally to achieve mutual benefits. Although intangible benefits are more likely the outcome of a conversation, purpose and worthwhile goals are important considerations by the participants. Without purpose, conversation can meander aimlessly like a lost orphan and come up empty. Whether the occasion becomes an opportunity to meet strangers, win friends, or influence people, the approach used and how the conversation develops are also significant to consider. Like most situations in life, some planning, as against leaving things to accident or spur of the moment, pays off dividends towards creative conversing.

Conversation encounters can range from those with strangers to those with ongoing or intimate relationships. Since this is a major form of communication that can have considerable bearing in the conduct of one's life, one must measure the effectiveness of one's ability to converse, as well as seek ways to improve in various situations and among various relationships. Conversation can proceed at various levels: informal, official, professional, or social. One may play different roles or wear many hats, however, it works best to be yourself. Conversation is neither an exercise in pretense nor game of acting.

The best conversations involve the exchange of ideas that stimulate responses and produce something worthwhile for those who participate. One who has mastered the art of conversation rarely bores others, knows how to listen, promotes understanding, and involves the listener without doing most of the talking. A pleasing voice and the use of tone quality where appropriate, as well as gestures, are characteristics of a good conversationalist. It is not necessary to be a wit or a personality gushing with superlatives. It is often a matter of etiquette to set others at ease by being relaxed, natural, and considerate.

Although a pleasing voice is an asset, as well as one that is well modulated and under control, it is also important to speak with sincerity and intelligence. It is the considerate conversationalist, who speaks plainly and clearly about what he or she knows, that attracts others. Good manners and a desire to give others opportunities to speak generally reflect the philosophy of talking about what is agreeable to others. Since people like to talk, especially about themselves, the person who speaks excessively is apt to bore. On the other hand, the person who doesn't say much can do little to contribute to the value of a conversation.

Conversation can flow like a stream, change its shape like a cloud, or run a straight course, like a canal. Much depends on the purpose of the gathering, the mixture of persons present, and the environment or locale. A good rule to follow is to suit the subject to the occasion and the treatment to the group. Informality promotes conversations that run smoothly. If too many subjects are discussed, some persons get carried away emotionally and make value judgments about sensitive issues. Not only are tact and caution important in a social gathering, but also, personal questions are out of place. Attaching labels or descriptive terms to those present may backfire, and in these instances, ignorance is no excuse.

Making others feel at ease encourages them to warm up and participate in conversations. It is generally better to say something, than stare, especially if you are attracted by a member of the opposite sex. There is nothing wrong with an approach that introduces oneself by name and follows it with a genuine compliment. A closed mind blocks the possibility of sharing the experiences and ideas of others. A bold or aggressive approach, on the other hand, may display the wrong impression in the interest of starting a conversation.

If you're going to spread information or gossip around, consider the possible good that can be accomplished. One need not exhaust a subject or resolve an issue forever. There is also no reason to switch from topic to topic in an effort to get things moving conversationally. A good way to stimulate participation or response is to ask the right questions—specific ones that reflect genuine interests. A little praise or remark may be necessary to draw out a modest or reticent person. It also takes tolerance to refrain from cutting a person short.

INTERPERSONAL COMMUNICATION

Our daily routines bring us into contact with many people with whom we maintain some type of interpersonal relationship. This relationship becomes more defined and productive as we exchange messages which we know as interpersonal communication. Most people with whom we communicate use a common language and culture. Those who speak in same languages interact as if they have more in common. This develops stronger relationships and more acceptance. In the process it emphasizes differences between other cultures.

During interpersonal communication, we act *as if* what we communicate to other persons is what they mean to us. We make *as if* assumptions, such as acting as if we trust one another. As we listen to others, we display behavior and verify our initial *as if* assumptions. If our *as if* assumption turns out to be incorrect, we make another assumption which fits the pattern of behavior being displayed and what we interpret from listening.

At a given moment for speaking and listening in an interpersonal communication, any one of the roles will dominate. The importance of listening cannot be overestimated. Even when speaking, one can "listen" for feedback in terms of reactions. People make many friends simply by listening, and necessarily reducing their speeches to a minimum. Listening is the better half of conversation because one can learn by listening, and will also be in a better position to know what to say and how. In addition, a speaker will always appreciate a good listener.

NOISE AND DISTRACTIONS

Conversation is often subject to distractions or disturbances beyond the control of the participants. For example, a party can get too noisy to sustain an intelligible discussion. Unfortunately, some locations are subject to noise pollution. Sounds from loud amplifiers or high powered stereo systems are particularly objectionable, since loud rhythmic beats drown out any sounds or speeches for the discriminating ear. There are many instances of deafness early in the careers of truck drivers, motorcyclists, machine shop employees, and those who listen to loud contemporary "music."

Noise and distractions not only affect listening, but also limit the ability to think, work productively, and control emotions. Any conversation, interview, or meeting must anticipate possible distractions from noise. Some people feel at home in a noisy environment or must have a radio going while they work. Common sense dictates that any activity that involves creative or professional discussions be confined to a quiet room or office.

Various speaking situations, such as telephone conversations, conferences, and presentations demand freedom from noise, and an environment that's free of distractions. Where and when possible, the communication environment must be considered for optimum conditions conducive to listening and conversing creatively. There are times when even the ring of a telephone or the blare of a public address system is forbidden, so that the participants in a productive exchange of information are not disturbed.

USING THE TELEPHONE

We take the telephone for granted, especially since it has become so much an integral instrument in our lives. One cannot imagine a day going by without the use of a conversation by telephone. Over a period of time we develop a telephone personality. We use the telephone a lot because it saves time, travel, and needless running around to locate people. It's useful, convenient, and well worth the price we pay for its service.

There are always important elements to consider when using the telephone, such as voice, manners, and extended conversations. Knowledge of the telephone's many uses and practicing in exploiting it as a medium of conversation or communication are very valuable. In a telephone conversation, consider what the speaker on the other end of the line reveals or suggests. As a listener, can you detect any combination of attitudes and attributes that the speaker manifests through words, tone, and other forms of feedback? How do you think you sound to others? Have you listened to your half of a conversation as recorded on tape? Have you analyzed telephone conversations in terms of these?

Alert; lethargic	Pleasant; disagreeable
Friendly; cool	Helpful; hindering
Natural; stilted	Considerate; unkind
Distinct; obscure	Clear; vague
Tactful; blundering	Expressive; dull
Warm; apathetic	Courteous; rude
Simple; technical	Reserved; talkative
Specific; general	Thankful; ungrateful
Careful; careless	Sincere; untruthful
Calm; excited	Inspiring; defeatist

It doesn't take much to examine and analyze your telephone personality. Every time you use the telephone for a day or week, turn on a tape recorder placed nearby. At the end of a period, listen to yourself and how you sound during telephone conversations. Check off your list of attitudes and attributes. If you think of other characteristics noticeable in your speech, make a note of them. This will also be a test of qualities or defects you recognize in your telephone voice and manners. In the process, you will understand others better. Literally, you'll be able to "see" their voices and faces as they speak to you by telephone.

In a booklet entitled, "Your Telephone Personality," the Bell System recommends five ways to sound as good as you really are:

Alert—Ready to help the person on the line

Pleasant—Putting a smile in your voice

Natural—Speak in simple language; avoid technical terms

Distinct—Use microphone and pronounce words clearly

Expressive—Moderate speech with proper emphasis; varying tone adds variety and vitality to what you say

There are also such important practices as answering promptly, returning calls, and identifying yourself. Being friendly and considerate will be appreciated by your caller. The use of the telephone provides another opportunity to practice the golden rule; i.e., speak unto others as you would have others speak unto you. In addition, some insurance against noise and distractions is generally appreciated by your partner in the telephone conversation. Can you put a smile in your telephone voice and keep it there? Can you be responsive? Can you listen with undivided attention? Be helpful? Can you limit conversation from dragging on or reverting to unproductive gossip.

MAKING CONVERSATION CREATIVE

To start off a conversation, address the person by name and come up with a genuine word of praise or flattery. For example, "I've heard so much about you, Mr. Jones, and have been wanting to meet you." Speak more of others' interests by asking a specific question, rather than dispensing unexpected information. You can establish a better conversation by concentrating on others, than by thinking about yourself. Many people have struggled to reach positions of fame or recognition. Expressing admiration for something or for what you appreciate as an accomplishment is a sincere form of flattery.

The subject you bring up most indicate some knowledge of what you're talking about, as well as reflect some positive aspect of things that concern you. If you ask a question, wait for an answer. Some people have the habit of impatiently responding to the very question they asked. Putting words in the mouths of others is not only impolite, but it also defeats the purpose of the question. You can drop the bottom out of the question and perhaps the relationship.

Tact must prevail throughout the conversational situation. Instead of asking someone when he or she is leaving, ask how long that person is staying. Self-confidence helps in your contact and conversation with others. You can't just stare at another. When you say something, do it with a smile. It should be easy to ask an unusual question, like "Do you remember the first person with whom you fell in love?" Conversation can be stimulated by saying something provocative or by asking a question that means something to the listener.

Listening is the better half of conversation. Why? Because you can learn something by listening. In addition, you can pick up clues to know better what to talk about and how. Here are a few suggestions:

1) Concentrate on listening with attention and objectively.

2) Be a patient listener. Wait until the speaker is finished before making remarks. Try not to interrupt unless it is absolutely necessary.

3) Ask specific questions of interest to the speaker, rather than general ones, such as "How's things?"

4) Before you start to bore listeners, encourage others to take part by asking questions.

5) When telling a story, don't extend its length by filling in all the details.

6) Don't contradict on small differences, such as age or a date. Practice tact and tolerance.

7) Use eye contact with your listeners or the speakers.

8) Disagree with discretion, not emotionally. With good reason, you can even remain silent on occasion.

9) If you agree, say so. Don't try to have the last word.

10) Speakers appreciate acknowledgments and compliments.

11) Speak with a purpose about something new or different.

12) Try to speak with clarity and precision, not with authority, as if you were the expert on the subject.

13) Refrain from passing judgment or giving advice, unless you are asked.

14) Avoid making a general summary of what someone else said.

15) Consider subjects that are of general interest to the listeners present.

16) Try not to be opinionated or express an opinion on every subject.

Whether you're making contact, conversation, or friends, you're not going to win them all. Avoid the appearance of a struggle to strike up a relationship. If you feel out of place and can't seem to break the ice or open up, relax and move on to another environment. The chances are you're lingering in one of the polar regions and you're not going to change the frozen or entrenched establishment.

Although it is conceivable that life can exist without conversation, it is virtually impossible to exchange information or conduct business and social activity without some form of conversation. When speaking and listening are interrupted to discuss things of common interest, the participants may go beyond the level of ordinary communication. Conversation is the most common and most important form of communication in which human beings can engage.

Any contact that represents a social gathering, business activity, or politics presents opportunities for conversation, one of the many blessings of a free society and a reflection of one of the many guarantees of the Constitution. Marriage, parental, and friendly relationships cannot exist without conversation, a practice that we enjoy automatically. It is through conversation that we make agreements, share thoughts and feelings, put life into meetings, and even resolve international differences. We cannot imagine a legislature, a company, or an educational institution operate without discussion or conversation at a professional level.

The question to ask is how can we make conversation creative? Although creativity in conversation is more likely between and among persons who are educated and trained in communication skills, there are certain guidelines that characterize the nature of a creative conversation.

First, there must be preparation, a sort of background on the subjects under discussion. Preliminary talk or idle conversation should be avoided, unless it has the purpose of establishing rapport or common ground to promote conversation directed towards a goal or a decision.

Second, since thought is creative, in one way or another, it becomes a matter of how much effort one applies to a situation. On the one hand, you can develop consistent effort to apply a way of looking at things from a detached point of view—elevated and objective. On the other hand, you can color your thinking about conversation from an emotional or self-centered point of view—distorted and subjective.

Third, participate with self-confidence and a positive approach. You can relax in an elevated atmosphere with an awareness that you can fill at ease by being natural and yourself. With a presence of mind, you can concentrate on several levels of progress: from a purpose, to a plan, and to action in terms of words or messages that mean something to others.

To summarize, creative conversation can be reduced to preparation, the application of positive and thoughtful efforts, and communication, in a language others can understand; that has goals, plans, and meaningful messages.

Observing
Creatively

The ability to observe creatively can be interpreted in many ways, such as detecting a flaw or a clue in a simple visual inspection; distinguishing between a work of art and a fake; and, understanding the difference between reality and fantasy. The disciplined observer double checks his vision to see what's really out there rather than injecting something or coloring things with emotions. The creative observer takes a keen, analytical, and purposeful look beyond the representational or two-dimensional aspects of a visual situation.

Whether observing a person, a place, or an object, can you see the parts if they can be separated, the whole, the physical and functional relationships? The traveler who observes with a meticulous sense of order, takes nothing for granted. The sculptor, architect, painter, designer, or scientist, by reason of their training and practice, are conditioned to observe more creatively than the average person. One can go far in observing creatively by learning how to draw, take up professional photography, and learn various techniques of visual expression.

The creative observer does not grow out of a host of experiences, but through development and learning how to approach the recognition of line, form, arrangement, texture, and the many uses of color. We learn to observe creatively by looking at the world around us from different perspectives; from enlarging and widening the scope of our visual activities. The mismanagement of stress and excessive viewing of video screens or television has the effect of weakening our creative perceptions.

Curiosity does not kill and familiarity does not breed contempt. Strangers may appear odd or funny, until we get acquainted. From the face, figure, walk, and dress, we move to the voice, gestures, and content of messages. Eventually, a warm personality may surge forth. We are observing and getting to know a complex human being, who in the semantic sense, is more than a physical person. In addition, he or she can be considered a biological, mental, emotional, chemical, and electrical entity with wants, needs, and with problems that many of us have.

Our observation modes can be switched when we see plants, animals, and works of man. In a world that teems with various materials, metals, alloys, plastics, mixtures, and compounds, the obvious suggestion raised is the value of a formal education. However, if we think of education as an organized shortcut to experience, nothing can really stop us from taking courses, using the libraries, and asking questions of professionals. One can train the senses to grasp or seek information, which can be a great deal more useful than the gossip with which we are constantly bombarded by radio and television.

VISUAL PERCEPTION

The complex society in which we move about competes constantly for our visual attention, which amounts to a strain on our eyes. Among other things, we use our eyes to drive, work, read, observe the real world, and watch television. It is no wonder we are subject to tired eyes and visual confusion, even with perfect vision. If our eyesight becomes a victim of tension, emotional strain, or distortions due to drugs or alcohol, we really have problems taking advantage of one of the most remarkable senses we enjoy. Do we really appreciate our windows to the world, these treasures that open up the universe to our consciousness?

Even though formal or symmetrical balance gives us a feeling of satisfaction or ease, it is not as interesting to the viewer as dynamic or asymmetrical balance. Balance by weight can be done with size, color, and apparent differences in strength. Psychologically, interest can generate balance, especially if there exists complexity, and symbols included arouse meanings and associations in the viewer. When there are contrasts or dissimilarities, interests develop and some new dimensions appear. Conflicts or contests attract attention and often they are included so that viewers take sides.

What we see is not only what enters our visual system, but also the influences of information from our other senses and from our memory. Through the visual system, the brain is capable of storing lines, shapes, colors, moving images, and complete pictures of events we have observed either in real life, or in some medium, such as motion pictures, television, graphic arts, signs, and symbols. What we "see" is influenced by simultaneous information from other senses and memory.

We live in a visual culture in which approximately 80 percent of our information is processed through our eyes. With the advent of data display systems, multiple channel television, and the paper explosion, characterized by tremendous amounts of direct mail and documents, we're caught in a visual web of confusion. We see more and remember less. Things move so fast, we cannot think visually. We are victims of visual persuasion. The commercial television packages on most channels inhibit our impulse to create visual images.

The act of perceiving a scene or an object can be psychological. It is as if we make a subjective evaluation of an experience. However, it is objective by nature, since it exists in the same visual form for all who perceive it from the same perspective. We know that different viewers perceive the same work differently. In fact, the same viewer perceives the same work differently at different times. If you have visited a former neighborhood or a home you occupied as a child, you wonder at the apparent changes. Surely, you see it differently than you did years ago.

Artists trained in perception enable them not only to see images more subtle and complex than viewed by untrained observers, but also isolate the visual elements, such as contrast, color, line, form, texture, etc. Like verbal communication, in which context specifies meaning, relationships and arrangements of visual elements characterize the message and impact of the experience. It represents an awareness of the content or substance and style of an object, an event, or a work of art.

We see color in contexts and relationships. The importance of color is as much a matter of hue, such as red, blue, or yellow, as it is of values, intensities, and psychological associations. Once we understand the language of color, its use of opposites and related members, their symbolic association and tonality, or the overall effect of a dominant hue, we can understand much about the functions of a work or an illustrated message. Often we touch or feel a surface to identify or reassure our perceptions. We attempt to clarify what appears ambiguous, mysterious, or illusionary.

Whereas art is organized to be observed as an experience, design is seen to persuade the viewer. In both instances, the elements are organized for visual effect. Various principles of design have been incorporated in a wide range of works (artifacts, structures, paintings, and sculptures) and one or more of the following are present in all: unity, balance, rhythm, and proportion. These principles are the artist's vision of the organization of the work. In some instances, unity is achieved in various ways, If we see coherence; i.e., a sense of various parts belonging together, the organization appears natural to the subject.

With the development of photography and the increased use of abstractions, the artist speaks a new language to describe, manipulate, and compose the visual elements. Lines become tools for movement and forms develop meaning in the context of the work itself. Whereas writing uses language symbols to contribute to widely accepted meanings, art uses visual language, with infinite variations to achieve intended effects. These can be movement, suggestion, quality, symbolism, or special meanings. For example, curves are considered feminine; sharp angles are considered more masculine. Lines can depict growth, decay, opposition, conformity, fluidity, etc.

It is remarkable how artists, with their skills of imagining and depicting, can do so much with lines, shapes, shadows, and color, whether it's the precise representation by the photograph—or suggestion and depiction of qualities. We recognize line because it can be precise and easy to relate to experience. Shapes, on the other hand, suggest geometric figures, such as squares, rectangles, triangles, and circles. In addition, we often relate solid shapes to parts of the body, including the breast, the leg, or the head. Our interest is drawn often by contrasts of geometric and biomorphic shapes, serious to amusing, and mechanical to poetic.

VISUAL THINKING

It was Napoleon, one of the great innovators of strategy and communication, who remarked, "The sketchiest pen drawing tells me more than a long report." An effective drawing or photograph describes a plan or an event a lot quicker than a detailed report. Equally, we can relate what we perceive more efficiently than what we must read, interpret, and visualize. Four hundred years after the discovery of printing, text gave way to the photograph, which also satisfied the requirement for an exact reproduction of visual reality.

Sense impressions can take over the mind, change it, and inevitably reduce its ability to analyze logically and clearly. There is also the melting pot of news, rhetoric, and all kinds of information, written and oral, that fill our minds. Language is losing its function of expressing what the individual perceives and feels. The image does it all and there in lies the danger. Many of us have heard this, "I don't know how to explain it, but when I see it, I can identify it."

The mind's rational areas are easily bypassed as the sensory stimuli are directed to instincts and emotions. The intensity of the sensory stimuli is almost shocking, as violence in wrestling, football, boxing, and hockey indicates. In a shakeup for attention, we see blood, explosions, crashes, and agony more frequently on television and in motion pictures. We have moved away from delicacy, nuance, and refinements. Sensation is dramatized in action as it overlooks reason and judgment. Why read the book when the movie of the story full of shots and scenes will appear on television or on the motion picture screen?

Motion pictures switch images at a fast clip and envelope the mind as they are subject to cuts, pans, dissolves, closeups, etc. Unfortunately, this form of entertainment spreads an iron curtain of perceptions that are filtered and standardized by actions in frames. The eyes are guided and tamed to follow the pace set by the motion picture, with no rest between visual impressions. The eyes are hooked. To coin a term, we have become "visiholics," hungry for more images to satisfy visual appetites.

The eyes receive thousands of sensations which we must transform into something meaningful about ourselves and our environment. How can we make meanings out of our perceptions and escape from the prison of artificial images? We have a responsibility to learn visual communication through passive control and active exercise of our resources. We can learn more from practicing the skills of the artist, the painter, the photographer, and the sculptor. In the process, we can slow our sensory operations to search for truth, reality, and visual poetry that can enrich our lives.

People who are good at visualizing; i.e., whose powers of imagery are well developed, approach problems spatially, with awareness of details, textures, movement, and sensory characteristics of an event. After one learns to control images and emotions, one can develop the ability to switch emotions and images at will. If a person has never been on top of a mountain or alone in a boat surrounded by miles of ocean, that person cannot recreate those specific environments. Experience and a sharp sense of vividness and control are necessary to recall scenes and reproduce unique features.

Children possess more vivid images than adults, even though the images often seem farfetched and full of fantasy. Artists generally maintain childlike curiosity toward the external world by observing, concentrating, and imagining. Persons deprived of sensory experiences will often be troubled by spontaneous involuntary images that are mostly visual, but also kinesthetic or auditory. The important factor about imagery is the degree to which it is vivid, available, and controllable—not simply achievements that depend entirely on the ability to store or recall from memory.

Visualization training, through looking, drawing, and comparing, includes exercises in forms and colors followed by drawing from visual memory. In the process, one may ask what an observed object reminded the visualizer; what it suggested or resembled. The person who relaxes can remember more. Likewise, in observation, the ability to relax enhances the ability to visualize colors. Their associations also play a major role in sensory thinking and visualization of images.

People who share, exchange, or communicate their perceptions must make adjustments in any collaborative effort to create a work of art. In this approach they can build on a foundation of shared experiences to entertain and enlighten with originality. In television and motion pictures, we are often faced with the integration of second hand, or later material, massaged many times to become cliches. Imagery must be considered not only a province of the visual arts, but also as an element in the quality of life, experience, and society.

We can enhance our visual system and improve visual thinking as follows:

1) Check the lighting, as we do when we use a camera. Poor lighting puts the eyes at a disadvantage. Why squint?

2) Learn to draw, sketch, and diagram. This trains the visual system to be thorough and accurate. Fewer elements are taken for granted.

3) Try to translate into words what you see. This ability reinforces your critical faculty and helps remember more vividly.

4) Relate or associate visual experiences with similes, metaphors, or analogous situations.

5) Try to clarify, isolate, intensify, or bring to life what you observe by using empathy, identity, or objectivity.

6) Isolate components, analyze, and manipulate two-dimensional blocks or representations through rearrangement, substitution, addition, or elimination.

7) When visualizing a building, a scene, a layout, or an object, try to include significant details. This helps develop accurate thinking in images and train new faculties.

ART AS A LANGUAGE

The visual arts constitute a language to communicate ideas, feelings, statements, and events. They combine visual expression with colors, shapes, lines, textures, and design into messages to move, sell, or evoke response. Artists through the ages have expressed a wide range of feelings, subjects, effects; varieties of experience. The need to represent, satisfy aesthetic interests, make sensual appeals, and demonstrate pure visual delight are all within the province of the artist, painter, photographer, and sculptor.

Art does more than entertain or gratify the senses. It can make visual commentaries on social, political, and idealogical conditions. It can voice propaganda, sell products, portray institutional images, and make protests. Through satire and caricature, often through cartoons, art can ridicule with a purpose or make fun for its own sake. Satire becomes especially effective during wars or when excesses of leaders become apparent.

When products or services are promoted visually, often with symbols and short verbal statements, they must arrest attention, identify the subject clearly with the group addressed, then characterize the benefits of the item merchandised. As in most instances of commercial exploitation, the design must be arranged artistically within the limits of cost, media, and product/copy requirements. The flexibility of the message to sell is enhanced by the use of abstractions, color, and graphic arts techniques.

The many styles expressed reflect various periods through what is visual, as well as, through the overall feeling of quality of the techniques. They may be objective and accurate as representations; formal to demonstrate balance and stability; show feelings of various emotions; or, through unreal forms and representations, experiment with fantasy for effects. American art has tended to foster matter-of-fact representation, whereas the European experimenters have tended to be more decorative and inventive, with emphases on abstract qualities.

Objective realism of America developed independent of impressionism in Europe, with its fascination for light and color. Americans are less prone to distort visual reality. The relationships of size and shape, as well as management of light on various areas and shadows, are essential devices for convincing the observer of reality. Focus, perspective, and the use of colors by hue and intensity, even with some exaggeration, are also devices to recreate reality.

The Greeks developed order through proportions that produced harmony, balance, and classical concepts of beauty. The human body was exalted as a symbol of visual harmony and this model of order could be applied to architecture, music, and poetry. The idealization of the human went as far as necessary to achieve the proper and harmonious measurements. There is something stable and permanent about formal order. However, simple geometric shapes and solids can be dull—even distracting. What makes art and architecture interesting are the methods by which challenging problems are solved and the designers' uses of interrelated line, color, shape, materials, and ornament.

In methods the camera cannot record, the artist can express feelings with a unique language and style—to show excitement, love, or anger, for example. Energy for emotions comes from the observer who experiences feelings in response to the subject, the form, and treatment displayed by the work of art. Here we have communication between the art object and the viewer. Although much depends on the artist, more depends on the viewer, because something more than is there can be injected. Response can come from signals generated by a work of art, signals triggered by organization of design elements, and subject matter.

When elements recur, a rhythmic quality is evident. In poetry, music, and dance, rhythm is related to time sequences. Variations in rhythm even make many sports dramatic and absorbing. On the other hand, repeated motives in fabric patterns and wallpaper lose appeal, unless there are subtle variations, changes in emphasis, or occasional surprises. Repetition with variations in the form of a feeling or patterns of alternation, progress, or movement sustain interest to relieve the monotony of decorative art. There are few reasons why motion pictures appear dull, since the medium has inherent opportunities for rhythmic flow and sustained interest through variety, action, and surprises.

Size relationships establish visual contexts for proportion. In the absence of dimensions, size becomes relative. As we approach a large building, we change our perspective and perception of the structure. Its relationship with the surrounding buildings changes and details emerge. For example, a house or human figure in a landscape establishes proportions of an object. This makes relationships and proportions more important than actual size.

In real life, drama, dance, and naturalistic environments, we feel closer to the events and identify with the characters in the situations. Architecture, abstract art, and stylized performances reduce identity and tend to maintain a distance in our unwillingness to suspend disbelief. Having perceived a series of events, we automatically develop a condition which we use to make a decision or take action in a new or similar event. By habit, we may jump to conclusions. By training, we may withhold judgment or become indecisive. As time and experience accumulate, later perceptions of data change the accumulated evidence, and we modify our evaluations of events. We interpret differently based on changing perceptions of the event or form that immediately commands our attention.

As we perceive, we make qualitative judgments partly determined by what we see and partly on what is stimulated in the brain, which we label conveniently as previous experience. How often do we pause to examine closely—to extrapolate and interpret an event? Are we isolating ourselves by the use of autos, television, and compartmentalized occupations? Will work stations and automated services isolate us from our fellow men and women? Finally, will we become manipulated numbers with no opportunities to communicate with others or have our voices heard?

We can always ask of the work of art. What did the artist try to accomplish? How was the purpose approached and arranged?

Seascapes are good examples of the variations in approach to generate response: turbulent, romantic, mysterious, powerful, calm, or noisy. All response to observed phenomena, including works of art, vary with the object and viewer. When stated in words, the initial reaction to an event will differ with the person. Descriptive phrases may not be accurate, but they reflect what is going on in the mind of the perceiver. "It's cute." "How beautiful!" "Well done." "What is it?" "What a waste!" "This is art?" "How much?"

We can finally ask what is the value of what the artist tried to accomplish. When there's unity of form and meaning, and the title identifies the work, we have broad appeal. It can be a persuasive message designed to stimulate action, as demonstrated by advertising displays. Gradually we can unravel the artist's universe by examining the various styles of emotion, treatments of subjects, symbols, and other devices designed to attract, evoke, disturb, or provoke thought. Like background music in offices and industry, paintings and other artistic forms are used to create restful, secure, and interesting atmospheres to offset the hectic, insecure, and dull.

The uses of fantasy are most often exploited in motion pictures, which have the reinforcing effects of trick photography, montages, music, sound, and various types of shots. The worlds of fantasy, illusion, and the provocative on the canvas exploit the language of art in terms of color, distortions, illusions, and decorative touches. The visual creations of man, the artist, represent manipulations of natural forms, abstractions, and scientific discoveries as commentaries of the future and the consequences of our conduct on earth.

THE POWER OF PHOTOS AND PICTURES

A picture is not necessarily worth a thousand words. Some pictures are worth less; some more. Some pictures have powerful and immediate impact; others have little to portray that is significant in content or form. Regardless of headlines and important statements, we are apt to recall flashes of photographic images more often. For example, we are often struck by the emotions of witnesses or victims in a scene frozen on the occasion by the photographer on the spot. A photograph of squalor, terror, or destruction by nature can make a point with a lot more impact than several hundred words of an editorial.

The power of language, which prevailed through Greek, Roman, and Elizabethan times has been relegated by the power of photographs and motion pictures. Can anyone describe a rose in words better than a photograph can? The eye captures, in one blink time, the rose in its whole form, beauty, and vivid color; whereas, words must be understood, interpreted, and converted to a visual image in the brain. In addition, unless a photograph is doctored, it represents a visual event that captures truth at the moment the shutter was snapped. Words cannot alter photographs of horrors perpetrated in Nazi concentration camps during World War II. People can use words to lie and distort truth, but pictures tell the story as it happened, and do it with impact.

Although photojournalists are more concerned with content and studio photographers deal with aesthetics, the elements are most often fused in photos of enduring value. On a reporting assignment, a photographer can capture abstract qualities while recording a major news event for immediate consumption or posterity. The studio photographer concentrates on form, texture, arrangements, lighting, and colors. However, content is not ignored in the treatment. There may be a point at which a photograph ceases to be a visual document and appears like an abstraction for an effect or a pattern with little significance.

Some photographers perceive a print while taking a picture; i.e., see what's on paper as accurately as what they perceive on the rangefinder. Other photographers visualize and see the print at the same time before exposing the film. Some few take many pictures, each of which provides a cue to the end product or photograph. The latter experiment as they capture items on film in a postvisualization scheme.

Newspapers give us headlines and occasional photographs. Magazines give us summaries and photographs to spice up the breezy prose. When one considers the power of moving images with voice, music, and sound thrown in, almost a recreation of reality, you wonder how long it will be before we do everything with control consoles and visual displays, all electronic. It's not difficult to visualize a home with three screens for audio-visual uses: a multichannel television set which includes the projection of videotapes; a personal computer with display and printer for typing letters, reports, and stories; and, a telephone system complete with videoscreen and answering service. We are relying more on audio-visual systems for transacting routine affairs, for entertainment, and commercial operations.

In the competition for the viewers' attention, so much seems to go on and so much is published in newspapers and magazines. We are told photojournalism has an obligation to bring us events of the day and week. The real purpose is to hold our attention long enough to pass on a series of commercial sales pitches in print. This is done by making promises and keeping the conflicts going until our insatiable curiosity is satisfied, or just saying, "Don't go, away. We'll be right back after a few messages."

The results of political strife and violent demonstrations in unstable regimes are etched in the faces of those captured by daring photographers. Much of what's printed, however, is gossip, or trivia in visual form. Some photographs are sold as "news" on the theory and practice of the "public's right to know." When spread across the country, these pictures of "events" have impact on the consciousness of the public. Some photographs have more impact than the television camera that captures moving scenes for viewing on a receiver.

Pictures in journalism have communication as a prime function. In many situations, photographs alone cannot tell the whole story. They need verbal reinforcement or support. Often the photograph is the first step in the collaborative efforts of editors, layout artists, and production personnel. Genuine efforts for natural and spontaneous reporting give rise to credibility. We believe what we read; more so, if we can see the event in a picture which we trust as a visual document bearing the stamp: implied truth. When truth is communicated, we can make judgments and decisions that can improve our lives and suggest changes in proper directions.

IMAGES IN MOTION

Motion pictures and television, when developed for dramatic works, display moving images as illustrations or imitations of reality and portray life in time sequences. In structure and perception of reality, they are intimately related to the real space-time perception of the viewers. The cinematographer controls segments of reality through shot sequences, slow motion, trick photography, and special effects. Through the editing process, the film producer controls the viewers' perception of action and life. The editor takes the raw film, selects, and rearranges the film, which has been shot under the director's control.

The camera can focus on details as no human eye can. Although the viewer cannot touch the image to sense texture and temperature, the sensual qualities of images can be accented and draw attention. Through continuity sequence and orchestration of images, the film maker manages the viewer's experience. Time is manipulated and it results in controlling mental activity. The response generated comes from impact, movement, music, sound, and a variety of filmic devices, such as dissolves, cuts, and montages. The live performance of a theater cannot be duplicated, nor can the actor on stage match the powerful and sophisticated techniques the motion picture screen can portray. The basic element is the frame. The visually represented screen, demands action, movement, variety, and a complete understanding of the various techniques available to the medium.

Television comes closer to immediacy and reality because of its ability to present live events as they are happening. There is some processing and editing, but nothing like what goes on in film production, especially the time span between shooting and screening. Whereas films are planned for large groups, television is intended for mass viewing audience and exploitation by advertisers.

The dynamic nature of the collaborative media, film and television, require huge staffs to present programs that combine visual, dramatic, and literary elements. The specialized personnel are funded by advertisers and many are at the mercy of rating systems in a game of numbers. It's generally a question of how many are watching and which show or program to satisfy the requirements of the sponsors.

How many readers of a magazine or a newspaper, net paid circulation, becomes a question of how many viewers of a given channel at a specified time slot. Often the hours of the day and days of the week determine the type of program. Program managers, producers, and directors participate in the selection and manipulation of images supported with sound, speech, and music to generate enjoyment, excitement, laughter, and information to an audience of tremendous size and various tastes.

Background music in film and television perform major functions: support or reinforce various emotional and dramatic meanings; establish moods and anticipate crises; and, make transitions or segues. Some institutions, such as law, church, and governments, use visual backgrounds and symbols to support establishments and emphasize authority. Communist governments are notorious for exploiting masses, using visual propaganda to enhance leftist views, censoring communication in various forms, and further entrenching established doctrines.

An analytical approach to criticism of film and television may appear cold and mechanical. However, breaking something down and offering reasons makes it easier to interpret relevant meanings. By asking questions, we can arrive at plausible explanations. We can try to discover and reveal the author's or artist's purpose, as well as evaluate how well the job was done in terms of quality. Generally, differences in interpretation or lack of agreement suggest that the artist did not succeed in what he or she tried to achieve. At the same time, it is possible for the critic to inject ideas that represent the person's own attitude, ideas, or experience.

There is nothing wrong with comparing and rating visual works, in the process of exercising judgment, as long as we stick with the same class of products. One cannot compare a portrait painted in oils with a photograph; nor a movie with a television drama. In the latter case, the audiences and the production techniques widely differ. If we seek excellence to advance civilization, we must favor originality, relevance, and quality, depending on the medium and function. We can also include such features, as performance, utility, and impact. The observer must select language and usage that adheres to the context of the subject being evaluated.

In this dynamic age of materials, processes, electronics, satellites, and visual communication, we can't turn backwards. We must free our minds of fundamentalist doctrines and learn to control our lives from mechanizations that will surely paralyze our critical and creative faculties. Freedom to visualize, imagine, interpret, create, and test are some of the many possibilities available to the creative observer, an essential aspect of creative communication. We can always remind ourselves of the scientists and engineers who literally and figuratively make observations, doing much of it through selection, measurement, and test.

Reading
Creatively

Reading creatively is a process by which the reader fuels the imagination, generates ideas, and relates experiences to those of the author. This is done while reading and could include a view to corroborate, contradict, or come up with other ideas. As a practical approach, the creative reader will read for ideas and think as he or she proceeds by sentences (statements) and paragraphs (coherent groups of thoughts). If the material is treated as a stream that flows with the writer, whose thoughts and messages make sense to the point of stimulating new ideas, the reader enjoys an enriching experience.

Unfortunately, many people consider reading as a simple perusal of information in print. In the creative or highest sense, reading, like listening, involves the skills used in learning and discovery. These include keen observation, an active and useful memory, the power of imagination, and the ability to think in several ways. Thinking, especially during reading, can involve analysis, reflection, logic, and the ability to construct a dynamic image of a concept or develop an analogy in abstract or concrete terms.

A creative person interrelates facts and concepts or theories to come up with a coherent structure. Variety of activities that sustain each other characterize the creative thinker, who may also engage in or pursue metaphors. Processes are viewed as implied similes; a search for analogies or similarities. We have a "whole" or comprehensive thinking person with a guiding purpose. Energies are directed towards a goal or a group of activities, which can be picked up and dropped, to make a fresh discovery. As efforts are directed towards many interests, the creative person often comes up with new problems to solve.

A book is an extension of the real world, especially the world that has been experienced by others and the results of observation. Writers try to organize those areas with which they have become familiar through contact, research, and help from others. A book cannot answer all the questions readers may raise. However, the reader who analyzes the questions and whatever answers are found in a book, can refer to other books on the same or similar subjects. You may not learn to play piano or golf by reading a book about these complex skills, but you can develop and approach to take for lessons, learning, and practice.

For learning, a book does not take the place of a teacher. Rather it supplements the work of the teacher, who has the responsibility to answer many questions, recommend a list of other books for study, and guide the progress of a student. Education is an expensive service for the user and one cannot afford formal training throughout a lifetime. Likewise, reading does not automatically make the reader a creative individual. Creativity is the outgrowth of motivation, varied interests directed towards goals, and general fluency in a major area of interest. It's a matter of discipline, depth, exposure, curiosity, and experience.

To learn anything, one must be able to read, a skill that can be acquired through training, motivation, and practice. Not enough children supplement reading skills acquired in school with a reading program at home. Too much television, outdoor activities, and games serve to develop handicapped readers. Those who expect to attend schools of higher learning, pursue professional careers, or perform routine responsibilities of adults, must not only learn how to read with some speed, but also understand clearly what they read.

Failures in reading, like those of writing, can be attributed to the rapid growth of visual media (mostly television and video games), reduced academic standards, and lack of discipline in elementary schools. These are often coupled with general disinterest by parents regarding reading skills. America can flex its muscles, talk about freedom, free enterprise, and economic self-sufficiency, but the real fact of life faces us: an illiterate society cannot compete with nations that are strict in educational requirements and practices. Many of the European countries, including Germany and Russia, rank high in literacy. This can also be said of Japan and China.

There was a time when novels were read in anticipation of a motion picture release that featured favorite actors and actresses in leading roles. More recently, some people will read novels after the production of motion pictures. Unfortunately, most people are not motivated to read, unless stimulated by gossip, newspaper headlines, or controversy. Among the many weak links in our society is the fact that at least 10 percent of the population has not learned to read. Most people consider reading dull when they compare the activity with watching television or attending sporting events.

The problems with reading, as with problems involving other communication skills, is that we realize the need for training and practice when it's almost too late. The comments sound like this, "I should have worked harder. We didn't have any homework." Reading skills have a direct relationship with literacy. If you can't read well, you are a potential loser. If you can't read rapidly, you can lose time and trail the pacesetters. If you can read 600 words a minute or better and understand the essence of what you read, you can go to the head of your class. Thomas Babington Macaulay, the English author and statesman, is a prime example of a world class reader. Not only could he read over 600 words a minute, but he could also remember the essence of what he read at a glance. His comprehension was phenomenal.

The craze over physical fitness appears to permeate our society to the extent that the newspapers promote athletes almost exclusively. Baseball, football, and basketball players, as well as hockey and tennis get the most publicity, whereas communication skills and education take the back seat or luggage compartment. Bombardment by the visual media, with stress on action in melodramas, coupled with the obsession about murder mysteries, horror stories, crashes, explosions, and other visual mayhem give the impression that there's little else in life to concern us. Graphic images, designed to satisfy the lust for sadistic, and the thirst for violence represent destructive substitutes for significant messages and satisfying experience. One wonders whatever happened to the emphasis on literature, meanings of life, and other aspects of language used to communicate intelligence, emotion, and rhetoric.

USE OF THE EYES

Eyes are too valuable a resource to burn out staring at lighted screens. When it comes to reading, many people develop a mental block with not enough motivation to overcome the artificial obstacle. Studies have shown that the unpracticed or illiterate reader will struggle at a rate of about 100 words per minute. The average reader reads at a rate less than 250 words per minute. The highly capable reader can plug along at 500 to 600 words.

Fortunately, improved reading ability and speed is a matter of concentrated training over a period of six to eight weeks. This training consists of spending the time to read more material at an increasing rate each day; reading for main ideas and comprehension; learning to skim; and, concentrating on building a larger vocabulary. If we accept the fact that we are weak or deficient in reading skills, then we can either take a course in speed reading or follow a program of self-improvement in reading skills. Like any worthwhile program, the program requires a plan with a schedule and motivation to achieve a series of goals, like milestones.

A first step in the program could be an examination of the eyes. Even though the brain actually forms the image and translates the words into thoughts, the eyes, as sensors, transmit the symbolic messages. Like a camera, they focus on objects by adjusting the focal length depending on the distance. The farther away the object, the shorter the focal length. When reading, the eyes adjust to the proximity of the material by lengthening the focus. There must also be adequate light to produce a clear image of the text. The retina, an extension of the optic nerve, is like the film in a camera. The eyeball automatically adjusts itself so that the image is focused sharply on the retina. If one is near-sighted (myopic), glasses are prescribed to enable the eyes to focus on distant objects. Far-sighted persons need lenses that adjust the eyes for reading and other close work.

Glasses adjust for defective vision by correcting the refractive error, which gradually changes. Since the lenses remain constant, the eye muscles get weaker through lack of use. Consequently, glasses are not the complete answer, since they must be changed as refractive errors change. Even though vision is 90% mental, corrections must be made through the eyes. A visit to an optometrist is an important investment. It's possible that exercise and massage will be recommended.

Tired eyes, irritated by smog, smoke, dust, and bright objects can't stay in good shape for reading. Eyes that are relaxed, free of refractive errors caused by stress, can produce proper vision. Stress relates to improper nerve impulses with the brain as their source. Defective vision can cause one to squint in efforts to produce sharpness and clarity. Television and driving carried to excess, as well as emotional strain, directly affect the performance of the eyes. The fact that few Chinese wear glasses is attributed to special eye massage exercise, according to a recent article in the National Enquirer. According to the report, based on researchers in the United States, twice a day the Chinese stop whatever they are doing to massage four areas:

1) Inside corners of the eyebrows;

2) Bridge of the nose;

3) Around the eyebrows; and,

4) Both sides of the nose, away from the nostrils.

When we want food, our body instinctively produces the drive coupled with secretions in our stomach to satisfy our hunger. The same is true of sex, thirst, rest, etc. When we want to improve our abilities to read, write, speak, etc., it takes self-motivation to generate the energy for the work required to achieve our objectives. Anticipating the benefits of improved reading skills, such as problem solving, learning, and enjoyment provides the emotional energy to accomplish the necessary reading tasks.

APPROACHES TO READING

After having the eyes checked, one can set up a plan for reading on a daily basis. This should allow time for required reading, as well as voluntary, or reading by choice. Your plan should be determined by needs, priorities, and available time. The schedule should be flexible enough to allow for other needs, changes, and approaches that respond to the purposes selected, such as ideas, information, enjoyment, and self-improvement.

Reading for ideas is a process of thinking as you proceed, by sentences and paragraphs. The reader thinks in terms of a stream that flows with the writer's thoughts and messages. The reader may miss a word or two, but rather tries to think with the author, even anticipate the author's train of thoughts, as presented.

Skimming or scanning is generally a rapid perusal of lines, paragraphs, or pages in the search for specific facts or items the reader can use. Once you have made up your mind what you're looking for, the object of your scan, if there, will stand out and make its presence noticed. Scanning saves time for the reader who is interested in research, information, statistics, etc., that relate to specific subjects.

Critical reading can be reserved for the examination of reviews, propaganda, or persuasive messages. In the process the reader looks for loaded words, faulty logic, and inaccuracies. Is the reader confused by irrelevant facts or led away from the principal issue? Is the reader aware of superlatives, exaggerated rhetoric, or false metaphors? Is the motion picture a "colossal success?" Do we need more defense dollars because the Russian submarines are "crawling like ants near our beaches?" Are things good or bad; true or false; and, black or white?

In all approaches to reading, one should avoid verbalizing; i.e., reading with movements of lips and tongue or in a subdued form of reading aloud. This slows down reading speed and reduces concentration on the ideas. Continue reading silently unless you're bored, lose motivation, and feel as if you're not getting anywhere. Skim through nonfiction by trying to identify main ideas which are usually supported by details and with examples. Skim through fiction by finding out who you're rooting for, what the conflict or struggle is about, and how the characters are developed towards the crisis and climax.

Before starting on daily reading practice, ensure adequate lighting. Control reading environment for freedom from noise and distractions. Get comfortable. Even if it's research, make an interesting project out of the effort. Browse through as many books as possible, skim, and look for useful material. From generalities and abstractions, locate specific subjects to correlate and corroborate.

Read critically in terms of the value of subject matter researched and question the author's ability to communicate clearly and effectively. You may find outdated or inferior books languishing on shelves of libraries. Look for newer books on the same subject and reading material recommended by librarians. Occasionally, you may want to check the reference shelves. Reading leads to learning by remembrances of facts and their relationships; through evaluation and association. In some way, try to associate what you read with what you know. As you memorize and condense information, you may even want to read aloud important passages to retain essentials.

BUILDING A VOCABULARY

Coupled with a reading program is the important task of building a vocabulary. A large and useful vocabulary results from broad interests and reading a variety of material. It boils down to a matter of exposure and being alert for new words as you read, as well as getting familiar with their meanings in context. A dictionary nearby is essential, but it's not necessary to look up every word one runs across. Some words are best learned by noting how they are used in their connotation and context.

In building a vocabulary, how a word is used properly is the most important lesson one can learn. When running into a new word, let it register in your mind a few seconds. Then, from the context in which the word is used, try to understand its meaning. If you must look up a word in a dictionary, try to understand all other possible meanings, as shown by examples. Then, come back and review the meaning of the word, as used in the context intended by the author. To reinforce the learning of new words, make a list of those you looked up and keep it with the reading material or book.

Good readers develop larger vocabularies by studying word builders and looking up words for usage. The important point about enlarging a vocabulary is to try to interpret meanings in the context of usage in the reading material. The improvement of vocabulary helps increase reading speed for various purposes: ideas, facts, and skimming. Some people go so far as maintaining a notebook which lists words and uses recently learned. The completion of crossword puzzles, multiple choice vocabulary tests, and the practice of writing sentences that include words recently learned contribute greatly to success in building a large and useful vocabulary.

Your brain has the capacity to put together the usage you run across in your reading and comprehension with the words you learn as a separate effort in vocabulary study. In your reading material, every so often, you'll run into words you learned individually on some previous occasion. When you decide to increase your ability to read with greater speed, your progress will be greater because of your comprehension supported by your larger vocabulary and better understanding of words—especially when used properly.

READING SPEED AND COMPREHENSION

Increases in speed and comprehension during reading are basically the outcome of setting goals and practice. The goals consist of increases in speed. A sprinter who wants to run better and faster runs against a stop watch and gradually conditions the body and mind for improved performance through practice. Practice reading any material and set a time for about 30 minutes a day, five or six days a week. Start with something easy to read and read as fast as possible, without regard to comprehension at first. Make a note of how many words per minute and continue the practice for about six weeks. This can total thirty sessions at a half hour per session, or about 15 hours of actual reading to increase speed.

Comprehension will follow with increased ability if the speed reading program is supplemented with vocabulary study. The effort to increase reading speed must be sustained to the point that if a session is missed, two sessions are used to make it up. Basically, reading speed is increased by increasing the eye span, increasing column speed, or vertical reading, and word recognition. The reader must remain alert during the practice of rapid reading and try to understand without slowing down or going back over the material.

The rapid reader first is training the eyes to move fast, and from the practice of going from word to word and sounding them in the mind, to an approach that concentrates absorbing information at a faster pace. Phrases and sentences replace the word-to-word movement. Some people use fingers to race across the lines and others use an index card to move down the page, line by line. As one moves across with the finger or down with the card, the reader is forced to read faster. It's important to read faster than your rate of comprehension. It's this approach to practice that helps increase your reading speed.

When reading to increase speed and comprehension, select material that increases your knowledge in various fields. Vary your reading material with respect to ideas, information, and critical evaluation. Base selections for subject value, for messages that represent something to say by an authority, and for material that provides pleasure in the form of humor, adventure, and fiction. Newspapers and magazines help us keep up with what goes on in the world. Besides information and pleasure, books can be considered vocabulary builders, especially history, biography, poetry, drama, and novels. "Summary of Tips for Increasing Reading Speed and Comprehension" suggest what to practice and what to avoid.

It is the sustained, positive, and uphill effort that will achieve the most productive results. A pianist can't progress by playing simple tunes. It takes motivation and effort working on increasingly difficult pieces. Learning consists of continuing efforts to accept new challenges to achieve mastery of various skills.

Accept with enthusiasm and determination the challenges to your ability to read faster and comprehend more through practice and exposure to a variety of reading materials. Test your ability to concentrate, to pay attention to what is before you, and to switch to the immediate problems at hand. Make a selection and treat what you're reading as the most important material to comprehend at the moment.

To summarize, you can double your reading speed through practice on material that's easy to read and progressively more difficult. First you sacrifice comprehension for speed. Keep a record of words per minute. Try to increase your reading speed each time you sit down with new material; expand your recognition span by covering more words as your eyes move across a line. In this way you train your eyes to move faster and cover more words. Trust your brain to do its job of grasping content or comprehension.

Summary of Tips for Increasing
Reading Speed and Comprehension

	PRACTICE	AVOID
SPEED	Try to read faster each time on new material, using fingers to lead eyes across lines or a card to move down a line at a time.	Reading at the same speed, rereading the same material posing no challenge or difficulty.
TEST	Test your reading performance in wpm each time, and keep a notebook to keep a record of progress.	Sloppy habits and guessing at progress. Worry about comprehension at this point.
SPAN	Increase perception by widening recognition span, shortening fixation pauses, and reducing regression (going back over words). Use peripheral vision to widen span from syllables and words to phrases and short sentences.	Short recognition span, long fixations, and regression; going back over same lines. Focusing on individual words and details, or parts of a whole.
MAIN	Look for main points. Concentrate for quicker understanding of main points. Think as you read.	Meandering from word to word or sentence to sentence to dwell on unessentials.
PACE	Move forward at a relatively constant pace to maintain a reading rate, a little faster each time.	Regressing or going back over some material and varying rate significantly.
RETAIN	After you read something, try to write about the gist of the selection.	Tendency to dismiss something difficult or what you don't understand completely.
WORDS	As a separate project, build your vocabulary. Note new words, look up meanings and pronunciations. Use word in a sentence in proper context for sense. Note variations of meanings in synonyms.	Avoid looking up words you don't understand or without noting relationship or association with what you read.
READ	Read selected material for accomplishment and enjoyment, for fast interpretation of ideas in quick fixations. Increase variety and selection of books, articles, and important documents.	Dull material, old articles, or books and articles that don't appear to have some bearing on current events, technology, or significance.

The Use
of Language

Language is the vehicle of communication, whereas usage is the manner in which language is used. To maintain a consistency in discussing language and usage, we must define them. We talk about levels of usage, such as formal, basic, and low. The latter can range from faulty usage and illiterate speech to slang and profanity. Formal usage, as the adjective suggests, applies in important situations, such as a State of the Union message, the Constitution, and professional journals. We are primarily concerned with basic, informal, or standard usage, as used in conversation, correspondence, and various forms of mass communication.

Basic usage is appropriate for most of the needs of normal communication in which the meaning must be clear. In basic usage, speech requires accuracy, clarity, and correct pronunciation. Writing, on the other hand, requires organization, precision with words, variety, and correct spelling. In a careless environment, where standards of usage are ignored, everybody can suffer the consequences: poor communication. It's everybody's business to avoid faulty usage and to concentrate on maintaining the standards of quality in American English.

The American language consists of the rich English language with infusions of French, Spanish, German, Dutch, and American Indian. English, in turn, has its roots in Celtic, Anglo Saxon, Greek, and Latin. The resulting blend of American English has a flexibility and variety borne of various cultures. Like the ancient Greeks, we have become a collection of various peoples unified by a common language. We have modified British usage to American idioms and practices. We have developed a beautiful language with synonyms, nuances, and a variety of words to choose and arrange to express meaning.

At the same time, we suffer from sloppy habits, reflected by misuses of words, loose jargon, poor grammar, and other forms of language pollution. The practice of good usage is a matter of joint responsibility: first, by those who communicate from higher sources; and second, by those who receive the messages and recognize the need to improve the quality of usage. The former group can be identified as the pace setters, such as educators, elected officials, newsprint editors, television commentators, and professionals in positions of leadership. The latter consist of students, children, the general public, and special audiences.

A discussion of language can be more specific by concentrating on words, symbols used in a system to express thoughts in speech and writing. We think of words as being abstract or concrete, literal or figurative, slanted or loaded. Language develops through custom; good speech depends on the habits of the users of a particular language. Dialects, for example, spring from regional uses based on geography and customs. We also have ingrained habits, called idioms of the language.

Idiomatic expressions make a lot of sense and reflect some of the unique characteristics of English. Some idiomatic expressions may not sound logical or correct to a foreigner, and also may not be easy to explain. We are not bound by the strict rules that characterize some of the European languages. In addition, the English language seems to have many exceptions. We say, "the sun rises." Actually, the sun appears on the eastern horizon as the earth turns on its axis.

Spoken words preceded the written and have the advantage of making it possible for the speaker to adjust, explain, and respond to the needs of the listener. When you include action and gestures that can accompany speech, the result is a powerful medium of expression that is difficult to match. We can communicate directly, immediately, and allow for feedback. Since television and radio have a powerful influence on our language, politicians, newscasters, and commentators, among others, have some responsibility for maintaining a high level of quality in basic usage.

Mannerisms, such as "you know?" are heard often. The "ah's" and the "and-ah's" are also frequent. It is difficult to accept the use of the indefinite article "an," when used before "historic."

Many announcers and newscasters keep saying "an historic occasion." One would not say "an hit," because the silent "h" is preceded by "an." (an hour) The aspirate (or exhaling) "h" is preceded by "a." If we can correct this improper use of the indefinite article, it will be truly a historic occasion.

Newspapers and magazines are also guilty of embarrassing mistakes in grammar, spelling, and usage. Copy editors should be experts, more qualified in the skills of writing and revising than the reporters. What should readers think of a newspaper which prints thousands of copies before spotting differences in "flare" and "flair," "pore" and "pour," the use "whom's" for "whose?" The careless attitude towards usage is partly the outgrowth of lax educational institutions and national acceptance of reduced standards for our language.

When standards for usage have been reduced in our educational system, the victims are the graduates. Courses in English, composition, speech communication, etc., should be required for those who pursue a degree in any field. There is no reason why majors in engineering should not be able to write well. Like physical fitness, defense, and dieting, high standards in English and usage should be an obsession for the American people. The benefits from high standards cannot fail to trickle down to non-participants in our educational system and receivers of messages through mass communications media.

WRITING EFFECTIVELY AND UNMISTAKABLY

A few years ago, Newsweek Magazine ran a long article entitled, "Why Johnny Can't Write." The article was full of quotes from universities, organizations, and individuals, including Marshall McLuhan, Karl Shapiro, and Jacques Barzun. Mario Pei, the philologist and author of many books on the subject, was also quoted with a reference to schools controlled by "a school preaching that one form of language is as good as another; that at the age of five, anyone who is not deaf or idiotic has gained a full mastery of language; that we must not try to correct or improve language, but must leave it alone; that the only language activity worthy of the name is speech on the colloquial, slangy, even illiterate plane; that writing is a secondary, unimportant activity." Both the attitudes of our society and the neglect in our schools are some of the major reasons why Johnny can't write.

The skills related to writing are directly involved with our other communication skills: thinking, reading, listening, and speaking. If you want to write something effective, or clear and precise, you should have it formulated in your mind before putting it on paper. Your must think about the words you use, their arrangement, and exactly what you want to get across to the readers. If you know what you're writing about; i.e., you have ample knowledge of the subject, you are in a position to make it clear to others. However, you must also know enough about good usage, structure, and style to make your message readable.

Your thought processes rely on your memory. If you don't remember the right words, because you haven't used them enough, it becomes more difficult to express your ideas adequately for the intended reader. If you haven't read much, you rely primarily on what you've heard or experienced. If you have limited yourself to listening to rock and amplified rhythms, you can't depend on the little that your brain has stored in the form of words and expressions. If you can't speak well enough to be understood by others, don't expect to write material that makes good sense to your readers.

We are products of our parents, culture, associations with others, education, and how we use our spare time. The educational establishment has become proficient at developing short answer tests that are easy to score with sensors or scanners. On the other hand, we have neglected writing exercises and essay-type homework, which takes time to correct. Since most classrooms are crowded—a means of saving money and shortchanging the American taxpayer for our educational system—it's too much for a teacher to handle. When a teacher has 40 students instead of 20, the class becomes unwieldy and forces overwork; lapses and neglect in assignments.

We increase our allotments for bureaucracies, foreign aid, price supports, and tax loopholes, but reduce our aid to the system of free education required by law for public schools. Our attitudes, lack of support, and reduced standards for the English language have put us behind many nations of the world. We are even embarrassed, on occasion, by citizens of other countries who have better command of English than many of our native born.

There are thousands of instances of immigrants with a poor start managed to overcome difficulties with English. Using free time and extra effort, these citizens developed a facility with our idioms and the ability to use an adequate vocabulary with precision. The questionable quality of English used on some television programs, and especially low grade cartoons, contribute to lower standards for the nation. Most of the programs are subsidized by commercial sponsors, primarily concerned with merchandising products.

It's disappointing to listen to a star football or basketball player, interviewed on television, speak in a language that detracts from our respect for his fine athletic skills. From one's speech one can infer similar lack of skill in writing. According to Scott Thompson, head of the National Association of Secondary School Principals, "Our biggest problem is lack of reading and writing being done by students."

Jenee Gossard, an English and writing teacher at Culver City High School, recently stated, "Writing is particularly important, because it forces students to think. It is a way of discovering what you think." The emphasis on grammar and punctuation are not relatively as important as being put on the spot to think about what to say, formulating the message by selecting the words, and arranging them in the proper context for the intended meaning.

Now that we are familiar with the problem and convinced that we all have something to gain by accepting some responsibility for improving our own ability to write, how can we get started?

1) Build a reference library for writing that includes a standard dictionary, a text on usage, an English handbook (for grammar), a book of synonyms or a thesaurus, a book on writing, and a style manual. Your local library can help you select these books, some of which you can buy as an investment in self-improvement.

2) Plan to write at least a page a day on a variety of subjects. You can write in long hand or dictate to a tape recorder, but in the long run, you're better off learning how to type. Eventually, everything written will end up in some form of typing or printouts. Use different approaches and topics in your writing, such as:

   a) Narratives of personal experiences;

   b) Explanations of devices and how they operate;

   c) Descriptions of places and things;

   d) Descriptions of people, including dialogue;

   e) Essays on political and social views; and,

   f) Critical reviews of movies, plays, television, and concerts.

3) Try writing a letter or memo to a person about a subject that has been on your mind for some time. Get something off your chest with a letter to the editor of your local newspaper.

4) If you're proud of something you've written, get a friend or acquaintance to read it and tell you what he or she thinks about your effort.

5) To develop or stimulate ideas about things to write, read books, newspapers, and magazines. Include vocabulary study by looking up words for use in different contexts.

Practice writing just as you would practice a musical instrument, tennis, or golf. It's up to you to make, what appears boring, interesting by accepting a challenge to tackle a worthwhile subject. Learn what's going on in the world around you and make repeated attempts to discover your latent abilities. Some time later, you may have a real or required writing assignment. Then, you'll find the writing easier to manipulate and know how to go about it for positive results.

We should not consider writing as a simple process of putting words on paper. We should rather think in terms of releasing the products of thoughts and ideas expressed with a purpose, and possessing the quality of readability for the benefit of readers. An effective writer has useful, enlightening, and often entertaining thoughts that are generated by manipulating and arranging words. The effective writer must have knowledge of the subject treated, the ability to handle an approach to presenting it, and the skill with words to make the arrangements interesting to the readers.

Good writing involves something to say and the ability to know how to say it. How to say it takes knowledge, judgment, and experience with the tools of the profession: words, the symbols of language. Although creative writing refers primarily to fiction, poetry, drama, and other forms of literature to entertain, most forms of writing should be approached as products of creative effort.

Since writing is one-way communication, whatever is expressed, discussed, or illustrated, must be complete and unmistakable for the reader, subject, and purpose. There's no opportunity for feedback from the reader. If the readers' questions have not been anticipated or answered, only direct contact with the author can resolve the possible dilemma.

The reader obtains ideas, images, and impressions from the author. If the author has not been able to put across the information and ideas effectively, doubts and differences between the author and readers can emerge. One of the reasons writing is difficult is the burden of trying to sustain interest and satisfy readers' needs. To be an effective writer takes a strong desire to express oneself in writing, a command of the English language, and a plan or approach to a specific task that compels you to do your best. These are outlined, as follows:

1) Knowledge of the subject, necessary for all writing. The subject must be clear to you before you can attempt to make it clear for the potential readers.

2) Readership—Some concept of who the readers will be for the product of your writing efforts. By knowing your readers in advance, you can establish rapport and an appropriate level of usage.

3) Purpose—Knowing why you are writing on the subject and what you expect to accomplish. Is it primarily information, entertainment, excitement, enlightenment, persuasion, or explanation. A combination of these is often more effective.

4) Structure—The material must be organized in some recognizable format, which can be functional, chrono-logical, spatial, logical, journalistic, or dramatic. The structure is usually suggested by the subject, purpose, and format appropriate for the medium or form.

5) Diction—Knowledge of words and expressions, especially those that are unique and related to the subject. The idiomatic expressions and usage must be appropriate to the level of the intended readers.

6) Technique—This concerns the ability to explain, describe, illustrate, narrate, dramatize, convince, and use rhetorical devices.

7) Construct—This involves the ability to formulate sentences, develop paragraphs, and generally express original ideas with sense and style for the benefit of the readers. If you can express yourself with clarity, style, and precision, you can anticipate readability. This quality encompasses all others and reflects genuine interest by the writer to satisfy the needs of the readers interested in a specific subject.

8) Usage—Include grammar, syntax, and punctuation.

To summarize, effective writing is a matter of being aware of the reader and motivated to produce a fine product of the mind interested in communicating with other minds for important and useful messages.

READERS' NEEDS AND RESEARCH

The reader has needs and interests to satisfy. These can range from curiosity, solutions to problems, entertainment, and identification with people in situations, to special information. We can satisfy these needs by what we say and how we say it. A reader responds in terms of judgments about significance, something original, a current subject, or a new concept. If the writing is effective, one can expect the reader to understand, mentally associate, remember, and approve what is presented. In many respects, the writer can anticipate response by the reader.

To mean anything to the reader, the writer must bring new information into association with things the reader already knows. Familiarity with environments, as indicated by the writing, adds meaning to the words and material presented to the reader. Much depends on what engages the readers' minds at the time. Significant details must relate in some way to the images, convictions, and feelings that dwell in the readers at that moment. For this reason, the writer must find out all possible data about the interests of specific readers, such as their attitudes towards the subject, prejudices, and particular things they may want to know. Familiarity with readers' points of view on a subject enables the writer to prepare persuasive or effective responses to their needs.

During reading, new information is related to experience, implications are weighed, similarities and differences noted, and mental decisions are made. Information and concepts will be modified, as needed by the readers. Responses can be positive, negative, or indifferent, depending on the quality of the writing and the beliefs or backgrounds of the readers. If the author has something important to say, good response can be anticipated. Eventually, this response will reach the writer in a variety of ways.

In nonfiction, the reader seeks information about specified topics to satisfy interests fulfill professional requirements, and for enlightenment. The author satisfies readers' needs at levels determined by an unwritten agreement. This agreement sets the stage for the purpose, meaning, level of diction, and response expected of the readers.

In fiction or drama, the author provides readers with a satisfying emotional experience. To accomplish a purpose, the author invents situations based on life and provides characters with identity involved in conflicts that are resolved after a crisis and a climax. Here, the writer succeeds in involving the readers by generating humor, excitement, mental stimulation, or other forms of entertainment.

Research refers to any organized search into a subject to collect facts and ideas. Research may involve putting together material based on surveys, tests, experience, and selected efforts published by others. A definite purpose in mind helps plan adequate research on a subject. With respect to the subject and its treatment, mental preparation may have preceded actual research for the writing tasks.

After thinking about and organizing the material compiled, it's important to establish relationships based on the data and to develop a plan for the approach to the actual writing. The order you generate out of the real and apparent confusion depends on the purpose, the potential readers, and the data itself. At this point, one can start thinking about the outline or the topical structure of the project. A logical approach improves the quality of the message, provides the necessary discipline, and helps make efforts for writing more efficient.

Approaches to research vary. One can start by asking questions. What is the subject? Define it. What is your purpose? How are you going to present your facts and ideas effectively? The substance of what we express must come partly from what we have observed, heard, and read; partly from the related material we have collected on the subject. The more varied, interesting, and original the collective experience and research data, the better stockpile of material we have for selecting, manipulating, and organizing.

However, we must add to this effort an original approach and effective language for communicating our facts and ideas in writing. We must not lose sight of exactly how we want to express our thoughts and feelings on the subject. At the same time, we must keep in mind the needs of the readers and the responses we expect of them.

GENERAL WRITING APPROACH

The writer's general tasks include concentrating on the subject matter, selecting material through research, and arranging it in a structure which the reader can easily follow. The principles to apply can be summarized as an effort that reflects unity, coherence, and emphasis. For unity, the writing must concentrate on a single purpose and related subject matter. In this regard, the topic sentence reduces the concentrated impression on the readers' minds.

The writer makes unity apparent through selection, by limiting the area the subject matter covers and by selecting the necessary details that support the subject. The unity of purpose must meet the readers' level of awareness and present a clear idea of what the writer is trying to achieve. To help make the statement of purpose interesting, the writer can tell a story or illustrate a point with an analogy.

The writing is coherent when its arrangement reflects an orderly pattern and the elements within the pattern are linked effectively. The sequence of words and sentences entering the readers' minds help make sense when logical patterns are perceived in the arrangement or flow of words, sentence formations, and paragraph structure. Our minds perceive patterns in sets. We group familiar and unfamiliar data into patterns already established in our minds.

We pattern verbal data in order of time, space, cause, and effect, part and whole, definition, explanation, illustration, analogy, general to particular, etc. In addition, we use forms of transition to connect basic patterns in a longer plan of coherence. When the writing is coherent (or logical), we can concentrate on the ideas or message the author presents without distraction.

Through emphasis, we indicate what we consider important. We must help the readers know which ideas are more important and those of lesser importance. We can emphasize by placing things in the beginning or end. Anything proportionally large in size, volume, intensity, excitement, or duration, becomes emphasized. A repeated impression emphasizes it in the readers' minds. By relative placement of important ideas, by giving more space, time and attention to ideas, and by repeating them, we achieve emphasis.

Each paragraph should express a central idea and represent a pattern of development with supporting sentences related to the topic sentence. The substance of a sentence group can be summarized in the opening sentence. The topic sentence expresses or implies the development of a point. The topic sentence provides a key to patterns of sentence groups, with unity, coherence, and emphasis in mind. The writer must build paragraphs that have depth, promise, and satisfaction for the readers. You can be subtle, but you must be certain. Well-formed and effective sentences help sustain interest.

For a general writing approach,

1) Collect all available facts, statistics, and material on the subject. Then check the data for accuracy, authority and completeness.

2) Plan the writing for the needs of the readers and the requirements of the medium. Consider the readers' interests, intelligence, and backgrounds. Consider specific stimuli and appeals to evoke the intended response.

3) Outline the overall structure and note the emphasis, treatment, specific aims, and qualities you want to achieve. Jot down in capitals the main ideas and organize them with a purpose.

4) Get to the point and purpose immediately when you start writing. Write as if you are talking to a group of friends. If you think you've said exactly what you mean, read it aloud to yourself and listen to how it sounds. Is it clear and readable?

5) Before you approve the final version, read it carefully. If possible, get some help in editing and criticism about what you tried to write and how well you achieved your purpose. It is generally better to take longer to do the writing job right, than rush it through and worry about questions your readers may raise.

6) Ask the following questions:

   a) Is the message appropriate to the readers?

   b) Did you achieve the intended purpose for the medium?

   c) Did you stick to the subject and treat it objectively?

   d) Did you express yourself naturally and with clarity?

   e) Is your work original, enlightening, or entertaining?

You have prepared a first draft, based on an outline which you may have revised, as you transformed your thoughts into sentences and paragraphs. Your are now ready to edit your own work. This involves deletion, rearranging, and rewriting, unless you want to sit back and admire the results of your writing efforts as if they were exactly what you expected: outstanding. Incidentally, few can claim that expertise. Except for a few professionals, effective writing does not survive a first draft without revisions, deletions, or rewrites.

It takes guts and humility to change, but in most cases, it must be done. You are not committing murder, but sacrifices in the cause of justice: effective and readable writing. As a writer you'll take a broader view of your environment and a more objective view of your work. Just as one cannot be reluctant to do some surgery in the interest of saving a life, the writer should not be averse to cut, change, redo, and rearrange in the interest of saving a manuscript.

When you investigate thoroughly, you'll find that there are many ways and devices for expressing thoughts.

Since simplicity is the product of thought, your editing must reflect improvement in clarity and precision of meaning. In your goal to achieve a smooth or engaging style for the subject and purpose, use common sense, an ear for sentence sounds, and judgments. If you are knowledgeable about and considerate of the readers, you'll maintain good standards of language and usage. As an editing procedure, you may try to:

1) Quickly examine the first draft and check the content for purpose and how well this was achieved for the intended readers.

2) Check for accuracy of statements and effective presentation; make the changes necessary for improvement.

3) Examine the effect of changes when you read the draft carefully the second time.

4) Check for style and writing mechanics; make corrections as necessary.

5) If necessary, retype the material and save the original copy for future reference.

6) Recheck for accuracy of information before approving release of manuscript for publication or final typing.

STYLE AND READABILITY

Style is the effective use of language to achieve something, such as writing, with clarity and brevity. Style also refers to the qualities that endow speech or writing with charm or power. If one can add grace and sustain interest, so much the better. To express and convey emotion with meaning to others, and to evoke responses, requires the force and quality of style. Inspiration, character, the ability to think clearly, and to communicate effectively on a subject are the foundations of style. Good style is often found in simple language that comes from the heart of the writer.

When one attempts to inform and move others, the influence of personality intrudes. When emotions are involved, one must not only know how to address others, but also how to do it persuasively. The personality of the persuader has as much to do with acceptance as the intrinsic merits of the message. Through style you gain rapport with your readers; and, this helps make the handling of a subject acceptable and interesting.

If your readers question your attitude or approach, neither syntax nor carefully selected arguments will persuade them. If you bore others because of your arbitrary handling of a topic, or use a pompous style, your followers, the readers, will desert you. On the other hand, if one lacks the talent or possesses a limited vocabulary to convey important messages, no goodness of character will generate an attractive style.

Like personality, style is also a matter of taste, convention, idiomatic usage, and manner of treating topics of current interest. The writer can improve style and arouse response from readers by infusing the writing with the following attributes:

a) Clarity, so that meaning is unmistakable;

b) Brevity, courtesy and respect for the readers' time;

c) Variety, in length, mood, feeling, or tone; contrasts to relieve monotony;

d) Simplicity, freedom from pretense; Anglo-Saxon words help;

e) Urbanity, a true form of politeness to set the reader at ease;

f) Vividness, using figures of speech, imagery, originality, and color to bring writing to life;

g) Sincerity, as you write about what you know to be true and of value to others; and,

h) Restraint, the ability to hold back or understate; reserved or avoiding extravagance.

Readability can be defined as writing that communicates ideas exactly and with ease for the benefit of the readers. Some of the factors that affect readability are subject matter, readers, and treatment of purpose. When the subject matter includes complex analyses and scientific terms beyond the comprehension of the readers, readability suffers. If the readers are not motivated and the subject matter does not fall within their field of experience, the level of readability is significantly reduced.

Textbooks in schools are published for comprehension based on requirements of students in various grades. College students will often use several books to report on a topic, because they have a level of comprehension covering a broader base of readability. On the other hand, treatment of a subject, style, or level of writing covers many principles, techniques, and elements, which place control of readability in the hands of the writer. Some of the suggested tools can be applied to various writing situations.

VERBAL ELEMENTS:

- Size of words (proportion of long and short words)
- Derivation of words (Anglo-Saxon, Greek, or Latin)
- Use of words (usage, as modifiers, idiom, and context)
- Level of abstraction (general to specific)
- Familiarity (a function of reader, subject, and treatment)
- Active verbs and prime or root words (as against derivatives)
- Nouns and proper nouns (rather than pronouns)

STRUCTURAL PRINCIPLES:

- Length and types of sentences (simple, complex, and compound)
- Arrangement (order of subject, modifiers, verbs, and objects)
- Continuity (movement, logic, sequence, and detail)
- Punctuation (for clarity, emphasis, and functional pauses)
- Placement (key words, phrases, clauses, transitional phrases)
- Paragraphs (development, number of sentences, and organization)
- Transitions (continuity, connectives, and changes in subject)

TECHNIQUES OF STYLE:

- Forms (exposition, description, narration, dramatic, and persuasion)
- Dramatization (use of quotations, illustrations, analogies)
- Style (clarity, brevity, simplicity, vividness, sincerity, urbanity, vitality, variety, and restraint)
- Principles (unity, coherence, emphasis, consistency, and originality)

PHYSICAL FACTORS:

- Appearance (page layout, type size, type face, white space, line length)
- Headings (marking, size, frequency, and numbering)

SENSORY WORDS AND IMAGERY

Among the uses of language by writers and speakers are words that evoke sensory images and enhance the presentation of the persuasive force of a message. Sensory words relate to the senses of touch, taste, smell, sound, and sight. They are primarily used to assist the reader or audience in recreating the sensations experienced by the writer or speaker. Sensory words add color and life to a message as reflected in the user's ability to observe with discrimination and to translate details about experiences into concrete terms. The choice of sensory words can determine the feeling of touch, the kind of taste, the type of smell, the quality of sound, and the effect of sight, an experience perceived as a sensation.

Imagery, or figures of speech, refers to rhetorical devices that use words in a manner that enhance the force or quality of a message; highlight a description or an explanation. A figure of speech can give words meanings beyond their literal interpretations, so that the message conveyed is endowed with original and vivid qualities. Purposes of rhetorical devices can be accomplished by making comparisons, contrasts, exaggerations, or understatements. Although there are names for specific figures of speech, in essence they attempt to like one thing to another, whether it's done to bring words to life in poetry, prose, or speech.

Among the principal figures of speech often used are the simile, the analogy, the metaphor, the allusion, and personification.

Lesser used, but also effective figures, like comparisons, are the hyperbole, the synechdoche, and metonymy. The most widely used and most effective rhetorical device is the metaphor. Unfortunately, the metaphor, with its variations, is often used in political speeches to influence and occasionally deceive audiences.

Simile	a direct comparison that uses the term "like" or "as." (Swims like a fish) (Fast as a horse)
Analogy	an extended comparison in which one activity is explained by means of another. A familiar or simpler example can be used to describe a more complex operation. (A word processor is like a computer, which has a keyboard, a display, a processor that manipulates data, a memory, and an output device, or printer.)
Metaphor	A comparison that implies how two things are alike and directing attention to it with originality and appropriateness. Metaphors are often extended to increase their effect. Overused metaphors, after a while, become known as cliches. (America needs the armor of defense to protect the honor of its freedom.)
Allusion	A reference to a historical or literary event or person, with a similarity to the subject discussed. An allusion should be familiar to the reader or audience addressed. (Drunken drivers not only crowd the jails, but also keep Forest Lawn busy.)
Personification	The endowment of inanimate objects, animals, and abstractions with the qualities and abilities of human beings. (The flames devoured the house in minutes.)

Hyperbole
: An exaggeration, that is occasionally excessive, to emphasize or to make a point for an effect or response. (The cease-fire lasted three hours, a record.)

Synechdoche
: A reference to the part for the whole, or the whole for the part. (We now have a roof over our heads.)

Metonymy
: A substitution of one thing for another with which it is associated. (The administration is rattling sabers.)

Irony
: Saying one thing, but meaning its opposite. (We should reward him for his contributions to public service by asking for his resignation.)

Creative Communication in Sales

How does one communicate creatively for sales? The answer to this question can be found by identifying important characteristics of professional salespersons and their requirements for success. These include:

a. Training in sales and product; company and services

b. Possess intelligence and common sense

c. Motivated for hard work

d. Self-confident and enthusiastic

e. Proficient in communication skills

f. Persuade others with conviction

g. Sincere and empathetic

h. Solve sales problems creatively

i. Identify decision element and put it to work

j. Maintain attitude of service and provide it

The creative salesperson builds sales and good will with original ideas. As a creative thinker, the salesperson constantly comes up with ideas to improve and expand sales. He or she is not satisfied by putting in a full day's work or just taking orders. Rather, the creative salesperson uses an outgoing personality, communication skills, and constructive ideas to build images in the mind of the buyers to make an impact. At the same time he inspires others around them, exercising qualities of leadership. He thinks positively, constructively, and as optimist of what is possible, carries out his or her convictions in action with enthusiasm.

The salespersons who contact as many prospects possible in a working day will often find themselves in an office just when a potential customer has some questions that seek answers. Whether it's being on the road or on the telephone, the salesperson must be organized to remind the customers that his company is always around and ready to serve.

Large companies offer good sales positions after extensive screening and background checks of applicants. Putting a salesperson on the road is costly and the potential for productivity must be relatively predictable. The marketing of some products and services requires expensive training and investment. There is usually an agreement between the company and salesperson to ensure guarantees for mutual protection.

A professional sales job requires a mind clear of worries or reservations about the position, product, and company. If one's heart is not in the company or product, confidence and enthusiasm are hard to come by. Without motivation to achieve, communications skills won't be of much help. It can be like an engine without fuel or a body without energy.

Knowledge of what you're selling and the authority to make decisions regarding the selling of a product, enables you to communicate with confidence. Pride in the company, product, and service generates enthusiasm naturally. Motivation by a desire to attain goals energizes the salesperson to battle competition, knock down barriers of indifference, and overcome objections from prospects. A professional salesperson sells himself or herself, the company, and the product lines.

THE SALES PROCESS

Selling is the life blood of the overall marketing program of a company. Marketing includes advertising, sales promotion, distribution, public relations, and management. For some products and services, the marketing program is broad and complex, involving training, catalogs, research, trade shows, etc. Consequently, selling must be a coordinated effort and the sales representative becomes an integral member of the marketing team.

Everybody in business involving sales, whether a contractor, an attorney, a physician, or a teacher must adhere to the basic rule: to deliver reliable products and/or services that help establish a good reputation. Good news often gets around to bring in good business in the form of referrals. It stands to reason that one must be healthy, confident, and knowledgeable to gain the respect of a customer. In addition, one must be able to speak clearly, listen carefully, and show real interest in all customers. The list of *Attributes for Sales Personnel* not only applies to salespersons, but also to all who deal with the public in operating, professional, and management levels.

The selling process, which can also be considered as an interview for the benefit of a prospective customer, is outlined as a six-step process.

1. PREPARATION—Involves checking leads, making preliminary contact, collecting data on prospects, and setting appointments.

2. RAPPORT—Establish a common ground for getting better acquainted with the prospective customer on contact at the first meeting.

3. QUALIFY—Find out if the prospect can afford the product and/or service, has a need, or should be persuaded to buy. Generate interest in the company, product, and services to determine there's a reason to go ahead with the sales presentation. Otherwise, curtail the interview with a request for a referral or for a future interview.

4. PRESENT—Use an informal presentation that covers the major features of the product to attract interest. Avoid a formal or memorized talk that proceeds without interruption. It is better to leave out details and some features to concentrate on the main ones that have direct bearing on the needs of the prospect, even if you must repeat. Ask questions as you move along. Pause for the answers after you ask the questions. You must make points you can anticipate will make a logical and emotional impact on the prospective buyer. Remind yourself that you are not pushing a sale, but rather, creating a specific buying situation.

ATTRIBUTES FOR SALES PERSONNEL

1. HEALTH—Conditioned with interest in nutrition and exercise.

2. APPEARANCE—Neat, well-dressed, and comfortable, without flash.

3. MOTIVATED—To serve and achieve, rather than exploit.

4. POSITIVE ATTITUDE—Optimistic for good results.

5. CONFIDENT—Self-confidence that helps inspire confidence in others.

6. ENTHUSIASTIC—Enjoys work and contacts with people.

7. ORGANIZED—Plans, schedules, and keeps appointments on time.

8. ABILITY—Skilled in profession and communication.

9. KNOWLEDGE—Familiar with company, products, and services.

10. WORK—Willing to devote time and effort required for tasks.

11. PERSISTENT—Determined to make all prospects customers.

12. PERSUASIVE—Can modify attitudes and convince people.

13. CUSTOMER CONSCIOUS—Aware, perceptive, and understanding.

14. RELAXED—Relaxed and able to make others feel at ease.

15. GOOD SPEAKER—Uses simple language and sounds credible.

16. GOOD LISTENER—Reinforces understanding through feedback.

17. EMPATHY—Able to evaluate from other person's point of view.

18. RESPONSIBLE—Accepts reasonable burdens and assignments.

19. SENSE OF NOWNESS—Accomplishes tasks as soon as possible.

20. IMAGINATIVE—Builds images for others and self.

21. LEADERSHIP—Sense of teamwork; pitches in for togetherness.

22. CREATIVE—Solves problems and comes up with ideas.

23. CHEERFUL—Smiles with a genuine sense of well-being.

24. CONSIDERATE—Exercises patience and avoids interrupting.

25. TOLERANT—Sincerely treats every prospect as a potential customer.

5. ANSWER OBJECTIONS—Which are the usual mental responses and emotional reactions to sales presentations or to the product itself. Don't brush aside any objection or look surprised. Accept the objection and respond to it as if it's a legitimate request for reassurance. Response to objections often help close the sale.

6. CLOSE—Try to close at any time during the presentation or interview. There are many types of closes, however, not all must be tried in the same situation. The proper type of close is the one that follows the objection overcome and fits the prospect's situation at the moment. Through experience, you'll learn to use the closing method that suits you and the type of customer you are interviewing. After asking a closing question, such as, "Do you like it?" or "How many would you like?" shut up. Don't answer the question you asked. Let the customer answer. Listed separately are Hints for Empathy.

THE SALES STORY OR PRESENTATION

You must help the prospect feel that the contemplated decision to buy is sound, voluntary, and in line with the person's best interests. Skill in making the presentation, to help the buyer realize his or her needs, depends on knowing your merchandise and capacity to meet the buyer's needs to satisfaction, as based on preliminary analysis. You might start off with an idea that will help the buyer's health, comfort, or business.

One must prepare, rehearse, and present the story with skill for a natural flow of facts, features, questions, and answers. This includes listening carefully. Show what you have with a demonstration that is personalized and incorporates, if possible, stimulations of the buyer's sense of sound, smell, sight, touch, and feel. As an image builder, you paint something pleasing for the buyer and suggest favorable results, savings, benefits, and examples taken from other customers.

The creative salesperson presents specific and constructive appeals directed to the mind of the buyer, essentially through the eyes and ears. There's no need to stress the obvious or visible; but rather, talk about savings in time, money; benefits in comfort, morale, or prestige. You can close with a plan for help or a specific suggestion that has proven useful in a similar situation. Stress advantages and benefits that promise to bear fruit in the future.

The sales story may be memorized, like a speech, but flexible enough to stop at any point to close the sale or answer an objection. You must know your story completely and include variations planned for the particular prospect. You can't tell the same story to different prospects and you must allow for participation. The sales story is an informal talk, like an interview, in which the salesperson encourages participation, but controls the demonstration.

If you're in the business of selling to the same customers, such as repeat orders, the sales story concentrates on service, new data, and provisions for changes in the story when confronted by a different buyer or new management. If you sell intangibles, such as insurance or investments, the sales story for services should be adapted to the specific needs and desires of the individual customers, depending on their income level. Product-oriented sales stories will generally feature price, quality, reliability, maintainability, and satisfactions to requirements.

HINTS FOR EMPATHY

1. Keep appointments promptly—never late—phone if tied up—plan everything.

2. Dress neatly—appearance (tie and jacket—always fresh).

3. Use quality language—simple, colloquial, sparkling words.

4. Mind your posture—straight and quiet—confidence and vigor.

5. Make use of pleasant facial expressions—reflect attitudes and meanings.

6. Listen well—share customer's point of view—never interrupt or delay answer.

7. Avoid nervous mannerisms—recurrent involuntary movements—negative habits.

8. Don't be loud or show braggadocio—use low confident voice.

9. Address others in a friendly but not overly familiar way—be dignified.

10. Show deference—thoughtful of ego and comfort of others—ask and be kind.

11. Agree and make your point—("May I suggest?" . . . "You may be right" . . .).

12. Be polite to secretaries and receptionists—express thanks—win them over.

13. Don't smoke unless invited to do so . . . to help create a bond.

14. Don't drink on the job; sparingly off the job, if at all.

15. Be careful of the stories you tell—free of bad taste.

16. Be a good conversationalist—learn to draw out others—give and take. Be free of fears of ignorance or originality—be interested.

17. Be at home in polite society—outgoing and thoughtful of the welfare of others. Take initiative without making a big project out of it.

18. Watch your table manners—as diner, host, tipper, talker.

19. Remember telephone courtesy too.

20. Watch your temper—a sign of defeat and loss of control.

21. Acknowledge communications promptly.

22. Keep that promise—as inviolate as a legal contract.

23. Say "thank you." Feel the urge to express gratitude and express it.

24. Say "good-by." Leave graciously—tuned to courtesy at all times—adaptable to social situations with tact, the sense of proportion; and humor, the sense of disproportion— in the spirit of the golden rule.

To pinpoint appeals or motives, the salesperson can ask questions, such as why there's interest in the product, service, or company. The story can be based on a plan or outline that concentrates on *reasons*.

A. Reasons why the customer needs or wants the product.

B. Reasons why the customer should buy your product or service (include demonstration).

C. Reasons why customer should buy it *now*.

At any time during the presentation, the customer may give you a buy signal. ("I'll take it." or "How much?") Close the sale at this point by switching to the sales contract or agreement.

There are three important points to remember:

1) Treat your participant in the sales presentation as a customer, rather than as a buyer. This brings you closer to the sale through assumptions and anticipation.

2) Think in terms of needs and wants; features and advantages of your product; and, why not now (while product is available; before prices go up; when waiting time for delivery can be reduced).

3) As you tell your story, ask questions to get participation and/or agreement.

The sales story can be outlined as follows:

A. Introduction (you, company, and product backgrounds)

B. (1) Statements about customer's needs and reasons why for each (motives or appeals, such as prestige, income, comfort, safety, convenience, health, future, etc.) to buy the type of product your company sells.

(2) Statements about your product and company, with explanations of the reasons for each, including demonstration that emphasizes each reason—features of the product and service.

(3) Statements about buying it *now* and reasons that back up statements. Include stories about how some missed the boat; waited too long; prices went up, etc.

C. Answers to objections and the use of closes.

Creative selling takes practice, which means work in front of customers. If a few sales are missed because of oversight or errors, don't despair. If you call back to find out what you did wrong, chalk it up to experience. Remind yourself that salespersons are made: mostly through self-motivation, organized effort, experience, and backup in terms of training, territory, and rewards for the results demonstrated. Review the Creative Sales Presentation, a list of suggestions.

CREATIVE SALES PRESENTATION

a. Prospect must instinctively feel that his contemplated decision to buy is sound, voluntary, and in line with his own best interests.

b. Thorough knowledge of the product and service your selling

c. Analysis of the buyer and his needs

d. Ability to prepare a personalized visual aid to use in the presentation

e. Skill in making the presentation—to help the buyer realize his needs

f. Capacity to meet the buyer's needs to his satisfaction

g. Prepare, rehearse, and deliver with consummate skill for natural flow

h. Offer an idea that will help buyer's business

i. Stimulate buyer's auditory, visual, tactile, and kinesthetic senses

j. Show and tell, using personalized visuals

k. Organize presentation around seven aspects of buyer's mental stream:
    1. Getting the buyer's attention
    2. Building the buyer's interest
    3. Arousing the buyer's desire to buy
    4. Supporting and adding to the buyer's confidence
    5. Helping the buyer to decision and action
    6. Providing the buyer with satisfaction
    7. Raising the buyer's respect for the salesman and his company

l. Enthusiasm needs first an idea which takes the imagination by storm; and second, a definite intelligible plan for carrying that idea into practice.

m. Image builder deftly paints a pleasant image for the buyer and suggests favorable business developments, dynamic suggestions of improvements, specific savings, benefits, examples... constructive specific appeals to the mind of the buyer...a professional, tangible visual aid...vistas of happy employees, fewer delays, prestige for the company...closing strong with a specific suggestion, a plan for help...advantages and better future.

ANSWERING OBJECTIONS

Objections indicate that the customer wants reassurance. They reflect emotional reactions or uncertainty. The customer has a self-image or what is expected of others. You respond to this image through courtesy and respect. You try to understand based on feedback of attitude, messages, and physical indications. You try not to project your set of values over the customer's, but work within the guidelines set through empathy and feedback.

The confident and reassuring salesperson, especially if enthusiasm is evoked, brings out equivalent or similar responses. If you're tense or fearful of losing the sale, you may evoke a similar feeling from the customer. Any indication of indecision or insincerity can produce a reaction of doubt or mistrust. You speak to a customer's self-image, interests, and concerns.

If you sense a stall or doubt, be reassuring and share your self-confidence with the customer. The customer may not be sure about exactly what is wanted or expected, a form of indecision. Avoid putting the customer on the defensive and show how your product enhances his or her self-interest. Appeal to wants or needs, the benefits that can result, and specific emotions that relate to the product, such as freedom from worry or fear, pride, herd instinct, and respect borne out of practical decisions.

When the customer weighs alternatives, show you're listening attentively or patiently. Sort out the real objections, whether they are emotional or logical. Check inflections in the voice gestures, or expressions for feedback. Swing the balance in your favor. Agree, when possible and try to understand. Listen carefully to each objection and encourage full expression. To lower resistance, first make a softening statement. You can even convert an objection to a question. For example:

"I can't afford it." (Could it be a matter of working it in your budget?)

"I want to sit on it." (Don't you see the advantage of starting on it now?)

"I can't make the decision." (Is it the company? Is it money?)

"I'd like to think about it." ("What is it you want to think about? Now is the time to ask questions. If you have any doubts, I can answer them while we're together. We may not have an opportunity like this. The sooner we go into escrow, the better we are. Is it financing? Delivery can become a problem if we waste time thinking about it., etc.")

Listen to the objections, one at a time. There shouldn't be many, unless there's something wrong with the product. Don't jump to any conclusions about what the customer is going to say. Negative thoughts from previous failures may make you tense or nervous. Relax and expand on a major objection to make a sale of it.

"If it weren't for this, you'd buy it, wouldn't you?" If the customer says "Yes," he or she has bought. If one exception is pinpointed, "I like it except for this," then the sale has been made. You answer the objection and reassure at the same time. The close with the final objection can be as follows:

1. Listen carefully to the objection;
2. Sell the customer the objection (I agree with you.);
3. Confirm the objection as a question;
4. Answer the objection and confirm the answer;
5. Use the objection and answer to close the sale.

Remember that the customer also gets feedback—from you. He or she will appreciate empathy or seeing it from the buyer's point of view. A show of impatience or condescension, even a patronizing attitude, will cancel the positive points you've made. Answer questions in terms of customer's needs with firmness, respect, and enthusiasm. Return to the presentation or demonstration and ask a closing question, such as "How much down can you put?" or "How soon must you have delivery?"

CLOSING THE SALE

Closing is the key to selling. If you've noticed in ads for salespersons, the demand is generally for good closers. The sales process is one big close. As soon as a closing situation develops, one must move in for the close using the best technique. The best closers are able to close the sale on the average of every fifth attempt. What you say or ask, and how you say or ask are essential. In closing situations, the words used and the meanings interpreted by the customers are critical.

By way of summary, ten examples of closing approaches are discussed. Some of them are used as they relate to objections which have become overcome. Answering an objection is one thing, but overcoming an objection means that you have made a breakthrough and are ready for the close. Much about closing depends on the product, prospect, and situation. An important point to remember is: whenever you ask a closing question, stop and listen. Remind yourself of the warning signal at railroad crossings: STOP—LOOK—LISTEN.

1. BASIC—This is otherwise known as the application or order blank close. It may even involve a credit form. Insurance agents, auto dealers, and investment salespersons use it often. They get out the order blank and start asking questions, such as last name, first, address, zip code, etc. Since the answers to this closing approach confirm the decision to buy, you keep writing. It's like shutting up after you ask a question. If there's no reaction to your basic close, keep writing until you have the contract signed.

2. ALTERNATIVE — Sears does it all the time. They ask, "cash or charge?" "Can you put 10 or 20 percent down?" "Which do you prefer? The coppertone or gold?" The answer to this closing question implies the product has been bought. You can help in this decision by offering a discount, such as, "If you pay this off in 90 days, we'll write off or cancel the interest charges. Do you want to pay it off in 90 days or finance it?"

3. PUPPY DOG—This is an approach in which the item is delivered on loan or for a low rental fee, charging for delivery and then billing for the full amount later. The principle behind this approach is that once the customer starts using the product (appliance, television set, mower, etc., the item sells itself). This is a good approach if there are no credit problems or delivery happens to be in a good neighborhood, rather than a motel.

4. BENJAMIN FRANKLIN—This is also known as the balance sheet on which good reasons are listed on the left column and the negatives on the right. If the customer is indecisive and can't offer an object, tell the story about the wise man who felt the same way, when confronted with a choice, and wanted to do what was right. Start off the sheet with the two columns and a line down the center. Head the left column with a "YES" and the right with a "NO." Give the sheet to the customer, hand over the pen, and start off by asking for a list of all the reasons to buy in the left column, under YES. Now switch to the NO column and ask for reasons the buyer can think against the purchase. The result is a convincing demonstration of a close, especially if you ask the customer to read you the many reasons under YES and the few under NO.

5. SUMMARY—This approach is used when you have a stall with no reason given. A little pressure is applied by asking questions through a process of elimination until you or the customer can pinpoint the reason. "Is it the integrity of my company?" "Do you doubt my integrity?" "Is there something about the product that troubles you?" If each question is answered with a "No," you then ask whether it's the price. The "Noes" eliminated the objections, whereas the "Yeses" revealed or admitted the hidden objections. Once you elicit the real objection, respond to it, and then write the order.

6. EXAMPLE—This is also called the "similar situation" in which you tell the customer how a problem was solved and the successful turn of events followed. In contrast, you may decide to tell the customer about the consequence of a wrong decision. For example, you can tell the story about what happened when the head of the family passed away, leaving children, a bunch of bills, and nobody to turn to. This approach can be used for certain products or intangibles, which have hidden benefits, and highlight the results of the right decision one of your customers made.

7. MAJOR-MINOR—This is also called the secondary question. In this approach you ask a major question and then follow it with a minor one before the major question is answered. You can also follow a major alternative question with a minor alternative one. "Can you pay 20 percent down and finance the rest? Do you want delivery as soon as possible or can you wait?" When the minor decision is made (or question answered), the major decision (or question) is considered made (or answered).

8. FEATURE-IF—If the customer asks for certain features, such as "Will it do this for me?" You respond by asking, "Do you want it if it does?" If the question is about the taxes on a house, "Are the taxes low?" Your answer could be, "Do you want it if they are?" As you respond with a question, which is answered in the affirmative, confirm the sale.

9. THINK ABOUT—If the customer wants to think it over, this is an indication that either there's no real interest or that this is an excuse to withhold the real objection. "Just to help me get it clear, what phase or part of this program (or product) do you want to think about." If you get an answer that sounds like an objection, respond to it. If you get no answer, use the summary question, asking what specific item it is. When "think it over" is reduced to a specific objection, YOU can handle it.

10. CLOSING QUESTION—This is like a close initiated by the customer and is revealed when you are asked, "Can I buy it with 10 percent down?" "Can I get it in gold?" "What is your interest rate?" You answer with a question, "Do you want it if I can get it for you in gold?" "The interest rate is no higher than the prevailing percentage with most lenders, etc." This approach is similar to the Feature-If close.

When you give up trying to close a sale, you leave with the customer an impression that you have doubts about your company, your product, and your services. The customer translates this into loss of confidence in you. This critical milestone in a sales presentation can make or break a sale. It often happens during the emotionally charged and dynamic sales situation. Try to relax and help the customer relax.

The salesman must exude confidence and warmth to answer all objections logically and then pursue the close as if it is a necessary formality. You can ask questions, such as: When would you like to start? (Don't answer the question for the customer. Be patient and wait for the customer to tell you.) Which system do you prefer? Can you afford to spend three dollars a day to save $2,000 a year and free your head from worries, because you know that everything is under control?

If the resistance is real, ask questions, such as: Is there something in particular you don't like about the service? Does the service sound too expensive? Do you want professional quality? If the resistance is artificial, then you can laugh it off as an attempt by the customer to be funny. You say thanks, but who has time to fool around with games, when real bucks, time, and quality are being sacrificed? Put on a show. Respect sincerity and make light of insincerity. Raise the customer up to a level of excellence and achievement, recognition and productivity, freedom, and success. Treat the customer as if he or she is about to become a member of an exclusive club.

Very few sales are closed on the first or second attempt. Keep trying to close five, six, or even ten times until one of the closing attempts succeeds with a bull's eye hit, the customer submits through sheer exhaustion, through persistence, determination, and unrelenting pressure. Make the customer feel glad you talked him into it. After all, at that moment you are his best friend, ready to do favors, answer questions, and deliver quality at a fair price. Try to end on an upbeat note.

THE CREATIVE SALESPERSON

The creative salesperson is a skilled communicator, sensitive to the problems and needs of his customers. Looking for better ways to do things, he or she manipulates a wide variety of thoughts. With breadth of vision and flexibility, the creative salesperson can easily drop one line of thought and pick up another. Relationships between seemingly remote things are observed and brought together in meaningful ways.

Alert to problems and situations that have previously escaped attention, these salespersons tend to have a variety of thoughts on any given subject. As they move around with contacts and exposure, they relate their work problems and apply ideas they have encountered elsewhere. They use initiative to set their minds on ideas. They get fun from work and rewards by earning them. They are relaxed and have a sense of humor. Their enthusiasms makes them aggressive in a positive manner. They become more than ordinary companions.

The self-confidence of creative salespersons is rarely shaken because they stick to high standards of performance and develop endurance. They are not afraid of looking at the customer steadily in the eyes with a strong sense of warmth and will. Their persuasive talents combine logic, imagery, emotional appeals, and the force of their personalities. They know their products, the benefits, and the advantages of the products and services they represent.

The creative salespersons present features from the customers' point of interests and combine them skillfully, offering reasons to buy. The customers' attention is attracted and held, the buyers' motives are made use of, and selling points are phrased with conviction in language the buyers understand. The salesperson asks questions with candor, not as if the customer is on the witness stand in court. As the buyer speaks, the salesperson listens analytically for meanings beyond the words and for their intent. As an adaptable and flexible representative, the creative salesperson helps prospects become customers and buyers to sell themselves on the features demonstrated.

The low pressure approach of the creative salesperson is rooted in integrity, based on representing the customer's interests and well-being. The customers' rights to accept or reject are accepted. Failure is equally accepted cheerfully with successes. Knowing they are not perfect, these necessary representatives for the distribution of goods and services don't stop trying to do their best. Like champions, they make their own lucky streaks. Their story or presentation is organized around seven aspects of the buyers' mental stream:

1) Getting their attention;

2) Building their interest;

3) Arousing their desire to buy;

4) Supporting and adding to their confidence;

5) Helping them make decisions and take actions;

6) Providing them with satisfaction; and,

7) Raising their respect for salespersons and the companies they represent.

The 25 Characteristics for Creative Salesmen are listed.

CHARACTERISTICS OF CREATIVE SALESMEN

1. Sensitive to problems and needs.
2. Look for better ways of doing things.
3. Usually get a wide variety of thoughts.
4. Can easily drop one line of thought and pick up another.
5. Have breadth of vision.
6. See relationships between seemingly remote things and brings them together in meaningful ways.
7. Notice problems and situations that have previously escaped attention.
8. Tend to have many alternate thoughts on any given subject.
9. Relate to their work problem ideas that they have encountered elsewhere.
10. Use initiative to set their minds on creative ideas or lines and get fun from work and many rewards from doing so.
11. Relaxed with a sense of humor and good fun to keep relaxed.
12. Good losers who bounce back with ambition and enthusiasm for work.
13. Aggressive leaders are priceless—not just good fellows.
14. Games are won in the field where results and scores are posted.
15. Champions make their own luck...no substitute for work, the price of success.
16. Deep-down interests surmount discouragement, gives them the basis of self-confidence and even enthusiasm.
17. Tension holds them to high standards of performance and they build self confidence by increasing and perfecting techniques.
18. Look customers steadily in the eye with a will that finds a way.
19. To persuade, they combine logic, imagery, emotional appeal, and the impact of personality...knows all the benefits of their products and advantages of the service they sell.

20. Present features from the customer's point of interest... skillfully offering reasons for buying...attract and hold customer's attention, making knowledgeable use of one or more buyer motives, phrasing selling points in language of conviction and enthusiasm. Ask questions.
21. Believe in what you say, sincerely...frank, honest, genuine.
22. Adopt a winning attitude...Your territory is like your own company.
23. Analyze buyer's temperament and listen beyond his words—for their intent.
24. Are adaptable, likable, and flexible...help customers buy and help buyers sell.
25. Low pressure selling is rooted in integrity, representing customer's interest and welfare...aimed at customer's dignity...right to accept or reject.

THE ATTITUDE OF SERVICE

In most types of selling, including tangibles and intangibles, the name of the game is service. Service begins with the salesperson's attitude and it means many things, especially doing useful things for and being responsive to the customer. The list is long and may consist of one or more of the following, depending on the product or intangible:

A favor requested
A "rush" order
Being available when needed
Responding to requests for quotations
Troubleshooting
Consulting
Solving problems
Coming up with useful ideas
Eliminating fears about making decisions
Bolstering confidence in product
Building trust
Making promises that can be kept
Putting customer interests above their own
Developing loyalty
Remembering the good things of the past as future pathways

If your customers don't feel important, one can't expect them to make important decisions that affect the livelihoods of salespersons. Performance by salespersons results from dedication, the ability to compete against tough opposition, and unremitting efforts to stay in shape through training in sales, knowledge about products, and new ideas that represent features, such as price, reliability, performance, and utility.

Sales takes contact, organization, control, effort, service, and a sense of humor, that lubricating agent in human relations. By developing a sales personality, with special goals in mind, salespersons easily overcome disappointments, while they find time for customers who appreciate those who tend to their needs. There's a lot to be said about checking a salesperson's batting average or exceeding goals so that the achievements more than reflect the rewards received.

Creative Communication in Business

Creative communication in business covers a broad spectrum of activities that begin with organization and include management, marketing, and operations. Experience as an executive with a company of management and merchandising consultants, specifically for department stores, provided valuable background in this area. Twice a year we staged fashion clinics (shows) and twice a year, executive clinics to forecast trends in the business. We dealt primarily with department store managers, buyers, and other merchandising personnel. Our services included advertising and sales promotion.

The consultants did well because everybody worked hard, communicated directly, and were motivated with promises of rewards. The attitudes were generally positive and profits were realized primarily by solving the problems of the clients, who were usually victims of ignorance and neglect. Their problems generally reflected lack of adequate communication among those in management, merchandising, and sales promotion. Deficiencies in the exchange of information exacted a heavy toll in the competitive arena of retail sales.

For some companies, things happen through reaction to events external to the organization, through acquisition and changes in the world of commerce that pass them by. Other companies make things happen through smart, aggressive, and active management. They recognize value and acquire other companies. Then, they show the former managers how to make profits and grow. The executives of such acquirers of companies anticipate trends. They read, listen, travel, and ask questions. Creative communication is involved.

The size and complexity of organizations in our society and businesses reduce the opportunities to communicate within personal levels. Since large businesses are engaged in specialized and complex activities, direct communication with employees and suppliers is limited. Most contacts are indirect, through supervisors and intermediaries. Many governmental agencies use public relations spokesmen to explain policies and answer questions of concern to the public, however problems are often not addressed. *Characteristics of Stagnant and Vibrant Organizations* are listed in tabular form.

The stagnant organization exploits employees by reducing benefits, while expanding salaries of CEO's and officers of corporations. The company may appear to thrive through government contracts obtained in a politicized environment by the use of campaign contributions or outright gifts.

Often to the dismay of long-term employees, corporate raiders and junk bond manipulators operate beyond ethical conduct and, in the process, destroy the character and reputation of an established company. Such practices have been noteworthy effects of deregulation in many savings and loans, airlines, and other large corporations.

Society thrives in progress, such as improvements in the quality of the lives of all its citizens whenever possible. Moving manufacturing operations to foreign countries, which have lower pay scales and standards of living, may appear profitable in the short term. However, there is a negative trade-off in the form of reduced purchasing power of our working force, fostering various forms of discontent, high unemployment rates, crime, and rising national debt because of the erosion of the tax base supported by the middle class.

Not long ago, a candidate for a Ph.D. in communications prepared a dissertation on, briefly, the school climate as related to communication with the administrative staff for the district. One of the main points covered was the difference in communication effectiveness in terms of solving problems, achieving goals, and working with students in a harmonious environment. On the one hand were the formal meetings and much in the way of vertical communications. On the other, there was the accidental, informal, and interpersonal methods which grew out of direct contact, generating positive relationships and productive ideas.

The research covered extensive literature and included a discussion of organizational climate, which applies to all types of organizations: business, government, and social. One survey covered teachers' behavior in their perception of school climate in terms of four factors. The additional four factors related to the behavior of principals.

CHARACTERISTICS OF STAGNANT
AND VIBRANT ORGANIZATIONS

STAGNANT	VIBRANT
Management is out of touch with broad trends and consider themselves "different." Company has ultra-conservative attitude, No view of what economy and competition are doing to them.	Keep abreast with economy, new technology, markets, and competition. On lookout for phasing in new products, dropping losers, and acquiring compatible divisions.
Unwilling to experiment or take chances; reluctant to give up old methods.	Accept new methods; try out or test new products. Decide with assurance based on facts.
Never look beyond own markets and can't handle hard times.	Seek new areas to market their products. Look beyond the horizon.
Demand conformity of their people. Resent mavericks and new ideas.	Allow mavericks to speak up and question current methods; respond to changing environments .
Like government, pays whether one makes a mistake or does an ordinary job; does not reward outstanding performance.	Rewards merit, ideas, and increases in profits; punishes failure or indifference. Provides incentives. Stimulates suggestions.
Staff does little training or self-development; no effort to learn new methods of improving operations.	Training and self-development are always going on to learn new methods, improve operations, and get together to trouble-shoot or help.
Limits communication, isolating company from new ideas, fresh viewpoints, and new people. Not interested in professional meetings, consultants, conventions. Smug and self-satisfied attitude build a wall of isolation .	Stimulates contacts at all levels, within reason by promoting communication (in all directions). Encourage seminars, professional meetings, and opportunities to exchange information with other companies and countries.
Obsessed with immediate profit and strong cash position; not interested in research and development; strictly hardware and production oriented.	Invest some of income in development of personnel, management, market research, product research, and development; have flexible and long range approach.
Attract passive and dependent personnel interested in security and retirement. Take orders like servants from vassals. Try not to upset or rock boat.	Attract vital and energetic manpower with ideas. Environment stimulates ambition; climate satisfies talents; management encourages creative pursuits.
Nothing exciting goes on. Everything is set, including seniority, authority, and policies in deep freeze.	Sparkles with innovation, change, energy, and activity, which often appears confusing. An exciting place to work. Things happen.

1a. Disengagement ("not with it") vs. participation

2a. Hindrance (burdened with routine duties, etc.)

3a. Esprit (morale) involving social needs

4a. Intimacy (enjoyment of friendly social relations)

1b. Aloofness (formal and impersonal)

2b. Directive (production oriented) and not sensitive to feedback from staff

3b. Thrust (leadership role by setting example)

4b. Consideration (treatment of staff in human terms)

According to the author, Dr. James T. Martinof, "A desirable organizational climate is one in which it is possible for leadership acts to be initiated easily by any member of the organization. This climate would also provide satisfaction and a sense of self fulfillment for those involved at any level. The climate must, of necessity, be one of interaction and communication among all levels."

It is interesting how communication was defined in this context. The term 'communication' refers to the process by which directions, information, ideas, explanations, questions, and feelings are transmitted from person to person or from group to group. It is a process of perception and interaction between or among individuals and may be verbal or non-verbal.

Dr. Martinof summarized findings, as follows..."Adequate communication enables members of an organization to remain conscious of established goals, their personal contributions, and the contributions of others. A feeling of belonging to an organization by participants can serve to promote the realization of the goals."

COMMUNICATION BY EXECUTIVES

In most business organizations, a typical executive's activities during an average hour on the job can be broken down, as follows:

Listening	21 min.	35%
Talking	18	30
Reading	9.5	16
Writing	5.5	9
Observing	3.0	5
Thinking	3.0	5

The nature of an executive's business, responsibilities, and operating habits are factors that determine the actual times spent on activities that represent communication skills. He or she sets the standards of efficiency with respect to the skills used and the times consumed on each. Most executives are not aware of this; i.e., they are more concerned with doing their job in terms of responding to situations, speaking on the telephone, etc., than dividing their available time more effectively. For example, reading and writing can be done early or late in the day to avoid interruptions by meetings and phone calls.

An executive communicates at various levels in the organization, directly or through his secretary. In communicating down from top levels, the accuracy of the relayed message reduces, as follows:

Chairman: 100%
President: 67%
Vice President: 50%
Plant Manager: 40%
Foreman: 30%
Worker. 20%

As we go down the line, not only is the accuracy of the message reduced, but distortions are also introduced. When messages cross organizational lines, communications suffer more; one reason, the words do not mean the same things as we cross levels or departments. Since meanings reside in human beings, interpretations depend on what are already there.

In communication between party A and party B, the common ground is the overlapping area, generally irregular, between the two. We sometimes bypass when there's no overlap or common ground. We can mistakenly assume, "I know what you have in mind." We can also overestimate knowledge of a subject by others. What's wrong with asking a question and relaying information at the same time? ("Did you know that we decided to merge Territories A and B under one representative?")

Just as a manufacturer gets feedback from sales personnel active in the field to know what is going on in the marketplace, an executive can get feedback from personnel beyond his or her immediate circle of activity. This often consists of a secretary and the top brass. Through recognition and interest, an executive can create a positive atmosphere for feedback and more productivity. Often it's a matter of sincerity over pretense. There must be support in the form of a friendly attitude and genuine interest in other persons.

BUSINESS COMMUNICATION

Business communication takes place when someone decides to deliver a message through a medium that suits the purpose or occasion. The message must have a purpose, such as selling, create understanding, inform, inquire, persuade, etc. In the process, the sender must gain acceptance from the receiver. In the military, we command; in business, we ask. The communication may try to motivate someone to do something determined to be in the best interests of the organization.

Creative communication is not just a matter of saying immediately what comes to mind, or writing "off the top of one's head." The initiator must figure out how to achieve understanding, acceptance, and motivation. Spreading the news is a job for newspapers and broadcast media. In business, we must be certain that the messages have been received and understood. The sender must think beyond "yes" and "no," or two-valued reaction, and consider what the words "understood" by different persons mean to them. Whenever possible, one should:

1. Be clear by selecting words carefully, in proper context;

2. Be specific; exact, as necessary;

3. Be redundant, for reinforcement or emphasis; and,

4. Ask questions, for feedback.

We can interpret words and actions with prejudices that reflect experiences. Words can be weighed, distorted, modified, clarified, clouded, or reinforced. We must ask whether we convey facts in our messages or offer conclusions. Do we interpret objectively? Do we go beyond the facts with assumptions? Is our purpose to inform or to influence? When quoting others, are we doing it precisely?

There may be situations in which we must ask whether we are trying to reach understanding or to react. If we're not aware of this, our response will surely reveal what we're doing wrong. Since management communicates with most levels of business operations through its staff and heads of departments, internal communication is a vital element of the total management process. All business actions must begin with communication, which in turn cannot be delegated or separated from the subject area of responsibility.

Companies must not only be conscious of the impact of internal and external communications, but also establish lines, media, and feedback systems. Some companies go so far as appointing a director of communications. Many authorize the public relations department to screen all sensitive and significant communications, especially as it concerns customers and the public.

Managerial work covers four broad areas: planning, organizing, executing, and measuring. The first step in planning is defining the objectives and goals. Objectives are broad aims or desirable ends which continue year after year. To measure accomplishments, it's necessary to specify goals and dates. The process of gathering information; the application of research, experience, and judgment provides data from various sources. This data is background information to plan and establish goals.

Effective internal communication is a major characteristic of successful management. Control of the sources help avoid the trap that some executives fall into when the formal communication pipeline is used to transmit information never intended for the whole company. When the climate for a message is unfavorable, its timing can cause repercussions.

As a company grows and communications become more complex, more information, paperwork, and personnel are involved. The communication process is ongoing and those in control must be familiar with what's going on, the media, and release of sensitive information. Typical *Internal and External Information* that may concern manufacturers and distributors of products are listed with major media for transmitting information.

Market, products, and program planning exploit various forms of communication, depending on the particular activities. Opportunities to exercise initiative and creativity to produce significant and effective communication are many. Advertising, for example, exploits various media to reach potential buyers through effective communication. It's usually designed to penetrate the forces of competition, memory lapse, and sales resistance by the creative uses of mass communications and techniques of persuasion.

From an awareness of the existence of a product to the comprehension of the features and benefits, an ad can move the consumer through reason and desire to action leading to a sale. According to Norbert Weiner, in his "The Human Use of Human Beings," the circulation of information is central to social order, since for human beings to live effectively is to live with adequate information.

The quality of management is a reflection of the quality of communication in an organization. Managers send messages, collect data, and get feedback from various sources. In this churning stream of information coming and going in the form of letters, memos, and telephone communication, we get interference, lapses, distractions, misunderstandings, barriers, and breakdowns. No one is completely insulated from problems associated with managerial communications.   Clarity, accuracy, and understanding are essential. When a manager wants something done, the person who is asked to do it must understand clearly what it is, and must be capable and willing to

INTERNAL AND EXTERNAL INFORMATION

PRODUCTS

Specifications and applications (new users)
Changes to models, types and pricing
Analyses based on markets and orders
Analyses of quality control, defects, and sales returns
Technical information from research and engineering
Competitive data on new products
Technical data from journals and trade shows
New and major orders from customers

PERSONNEL

Organization openings and changes
Training programs, job classifications and descriptions

FINANCIAL

Statements, budgets and projections
Credit and cash flow
Property tax considerations; property management (assets)

MARKETING

Sales performance and analysis data
Sales forecasts and results
Sales problems and feedback
Service bulletins and publicity releases
Advertising and sales promotion
Trends and projectsions; possible acquisitions
Government, defense, and international developments

MEDIA FOR TRANSMITTING INFORMATION

Interviews	Bulletins	Reports	Releases
Conferences	Memoranda	Manuals	Procedures
Meetings	Letters	Proposals	Presentations

accomplish it as directed or intended by the manager. After messages are received, they must be acknowledged. In most cases, the words are converted into action. Meanings must be dramatized as directed, not misinterpreted or treated as an intangible.

Once the message is clear and specific, or unmistakable, there's no reason for distortion or error. Occasionally, there's interference in the sending and receiving channels. There are also cases of foot-dragging, delays, or procrastination—even downright contradiction or insubordination. Interference can be caused by several factors:

1) Competition for attention, because there was no provision for sorting our information in terms of priorities;

2) Interruptions, which cause difficulties in concentration and getting things done on schedule;

3) Indirect communication, or the use of many channels that cause inevitable delays and distortions in the original message;

4) Lack of clarity in the message or its interpretation; e.g., the meaning of "Urgent" without specifying a deadline, or talking about a "Project" without identifying it.

5) Emphasizing status or emotional overtones, instead of facts and relative importance on an objective basis; and,

6) Use of gobbledygook, jargon, fuzzy words, or general terms that reflect muddled message formation and presentation, as if the receiver knows what the sender is talking about.

7) Presence of dishonest personnel in key positions, such as secretarial or telephone switchboard.

8) Lack of screening of material to reduce superfluous literature and establish priorities.

To ensure clear, responsive, and effective communication, the manager must ask the proper questions in simple terms. For example:

A. Replay or repeat the message. (Can you repeat the instruction as you understand it?)

B. Substitute or application. (What would you do if you were faced with this situation?)

C. Impact or effect question. (Can you tell me what effect this directive will have on your people?) (Will this request or procedure affect your regular duties?)

D. Test or performance question. (Can you try this procedure and let me know how it works out?) (Why don't we put this new form to a test?)

When an attorney questions a witness to elicit evidence, the questions are usually worded for a "yes" or "no" answer. In this adversary system, in which the litigation is overshadowed by the attorneys in a contest of wits, facts, arguments, and legal technicalities, the witness is often asked to refrain from explaining or volunteering information. Theoretically, a case requires proof to a jury, based on evidence that's permitted and testimony presented. Often the verdict is based on which evidence or witness was more credible. With this approach, most companies in business would fail through lack of adequate communication.

"Yes" and "No" answers leave no room for shades of gray and color in situations, exchange of information, and ideas. To cover a situation, one can ask various questions to cover a situation and give the responder time to think and answer each question. A manager asks questions in terms of the subordinate's point of view and comprehension. The questions are asked in a friendly manner. Occasionally, the "we" approach is used to indicate it's not a matter that concerns one or two persons, but the whole organization or department.

The tone used, attitude displayed, and even the words themselves can arouse flags of caution or fear in a responder. In addition, it's better to stick to the point or issue, than waltz around its perimeter. Keep in mind that one does not have a witness to cross-examine and the responder should not be put on the defensive. The best approach to ask for something is to use questions that reflect simplicity, candor, and a search for help. For example:

WHO   Who can best do this job? Whom should we contact to start the project?

WHAT   What should we consider first? What approach shall we use to reach our goals?

WHEN   When shall we make the announcement? When will you be ready to kick off this proposal?

WHY   Why do you like this approach? Why shouldn't we advertise on television?

HOW   How can we handle (or approach) this problem? How do you interpret this latest trend?

WHERE   Where should we hold our joint meeting? Where should we go for our raw materials?

Answers may not come easily. They may also come as remarks devoid of adequate thought to the question; even, reflect reactions. One should give the listener time to think and formulate answers to questions. One can encourage the other party to ask questions; put the asker at ease through attitude and response. If one does not know the answer, ignorance is no crime. If it's important to the issue, promise to get an answer. Time may be of the essence.

An effective manager may have a list of things to get done and a list of people to contact for various reasons. The jobs of communicating creatively for business or management is multifaceted; much more than a list of errands or things to acquire. Often obstacles must be removed so that things can be done. Problems develop, and depending on their importance or impact, the manager's communication skills must be warmed up to start tackling, approaching, or investigating through information, ideas, and decisions.

An effective manager:

1) Anticipates communication needs and accepts the tasks associated with the position and its responsibilities;

2) Makes notes of essential tasks and messages; practices and encourages written communications, as required;

3) Keeps an active or visible file of things to check periodically; confirms tasks with others and makes necessary changes;

4) Tries to resolve matters as soon as possible, unless there's reason to put something off. Facing piles of paperwork and unresolved problems can discourage or hold up progress in other areas. They may reflect procrastination, neglect, and the confusion of indecision.

5) Gets things done like an executive by establishing a routine for:

   a) Conveying information to all concerned;
   b) Performing scheduled tasks for the day;
   c) Initiating requests for information and action;
   d) Follow up activities on large projects and crucial items that cannot be completed in short time frames; and,
   e) Updating schedules and getting feedback to stay "on top" of projects and situations.

Companies interested in constantly improving communications will periodically review procedures, as well as assign responsibilities for specific areas. Listed are 20 *Suggestions for Procedure s and Practices*, which can be monitored, reviewed, and changed, as necessary.

20 SUGGESTIONS FOR PROCEDURES AND PRACTICES

1) Periodic review of communication practices
2) List of communication items to coordinate
3) Handling of employee feedback and complaints
4) Management training in skills and media
5) Eliminating waste in copy systems and duplication
6) Suggestions to improve organizational communications
7) Defining positions and responsibilities of personnel
8) Use and dissemination of management newsletter
9) Survey and measurement of organizational climate
10) Training and orientation of all personnel
11) Resolution of departmental conflicts and problems
12) Operating efficiency of company as an integrated unit
13) Use of available talents in organization
14) Measurement of pay scales and benefits for all levels
15) Protection of company confidential and proprietary
16) Review of forms and procedures for changes
17) Examination of possible cost reductions in all operations
18) Review of waste, pilfering, and absenteeism
19) Review of effectiveness of communication media
20) Review of personnel hiring and firing implications

INTERVIEWS

Interviews are identified by purpose, such as filling an opening for a position, presenting information, influencing behavior, or obtaining information. Participants generally determine the nature of an interview, such as talk-show hosts and commentators who invite guests to answer questions of interest to the public. Television interviews often present a mix of information and entertainment, with time out for commercials. Essentially, an interview is a meeting between two persons who agree to come together to discuss problems, answer questions, exchange views, or help arrive at decisions. Some interviews involve groups.

Most interviews are productive and informative when the participants are prepared to discuss the specified subjects and answer questions related to those subjects. This is especially true of talk shows, like the MacNeil-Lehrer Report on Public Broadcast Television. Here the principals ask the questions and the participants represent accepted authorities, public figures, or experts on issues of interest. In business, the interviews may range from discussions about personal problems and surveys to jobs that must be filled.

When personal problems of employees are revealed to supervision, often a representative of personnel or employee relations, with experience in counseling, will participate. In many cases, the manager will do the counseling. The employee-oriented counseling suggests a relationship which, like an interview, involves a one-on-one exchange of information. The need may range from a simple question or a seeking of advice to help solve a problem, which can be personal, marital, financial, or job-related. The manager or supervisor can listen and suggest alternative solutions, which the employee can use to develop further or resolve.

As the interview develops, a warmer atmosphere should result through understanding, empathy, and positive attitudes. As more alternatives evolve, choices can be made for tryout or test. Some solutions may create new problems. This is an area in which both parties can contribute to the process of elimination, evaluation, and resolution of the original problem. Both parties with open minds can learn from the exchange of views. In many situations, the counselee accepts the conclusions or realities of the situation.

In some instances, referrals are made to professional counselors or persons with higher responsibilities or authority. Managers cannot be expected to deal with all types of employee counseling situations. However, they should be prepared to make specific suggestions for referrals with reasons for and approaches for the counselee.

If the purpose of the interview is to *obtain* information, the preparer or interviewer can do the following:

1) Specify the type and amount of information desired;

2) Arrange a series of questions designed to obtain the information or to reach the objectives established.

3) Establish an attitude of respect and a climate of impartiality or objectivity.

If the purpose of the interview is to *present* information, the speaker can do the following:

1) Determine effective ways to present selected items;

2) Relate the information to the concerns of the receiver(s);

3) Obtain feedback through questions and listening carefully to the responses;

4) Anticipate reactions or responses and prepare some of the answers to possible questions; and,

5) Evaluate responses based on purpose and content of the information presented.

The job interview can be treated in two phases: preparation and presentation. To help prepare for an interview for a job you want:

1) Learn all you can about the company; what they do and what you can do for them; and, the types of openings available. It is better to respond to an opening than look for "any" job.

2) Have a resume ready. It should include facts about yourself, objectives, experiences listed with the most recent one by date first. Include in your briefcase a kit of work samples, letters of recommendation, names and addresses of references, etc.

3) Be ready to talk about your training and experience as they relate to the opening you expect to fill. As the occasion permits, talk about your accomplishments and your spare time activities. Try to be relaxed and answer all questions asked.

4) Dress for the occasion; be clean and well-groomed. Try to be there on time or a few minutes before the interview.

For most jobs, there are usually two or more interviews; at least one by personnel and one by the department with the opening. Some managers use a check list that rates personal characteristics, attitudes, appearance, and ability to work with others. Prospective employees, for example, will reveal personal concerns, such as fringe benefits and job security. However, the main issues are generally the salary and opportunities for advancement.

It's up to the manager to put the person being interviewed at ease, especially if the subordinate is involved. The interview is primarily a matter of adapting to the situation and persons involved. If it's a matter of influencing people, the interviewer should be able to accomplish it without the suggestion of force or threat.

The results of the interview should be conclusive enough to enable the manager to make a decision. Since there are time limitations, gaps should not be extended. A convenient method to avoid lapses and digressions is to have a list of questions to ask or subjects to discuss. Brief notes are not discouraged, but making a report or filling a form can detract from the productivity of the interview.

The climate should be one of relaxation with a candid exchange of views. Disagreements should not be escalated and points of accord can be reinforced. One may not want to agree on everything, but if there's total agreement or total disagreement, something's wrong with the interview and one or more of the participants.

CONFERENCES OR MEETINGS

Conferences or meetings are an essential activity of most organizations and demonstrate effective examples of group communication provided they are conducted properly. Although these "get togethers" take people away from their normal or routine responsibilities, no organization can operate productively, profitably, or effectively without regularly scheduled or special meetings that require physically convening around a table. In this setting, those present can exchange information, ask questions, and present problems.

Some of the more important reasons for a conference or meeting are:

1) Report on progress and confer on related problems;

2) Outline proposals and discuss new programs;

3) Discuss problems that can only be resolved by a consensus of principals in a joint session;

4) Announce plans, establish goals, and obtain feedback;

5) Survey opinions and solicit ideas;

6) Prepare answers requested by government, union, or industry;

7) Review effectiveness of systems, procedures, or designs;

8) Persuade management to change a policy or a decision;

9) Analyze and discuss suggestions to cut costs or try new ideas;

10) Motivate personnel, brainstorm, stimulate new ideas.

Whether they are special or regularly scheduled, all meetings or conferences should be planned adequately in advance. What each member is expected to report and ready to answer questions should be known. This may include an agenda covering topics and responsibilities. The chairman, or principal in this important project of group communication, must be adequately prepared to run the meeting through familiarity with the programs and personnel involved.

The chairman must ensure that key personnel will be present to make reports and answer questions. A conference must be more than an occasion to assign jobs, offer value judgments, or air grievances. Advance preparation for the conference should include time, place, estimated duration, participants, provisions for recording minutes, and a fact sheet distributed in advance.

The productivity of the conference depends largely on how well the chairman and participants are prepared. Under effective control of the chairman, the tone of the conference can range from restrained, natural, and sincere to enthusiastic, confident, and respectful. In a spirit of good will and attitude of cooperation, the chairman can stimulate participants to help accomplish the goals of the meeting. To begin, introductions may be in order.

To start the discussion, each subject on the agenda should be stated clearly and amplified, as necessary. The chairman must control the meeting by creating interest and stimulating response, yet ensuring that the discussion does not veer off the subject. Before introducing a new topic, it may be necessary to emphasize or summarize the topic previously covered. Regardless of the methods used, the greatest amount of business must be accomplished in the shortest time. Adequate preparation helps chairmen recognize the best solutions or practical decisions.

Some problems are not going to be resolved during a meeting. In this regard, the chairman should know when to cut off discussion and proceed to the next subject. All participants should be encouraged to make contributions in applicable areas. If a participant is not prepared, provision should be made for an input after the meeting. The chairman should try to conduct the meeting without creating an atmosphere of tension or strained relations. Distractions should be cleared and interruptions avoided. A checklist of *Reasons and Procedures for Meetings* has been prepared for reference or use by managers.

Questions are the foundation of a conference, since they can be used to open discussions, stimulate thoughts on a subject, and fulfill the requirements of an agenda. All principal questions, at least those that strike at the heart of an issue or problem, should be planned. To promote the proper climate and avoid emotional overtones, the phrasing and tone of the questions are essential.

Four basic types of questions used to conduct a discussion are:

1) Overhead—asked without specifying who is to reply;
2) Directed—indicating who is to reply;
3) Reverse—asked in answer to a question; and
4) Relay—transfers question to another or anyone willing.

REASONS AND PROCEDURES FOR MEETINGS

VALID REASONS

1. Provide integrated group judgment.
2. Promote coordination of interrelated efforts .
3. Obtain cross-fertilization of ideas.
4. Enlist cooperation.
5. Communicate in parallel.
6. Report and discuss problems.

INVALID REASONS

a. Delay actions; postpone reasons.
b. Mask individual incompetence.
c. Avoid or spread responsibility.
d. Provide an audience for the boss.
e. Get together for a bull session.
f. Make unimportant decisions.
g. Provide a "rubber stamp."
h. Ease pain of decisions.

PROCEDURES

1. Determine purpose and objectives. (Justification for meeting)
2. Organize committee properly. (Define duties and authority—limit)
3. Staff committee properly. (Qualified persons with authority and help)
4. Establish committee procedures. (Ensure bold and effective action)
5. Appoint the right chairman. (Efficient running; participation)
6. Know and understand participants (Personalities; interplay for action)
7. Indoctrinate members properly. (Know rules and agenda)
8. Be prepared for subjects. (Avoid detailed explanations; make references to data in advance)

RECOGNIZE AND CONTROL

a. Loud talker—squelch
b. Detached observer—drop
c. Wallflower—encourage
d. Take charge guy—remove
e. Antagonist—ask for the constructive
f. Hedger—manage and elicit
g. Yes man—unnecessary
h. Mediator—watch
i. Climber—disparage
j. Cynic—ostracize
k. Promoter—curb
l. Fanatic—recognize and depress
m. Emotional—sympathize
n. Belittler—reduce

PROMOTE

A. Objectivity
B. Open minds
C. Movement forward
D. Resolution of issues
E. Good will
F. High Standards
G. Discussions limited to subject

REDUCE

a. Distractions
b. Open debates
c. Long speeches
d. Boredom
e. Extensive taking of notes
f. Running overtime
g. Overloading individuals

The overhead question starts everyone thinking. As a *lead-off* it stimulates group responses, which can provide the basis for *follow-up* questions. In turn, this can lead to a *provocative* question, which may point to the root or the problem or issue.

The directed question is aimed at a participant in a discussion that is closely controlled. The reverse question may be used to ask the questioner or any other participant as a "throwback." This is a question related to the one asked, and is often used to clarify or pinpoint an issue.

Since the aim of the discussion is to clarify and resolve through contributions of information, the reverse question can be useful. However, it must be used properly. It's up to the chairman to see that the reverse question is not an evasive tactic or demoralizing ploy. The relay question, on the other hand, is a way of getting other participants involved, as well as getting more opinions and information.

Use *lead-off, follow-up,* and *provocative inquiries* in any of the four basic types of questions. The questions themselves should anticipate contributions by participants in terms of facts, actual experiences, or conclusive judgments. The participants should not be treated as witnesses being cross-examined. The chairman can stick to questions that promote enlightenment and friendliness; indicate genuine interest for purposes of reaching decisions through an attitude of confidence and mutual respect.

The chairman must be an excellent communicator, with skills to match the subjects and the importance of the conference. He must prepare, establish rapport, control, stimulate, and help resolve, without the impression of being a pushover or an autocrat. Toward the objective of summarizing suggestions for conferences or meetings, the following list is recommended:

a. Prepare for the group discussion. As chairman, make certain participants are notified in advance about the subjects and what accomplishments are expected of the meeting.

b. Introduce everyone, and after a few introductory remarks to establish rapport amongst members of the group, get the discussion started.

c. Establish ground rules. State problem or subject clearly and be prepared to deviate from original outline, as necessary, to accomplish aims.

d. After the problem is stated, submit for analysis, approaches, and criteria for solutions. A primary goal might be finding the best solution, through evaluation, with respect to the current policy or situation.

e. Accept contributions in the proper context and spirit. When necessary, raise questions of fact and value; avoid value judgments and premature conclusions.

f. Investigate thoroughly, impartially, and rationally. Clarify understanding in areas of agreement and disagreement. Be open-minded and flexible with a purpose. A responsible attitude, as reflected in attention, cooperation, and courtesy, will generate similar attitudes from participants.

g. Encourage participation from all present, but limit extraneous discussions and specialized subjects that can be handled separately. Handle digressions with tact, geniality, and humor.

h. Review and summarize the material discussed before proceeding to the next subject. Restate ideas in terms that the speaker and participants can understand. Then, move the discussion on to the next subject.

i. Encourage everyone to show respect for varying shades of opinion; acknowledge facts; maintain an objective point of view; and, observe the proceedings with a clear perspective of the overall purpose of the discussion.

j. Discourage emotional reactions, maintain firm control of the meeting, and provide for relief. Break up tension with humor and wit; boredom with breaks, variety, and refreshments.

k. Stick to time schedule and discourage interruptions.

l. Make provisions for recording (with secretary) or tape recording meeting for subsequent distribution. This often ensures attention and participation.

m. Encourage communication, coordination, and cooperation on a team and individual basis.

n. When assigning tasks, distribute responsibility equally, whenever possible.

TRAINING PROGRAMS

Training requirements of an organization can range from simple orientation to full time classroom and field training. Many companies cannot cope with the realities of competition, change, and new technologies, including the marketing of products and services without regularly scheduled training programs. New hires may be skilled enough to fit job requirements, but to assure adjustment and productive participation in operations, orientation and specialized training is essential. Job training, generally conducted by industrial relations, can involve management, staff, and line personnel.

Many young people, even those with degrees, ready for work should begin work with close supervision, and go through a learning period to become familiar with company practices, procedures, and sources of information. It's easy to take things for granted in work situations. It's like the situation in which you want to visit a friend living in a hillside tract. The house is difficult to locate even though you have the street and number. To get there, you need specific directions and occasionally a flashlight to locate the number on the right street.

It's standard practice for a member of personnel administration to take a new hire around, make introductions, answer questions, and release the person with a supervisor. Anticipated questions should be part of a check list of items to cover in an orientation session and tour of facilities. Whether it's a transfer to 'a new assignment or a new hire, job training cannot be overemphasized.

It's more than a matter of familiarity and knowledge of technical aspects of a job. It's also a matter of "feeling at home" and meeting the people with whom the employee must work and the interfaces at various levels. In certain instances, fellow employees are available to show the new hire how to do somethings, where to go for specific services, and even get something needed to do a job.

Learning requires effort to acquire facts, supported by materials, examples, and illustrations. Those responsible for training must go beyond lectures, and include experience in practices and monitoring of activities. Ways must be developed to measure results of training in terms of productivity and efficiency. In anticipation of possible mistakes, those responsible for training must be available for suggestions and to answer questions. What may be strange, confusing, or difficult at first, becomes, with patience and effort, easy to accomplish. Training programs require careful planning, dedication, and an atmosphere that promotes desire or motivation.

A working environment, in which there is increased mechanization of tasks, demands that companies take on more responsibility to train operators, service personnel, and technicians. For example, selection of personnel is important for operators of word processors and terminal devices. Errors, down time, and uncoordinated operations are costly. Competent training personnel are not easy to find.

It is generally better to have internal instructors and supervisors conduct training, rather than consultants. In special areas and for limited periods, consultants with proven credentials can do much for a company. Within a company, training specialists work better than supervisors. The latter may lose productivity when diverted from normal duties. Studies have shown that an experienced training staff can do a better job in certain areas than management or consultants.

Training must be systematic, well organized, and cover all the requirements of current operations. New technology or new equipment may require manufacturers' representatives to conduct the training. In planning the specific training program, the facilities, cost, logistics, travel, etc., must be considered. Before starting any training program, a complete analysis should be made covering:

1) Purpose of the specified program

2) Participants, including number and levels

3) Instructors

4) Number of hours and time of day

5) Location of training; site or facilities

6) Instruction outline and format

7) Materials, equipment, and handouts

8) Cost of program and projected benefits

Talk in the form of lectures can be expensive because of the time consumed. Limiting lectures may be practical in favor of using training materials, reference notes, and equipment. Sometimes a series of problems and tests, followed by a critique, prove effective. Question and answer sessions are always useful because the group can also benefit from the answers, as well as provide feedback for the instructors.

Examples of problems for trainees, with instructors available as coaches or consultants, help monitor progress. Discussion, on the other hand, may not provide easy grasp of information by all. Realistic training programs simulate actual operating conditions and real-time responsibilities. One cannot study how to perform on a musical instrument by reading a book on it. It takes practice under competent supervision, so that the procedures are correct and errors are not learned. Much training involves proper approaches taken under guidance, a form of technical discipline.

An atmosphere of warmth, established by rapport, will generate motivation and active participation. The instructor cannot just lecture about "things." The "things" must be demonstrated, manipulated, or operated so that the trainee can get the "feel" of the function, equipment, or tasks. Generalities and discussions about the wonders of a word processor cannot do the job of actually operating the keys and generating errorless printouts. In addition, terms cannot be tossed about as if everybody understands them in the context the instructor has in mind.

Knowledge of the subject comes first for the instructor, who must have experience in training and on the subject or technology. To ensure grasp of facts, a series of short quizzes can be used. At least the tests can tell the instructor about the progress of the trainees, even how well the instructor is doing. The missing links needed to complete the training, on an individual basis, are items each trainee can work on.

Group training has the advantage of cost per hour per trainee. The slower ones may have to catch up by doing some "homework" or additional study after hours. Effective learning is a three-way operation. This triangle starts with competent instruction, is followed by efforts to learn, and takes place in a warm and motivated environment. The instructor and students share together the process of communicating useful information and an experience which advances the productive goals of the company.

MEMORANDA

Memoranda are internal messages which document essential information. Primarily an organizational note, the memo communicates in writing an account of information to report, remember, or highlight. Like a news account, the memo presents facts in an organized format to one or more persons. When possible, it answers specified questions or anticipates possible ones. The memorandum can be a response to a request for information, a trip report, an account of a conference, or the nucleus of an idea or proposal. Whatever the purpose, it sticks objectively to a main topic.

In many organizations, reams of interoffice memoranda take up valuable space. The stacks of memos signal the impression that writing them represented the major activities of some employees. Confusion is the inevitable result of paperwork interconnected like a giant cobweb of originals and copies. Memos are important, but some organizations make incessant use of them instead of other forms of communication.

The files of many organizations are jammed with memoranda that could be summarized, shredded, or rearranged in more effective forms. The valuable storage space, in which memos lie undisturbed for years, could be used for more important papers and documents.

A memo should fill a need and justify its existence in writing. Like a letter, it should be short and to the point. A memo is not a statement addressed: "to whom it may concern." Rather, it's addressed to one person and include others for distribution on a "need to know" basis. Its format should be simple and logical; the message clear and unmistakable. There should be no doubt as to its purpose and justification for existence in writing.

Address it:	TO a person or distribution
Name the source:	FROM by name and title
State briefly:	SUBJECT, which implies purpose
Indicate:	DATE
Refer to:	Documents, previous memos, identification no., etc.

The first sentence of the memo summarizes the main story or the topic of interest to be covered in the body. The central point is presented as if it's of immediate concern to the addressee. If more than one person is to receive a copy of the memo, the writer must consider the impact of the message. Consequently, the elements of objectivity, accuracy, and adherence to facts become paramount. If the memo summarizes an important meeting, that requires a record as to date, place, participants, and subjects discussed, include actual remarks in quotations. Paraphrasing may be difficult and subject to more than one interpretation.

A memo that records conversations, without redundant phrases and casual remarks, will tend to be more readable than a wordy account that runs several pages. Develop the memo logically and arrange items in descending order of importance. If possible, end on a positive note. As applicable, ask for a personal discussion or reaction to the message.

Write the memo for your reader(s). Visualize the person(s) who will receive it. What would they want to know? If possible, open with the primary interest and build around it. Organize the facts so that they can carry an impact. You can write the way you speak, however, try to be crisp and to the point. When you have really thought things through, you can state them simply. Use whole sentences, but keep them brief. Journalists say that no sentence in a news story should average more than 32 words. Give your sentences the rhythm of speech and they will flow easily. Your reader will go along with the ideas because they sound natural; appreciate sentences with fewer words, but used with precision.

Treatment of the subject depends on the reader. In general, you are on the right track as long as you remain factual, terse, grammatically correct, and technical as necessary to discuss the subject adequately. Before the final draft, check out related facts, requirements, addresses, etc. If the memo replies to a previous message or request, make reference to it and try to cover the open items.

Here are a few suggestions to help prepare memos in a professional manner and for positive results.

1) Start with an outline of subjects to cover an purpose to achieve.
2) Write a rough draft with an introductory sentence which summarizes the main story.
3) Proceed with the logical development in one or more of the following arrangements:
   a. Descending order of importance
   b. Chronological pattern
   c. Spatial pattern
   d. Analysis of functions or physical breakdown

      e. Comparison or contrast pattern

      f. Cause and effect

4) Make brief references to other documents, as necessary

5) Be clear and candid as to what you want or expect to accomplish. If the memo contains proprietary or classified information, identify it accordingly. Limit distribution to persons who have a need to know.

6) Summarize by recapitulating the main ideas without excessive repetition. Emphasize the important elements.

7) Add attachments and any reference data essential to the memo and its purpose. After completing the rough draft, check the memorandum.

    a) Does it communicate what the addressee wants to know?

    b) Is it accurate, clear, and brief?

    c) Is it unmistakable in intent and meaning, yet provocative and pleasant?

    d) Does it stick to the issue, yet cover essential points?

    e) Does it have continuity and natural breaks in paragraphs?

    f) Does it read easily, like a friendly discussion?

    g) Do the attachments and references support the issues or main points made?

    h) Does it end on a pleasant note or in a positive key?

    i) Does it read like it can succeed in accomplishing its overall purpose?

BUSINESS LETTERS

A letter is not the easiest document to prepare. It must have a specific purpose and convey an unmistakable message to the addressee. In thinking about the letter you must write, analyze the situation, the reader, the purpose, and the desired response. Letter writing requires a command of the English language, knowledge of the subject involved, and the ability to respond logically, emotionally, and productively to the readers' needs or desires.

Whether the purpose of the letter is to raise funds, persuade, make an offer, acknowledge, or inform, it should have five major attributes:

1) Short as possible to accomplish its purpose;
2) Content that reflects knowledge of subject and the ability to discuss it naturally;
3) Originality through special treatment of subject;
4) Sincere in character and appropriate in tone for situation;
5) Positive and firm, geared to reader's interests.

Like a good speaker in a friendly conversation, the letter must present facts and relate to the subject. Since the letter can reveal much about the writer, what you are and how you express yourself on a specific writing occasion can evoke a positive response, a negative reaction, or nothing, like a cold shoulder.

How you present the message to the addressee and the tone of communication established are so important, the ability to achieve results intended often depend on them. Business correspondence is not a matter of dictating to a secretary or tape recorder. Until one becomes a professional at it, important letters require analysis, planning, writing, editing, and even rewriting. When you're aware of the needs, desires, and self-respect of others in various situations, you can do a better job of communication through letters. Through simplicity, clarity, and logical coherence of ideas, the writer can promote the effect of substance and treatment to persuade the reader.

Let's say you have a letter to write and have a good idea of the reader's need and what you want to accomplish. Start with an outline framed around an introduction, body, and conclusion. A worksheet, with two narrow columns and one wide one is suggested, with headings: *Outline —Accomplish—Draft of Text*. After you complete the outline and note the specific items to accomplish in the letter, start writing a draft of the text. This disciplined approach puts you on the right track.

OUTLINE	ACCOMPLISH	DRAFT OF TEXT

This arrangement of subjects to discuss, the ideas that require expression, and the results you want to accomplish in the letter, develops a better awareness of the purpose and the reader. This approach provides the writer with an overall perspective for an effective writing process. You may have to rearrange, revise, check meanings in context, and verify facts.

You can also keep in mind that the reader sees appearance, takes interest in anticipation of needs or desires to satisfy, responds to readability, and feels the good will if it's there. The reader can act when persuaded by a promise backed up with evidence or potential satisfaction. A checklist has been prepared in the form of questions and suggestions.

1) Is the opening sentence attractive, smooth, and original? (State aim quickly, as soon as an item of identity has been established. Avoid needless words.)

2) Do you call the reader by name in the salutation and body? (Unless the name is unknown, use "Dear Mr. Jones" or "Dear Bill" in the salutation. Mention Mr. Jones or Bill in the letter itself, as appropriate.)

3) Does the letter address itself as a message from one person to another? (Visualize the addressee's presence. A frank and conversational approach can be natural without the appearance of undue familiarity.)

4) Is the addressee played up, recognized, appreciated, or shown respect? (Be considerate and see the reader's point of view. Stress the "you" factor by mentioning specific benefits. Credit the reader with intelligence.)

5) Is the letter as short as possible, attractive, and to the point? (Eliminate the superfluous and stick to the subject.)

6) Does the letter make definite statements with positive attitudes? (Be firm gracefully. Be specific about what you want and leave the door open to the future.)

7) Do the ideas flow logically from point to point? (Develop each point in support of a statement in an organized sequence so that it flows naturally to a conclusion.)

8) Do you request definite action? Is there a promise, implied or stated, as of a specified date? (State exactly what you'll do and when; or, what you expect of the addressee and when.)

9) Do you close the letter with a request for a favorable result? (Ask for something reasonable; reduce it to a simple choice or decision.)

10) What kind of an impression does the writer make on the reader? (It should be firm, gentle, sincere, well-mannered, considerate, responsible; not unreasonable, demanding, unusual.)

11) Does the letter accomplish its intention in a positive manner and approach? (Reflects a personal interest in the addressee and displays it with a spirit of warmth.)

12) Does the letter read and sound like the best one you've ever written? (It's the kind of letter you'd like to receive and acknowledge; willingly do what it asks of you.)

TECHNICAL REPORTS

Technical reports are generally used to present information resulting from an investigation, feasibility study, tests, surveys, and formal inquiries. In preparing technical reports, accuracy of content and clarity of presentation are more important than style and appeal to a broad readership. However, in this form of communication to document a specified subject, there is no excuse to include jargon, to hedge, or subject the reader to an extended discussion of unessentials.

The report should be well organized and contain the elements that justify its existence for the benefit of the intended readers. Unless it's an extended memorandum or letter, a report should contain the 12 elements listed, described by function and material in the *General Organization of Reports*. A guide for *Typical Number/ Letter and Decimal Sequences is* suggested for preparing the report.

Once the requirements for the report are established; i.e., subject, purpose, and readers or authority for its preparation, a tentative outline is recommended. This helps determine the approach in gathering and organizing the data. After the important facts and supporting information have been collected, the writer can analyze the material. During this time, preliminary discussions, conclusions, or recommendations can be made.   This is a period of digestion and decisions to help establish the overall approach.

The actual writing begins with a firm outline in the form of headings or topic sentences. There is no reason why the subject headings cannot be changed during the writing and revising stages. From this point on, preparing the report is a matter of writing, reviewing, editing, and getting it ready for publication.

As a matter of standard procedure, the writer can approach the preparation of a report, as follows:

1) Write the rough draft and incorporate submissions of material for the various sections.
2) Check all content, revise, rearrange, and rewrite, as necessary.
3) Arrange to have a rough draft typed.
4) Make several copies for review by participants.
5) Consolidate changes and corrections; review and edit for structure, style, and writing mechanics.
6) Obtain approval for changes.

GENERAL ORGANIZATION OF REPORTS

ELEMENT	FUNCTION	MATERIAL
1. Title Page	Identify report.	Title, document identification, date, author's name, company name, address, logo.
2. Copyright Page	Notice of protection.	Copyright statement and year.
3. Foreword	Identifies subjects covered in report; acknowledges assistance.	Statement of purpose, names of contributors; requirement and authority for document.
4. Table of Contents List of Figures List of Tables	Locate topics covered. Locate illustrations. Locate tabular material.	Main headings and subheads Figure titles Table titles
5. Glossary	Identify and translate abbreviations, acronyms, and symbols.	Special abbreviations, symbols, acronyms, & notations
6. Abstract	Summarize report in less than 100 words.	Paraphrase highlights of topics covered.
7. Introduction and Summary	Introduce subject, problem, approach, and summarize findings and conclusions.	Purpose and limits of discussion background; extracts from various sections.
8. Body of Discussion	Discuss work in narrative, expository, and descriptive techniques; analyze data and develop logical support with facts.	Content of report as it presents main ideas, facts, and related support; analyses, experiments, or tests; results and other significant data.
9. Conclusion	Detail rationale for findings or results; make recommendations.	Results, proposed studies, or actions; recommendations based on findings.
10. References	Identify sources mentioned in text of report.	List numerically in order of mention: author, title, source, page, date, etc.
11. Bibliography	Recommend sources generally related to topics discussed.	List sources alphabetically, furnishing same data as used for references.
12. Appendixes	Give supporting data that is too bulky or specialized for use in body or which may disturb continuity.	Derivations of equations; case histories, complex discussions, source material, processor printouts, exhibits, etc.

TYPICAL NUMBER/LETTER AND DECIMAL SEQUENCES

I. INTRODUCTION AND SUMMARY   1.0

II. TECHNICAL DISCUSSION   2.0

    A. FIRST MAIN IDEA   2.1

        1. Fact Supporting This Idea   2.1.1

        a. Item Relating to 1   2.1.1.1

        b. Second Item Relating to 1   2.1.1.2

            1) First order listing   1)

            2) First order listing   2)

                a) Second order listing   (a)

                b) Second order listing   (b)

                    (1) Third order listing   (1)

                    (2) Third order listing   (2)

        2. Another Significant Fact Supporting A   2.1.2

    B. SECOND MAIN IDEA   2.2

    C. THIRD MAIN IDEA   2.3

III. TEST RESULTS   3.0

    A. GROUP 1 DATA   3.1

    B. GROUP 2 DATA   3.2

IV. RECOMMENDATIONS
(OR CONCLUSIONS)   4.0

    A. FIRST RECOMMENDATION   4.1

        1. Fact Supporting First Recommendation 4.1.1

        2. Fact Supporting Second Recommendation 4.1.2

    B. SECOND RECOMMENDATION   4.2

    C. THIRD RECOMMENDATION   4.3

    Appendix I   Appendix A

    Appendix II   Appendix B

    References   References

    Bibliography   Bibliography

    Index (as required)   Index

Craftsmanship, which is reflected in the end product, comes from practicing the principles, which follow, and making changes.

A) COMPLETE   Gives all information required by authority.

B) SHORT   Reports no more than necessary; avoids repetition.

C) CONCISE   Includes only essential words; simple; accurate.

D) SIMPLE   Sticks to subject; discusses it naturally.

E) GENUINE   Sincere effort to convey ideas.

F) CLEAR   Language fits readers; expresses thoughts exactly.

G) ORGANIZED   Information is represented in a logical order.

H) CORRECT   Information is accurate; free of errors.

I) APPROPRIATE   Tone elicits desired reaction from readers.

J) EFFECTIVE   Accomplishes purpose for requirements.

Before publication and distribution, report should be reviewed, approved, and signed by person(s) authorizing release of document. It has been found that delaying publication and distribution of a report is preferable to the late discovery of errors or necessity for changes. It's difficult to recall documents in the mail or shipped to meet a deadline, when date could have been changed for good reason.

TECHNICAL PROPOSALS

Technical proposals are principal forms of communication generated by organizations to obtain contracts. Responses to requests for proposals (RFPs) must adhere to the requirements of a program and offer, generally, something unique or extra. The document must propose an approach acceptable to the customer; offer to conduct the program at a realistic cost and reasonable schedule.

Being technically responsive does not mean rephrasing the customer's statement of work. Originality and responsiveness are evaluated along with reliability, personnel, management, costs, and schedules. A realistic cost is not possible if the contractor has limited background in the technology involved; needs new capital equipment; or, subcontracts a large amount of services. If key personnel in the company are occupied with other major projects, the contractor cannot be expected to perform or respond within a reasonable schedule.

Preparation of a technical proposal begins when management, marketing, and engineering agree to bid for a contract on a technology in which the company has the resources: manpower, experience, and facilities. The decision to bid is followed by the appointment of a technical or project director and members of the proposal team.

The makeup of the team depends on the requirements and magnitude of the program. The team examines the RFP, the statement of work, and all attachments. This is generally done before scheduling a kickoff meeting, where the proposal assignments and schedule for its preparation are made. Based on the approach taken in response to the RFP, the team prepares its own statement of work and a tentative outline of the technical proposal as represented by the document.

At the kickoff meeting, the RFP is reviewed by the proposal (program) manager. All questions, if not answered at the meeting, are assigned to team members for follow up. The questions may concern interpretations, deviations, requests for changes in delivery schedule, contractual exceptions, etc.

The responsive statement of work, to which the team agrees, is used to guide engineers for preparing estimates, inputs in writing, as well as schedules and PERT type charts for inclusion in the proposal. Structurally, a medium sized proposal (two to ten million dollars) will generally contain the following sections:

1) Front Matter (title page, foreword, table of contents)

2) Introduction and Summary

3) Technical Discussion (main body of proposal)

4) Program Organization (personnel, schedule, statement of work)

5) Qualifications of Contractor (experience; facilities)

6) Quality Control and Reliability (other requirements)

7) Appendix (supporting data, references, special reports)

The most important factor in preparing the technical proposal is its content: the ideas and facts documented to support the response to the request. Cost is important as it relates to the conduct of the program, amount budgeted, and delivery of goods and services, as specified. How the contributors treat the material in terms of presentation, graphics, and format are also important. However, if the proposal does not respond technically to the requirements and specifications of the RFP, neither a Nobel prize winner in literature nor an art director will help much in receiving the contract award.

A good grasp of the technical approach naturally leads to an outline of the technical discussion, which in turn reflects the statement of work. Some of the criteria listed for an outline can guide the contributors and team members in preparing the material for a rough draft, which:

a) Covers all the main points of the requirements and response, as appropriate.

b) Approaches program technically, stating the problem(s), discussing approaches, noting and supporting facts, and provide rationale for reaching conclusions.

c) Takes into account points of lower rank and reflects a consistent approach.

d) Avoids excessive details, faulty coordination, and over-lapping points covered elsewhere.

e) Creates impression of unity, coherence, emphasis, and proportion through logical development of structure.

More important than establishing paragraph or subsection headings, the outline identifies each subject or idea covered in writing and supported by data. All supporting sections of the technical proposal must reflect consistency, coordination, and responsive treatment. Specialists, experienced in preparing material on contractor qualifications, program management, reliability, etc., must be familiar with the program requirements and technical approach. This enables members of the team to furnish inputs consistent with the technical discussion.

After the main sections have been drafted, the Introduction and Summary can be prepared. For this, functions, approach, and structure have been outlined for use as a guide.

FUNCTION:

a) To introduce document

b) To present essence of technical approach

c) To summarize major features of subjects covered

d) Relate subjects to various sections detailed in body

APPROACH:

e) Persuasively promotes specific program capabilities.

f) Readable for management, customer, contracts, etc.

g) Point of view is customers interests and goals.

h) Like a presentation, tells story and explains.

STRUCTURE:

i) Relates proposal to problem or request in opening.

j) Briefly explains proposed response or solution.

k) Covers benefits to customer; performance, reliability, cost, and unique features.

l) Describes company capability in terms of qualifications, experience, manpower, and facilities.

m) Provides convincing reasons to accept proposed approach.

n) Establishes continuity for sections which follow.

The *Proposal Planning and Preparation Guide* recommended for personnel responsible for producing technical proposals, can be adapted for specific programs and organizations. The guide represents the minimum coordinated effort necessary to produce an integrated response to a request for a proposal. This approach helps put all concerned on the right track and increase the probability of acceptance and contract award. In addition, it helps evaluators reach the conclusion that the organization submitting the proposal knows what it's doing.

The guide for *Proposal Analysis and Review* helps evaluate the content and treatment of various sections, including the plans and estimates. It can be used by engineering, management, marketing, and contracts administration to ensure response to requirements.

When designs, technologies, and organizations compete for contracts, the common starting points are the requirements, as stated in the requests for proposals. The most extensive treatment of responses to technical problems and sophisticated management sections of proposals won't guarantee that a proposal will be the basis of a contract award. The reasons for an award may be reduced to costs, general capability, design, or innovative features. The reasons may even be minor or unknown to the bidding organizations.

Contracts are generally awarded after a presentation is made as a follow up to the technical proposal by finalists in competitive bids. The presentation provides an occasion for the procuring agency to ask questions to members of the team that represents the company submitting the proposal. On a large contract, the representatives will generally involve management, marketing, engineering, and contracts administration.

PROPOSAL PLANNING AND PREPARATION GUIDE

1. Kick-off Meeting (Preliminary conference)	Distribute and review RRP.	Team members
	Discuss approach and make assignments.	Proposal Manager
	Establish statement of work.	Team Members
	Establish proposal schedule.	Proposal Coordinator
2. Preliminary Effort	Research data and collect intelligence.	Team members
	Define technical approach.	Proposal Manager
	Prepare rough draft.	Engineering
	Prepare rough estimate.	Engineering
3. Technical Conference	Resolve technical problems.	Team members
	Review technical approach.	Team members
	Review rough estimate.	Team members
	Determine final approach, deviations, changes, etc.	Team members
4. Rough Draft	Organize technical sections.	Proposal Coordinator
	Organize management sections.	Proposal Coordinator
	Review technical sections.	Engineering
	Edit technical and management sections.	Marketing/Proposal Coordinator
5. Estimates and Costs	Prepare program estimate.	Engineering
	Review program estimate.	Marketing
	Review all estimates and schedules.	Management
	Approve subcontracts, travel, per diem, etc.	Management
6. Final Draft	Introduction and Summary.	Proposal Coordinator
	Complete sections; capability.	Proposal Coordinator
	Complete document (title page, schedules, resumes, etc.).	Proposal Coordinator
	Approve final draft.	Marketing
7. Art & Production	Prepare art work (lead time).	Art Department
	Prepare reproducible copy.	Production
	Check art work; diagrams.	Engineering
	Review art and reproducibles.	Proposal Coordinator
8. Publication	Approve reproduction.	Proposal Coordinator
	Prepare costs and contract.	Contract Management
	Approve and sign documents.	Management
	Prepare cover letter for mgt. signature.	Marketing

FORWARD AND DISTRIBUTE DOCUMENTS   Marketing

PROPOSAL ANALYSIS AND REVIEW

I. TECHNICAL APPROACH

    A. Reflects an understanding of the request and problem.

    B. Proposed solution is responsive to requirements.

    C. Approach reflects a significant technological advance.

    D. Alternate solutions are proposed, as required.

    E. Response is clear, organized, objective, and readable.

    F. Deviations and exceptions are justified and explained.

II. PROGRAM PLAN

    G. Is consistent with statement of work and schedule.

    H. Proposes realistic schedules and estimates.

    I. Statement of work, schedule, and time efforts are consistent.

    J. Various tasks reflect an understanding of the program.

    K. Subcontractors, facilities, and tests are covered.

    L. Program organization shows functions of persons assigned and relationships of principals within organization.

III. CAPABILITY

    M. Responsibilities of management are individually described.

    N. Resumes of key personnel stress background in technology.

    O. Facilities and equipment for program are described.

    P. Facilities and equipment owned by Government are described.

    Q. Related experience includes contracts awarded.

IV. COST

    R. Price is based on requirements, schedule, and type of contract.

    S. Price reflects realistic estimate of manpower and materials.

    T. Funding available for program is taken into account.

    U. Costs are emphasized in proportion to major tasks.

V. Price reflects a contribution by company towards program.

V. GENERAL

W. Requirements for contractor data, quality control, reliability and tests, as well as software and data are met.

X. Introduction to proposal effectively summarizes document, sells programs, states problem, proposes approaches, and effectively enhances image of company.

Y. Communicates factual and original information coherently; clearly.

Z. Uses illustrations, graphs, charts, and diagrams effectively.

TECHNICAL PRESENTATIONS

A technical presentation is generally an oral briefing that follows a proposal for a large contract. Since the technical proposal provides no updating for changes or new developments, this provision is conveniently satisfied by the presentation. The technical presentation helps bring various items up to date and enables the company to "sell" the program. In addition, the printed word does not provide sufficient emphasis on the decision issue; i.e., what often develops as the main reason for selecting one contractor over another.

The decision issue may not be known until the proposal has been delivered and some feedback about the program has been received. The technical presentation also makes it possible for the customer and contractor to make personal contact, discuss various aspects of the program, answer questions, and establish rapport for negotiations.

The technical presentation provides an opportunity to present an image in person and to stress the decision issue. The occasion makes it possible to analyze the audience, introduce new elements to supplement the proposal, and to persuade key personnel authorized to make the decision to award the contract. The impact of the speaker who represents the organization, as well as those with expertise in the technology, can be powerful. The expert can inform, persuade, and bring the audience up to date on the spot. Models and other visual aids can be introduced to support the presentation.

When used properly, the technical presentation is an effective means of communication to influence those who are authorized to make major decisions. To prepare for the presentation, the principal speaker should analyze the audience, the occasion, the speaker's impact, and the material. The speaker selects and arranges the material into four sections: introduction, purpose, body, and conclusion. An allowance in time must also be made for questions. An *Analysis for Technical Presentations* is recommended for its preparation.

The introduction tunes in the audience and establishes rapport. A captive audience does not ensure captive interests. The speaker uses rapport to get everybody on the same frequency so that interest can be aroused. The speaker may begin by talking about a major concern of the audience, such as a possible solution to a specific problem, performance, reliability, or safety. People take interest in how others respond to crucial situations.

A brief story, an illustration, or an example that relates directly to the subject at hand can accomplish several things in a nutshell to attract attention, establish acceptance of the speaker, and help move towards a decision. "Yesterday, around three o'clock, one of our engineers came up with an idea that changed an important facet of this program. We have the man here to tell you about it. He may point out some of the things you've been seeking for a long time," etc.

The purpose briefly states the function of the program or equipment proposed. Sometimes called the application, it relates the program or project to the problem. A colonel in the audience might marvel at the ingenuity used to package a module, but wonder how it is used and in which part of the system the module performs. To establish the purpose with clarity, it may be necessary to introduce background material. The relationship of the product to the system or program should not sound far-fetched. Unless there are high-level scientists or engineers present, formulas and references only specialists could appreciate should be avoided.

ANALYSIS FOR TECHNICAL PRESENTATIONS

AUDIENCE

1) Who are members of the audience, by name and title?

2) What are their responsibilities in making decisions?

3) What are their backgrounds and experience?

4) What are their interests and prejudices?

5) What do we know that is unique about each member?

6) What is their function at the presentation?

7) How much time do they have for making the decision?

OCCASION AND SPEAKER'S IMPACT

8) Where and when will the presentation be made?

9) Is there anything special about this occasion?

10) What impact will the speaker(s) have on the audience?

11) What does the audience expect of each speaker?

SELECTION AND ARRANGEMENT OF MATERIAL

12) In the light of the audience and the occasion, what is the best treatment possible for the material selected?

13) What is the best arrangement for the material?

14) What can be left out if time runs out?

15) What visual material, props, or media are most effective?

16) Can the presentation be presented naturally to make the subject easy to understand by those present?

17) Are the members of the team prepared for questions about high technology and support sections. Are the members qualified to answer questions with responsibility and accuracy?

The body describes the product and how it works. It covers the high spots and can be illustrated with sketches, slides or a film. Although pictures can be more interesting, introducing them with detailed explanations may cause interest to wane. The effective picture is the one large enough to see from a distance, that tells its story with clarity, and demonstrates some things that words could not do as well.

When using films, the speaker should comment briefly and ask for questions at the end of the showing. A list of specifications can be dull and easily forgotten. Features should be pinpointed out from different aspects, but size, shape, and weight stressed only as they relate directly to requirements. In building peaks of importance, something unique in the decision issue, emphasize the characteristics of the program. Avoid debate, but rather instill a desire to learn more about the program.

The conclusion summarizes the main points with a view to getting off the floor quickly. As the next step, one may ask for questions or suggest some action to take. Since we're all curious to see what the new idea looks like, the conclusion can feature a mock-up or an attractive artist's concept based on preliminary designs.

Introduce speakers with half-minute resumes of background, responsibilities or specialties. Rehearse everything to afford speakers practice in making individual contributions. Keep the presentation lively, moving quickly, and entertaining. Anticipate a favorable decision in making the presentation with enthusiasm. Use feedback to gauge response. Ask for questions. When preparation has been adequate, answers become easy and convincing.

Preparing Speeches

In modern times, Sir Winston Churchill deserves the honor of being called our greatest speaker. Franklin D. Roosevelt, his contemporary, was not far behind. Taking advantage of the radio broadcast addresses from the White House, Roosevelt unified the nation through some difficult years. Both Churchill and Roosevelt had responsibilities in adversity; mainly, World War II.

Great speakers are made—the hard way—through adversity, persistence, industry, and practice. Democracies offer better occasions for speaking to free peoples than dictatorships, which limit speeches to a few. Great speakers thrive in democracies, such as ancient Greece, Rome, and the United States. In the free world, speakers are faced with challenges to stimulate, enlighten, and inspire. In captive societies, speakers tend to harangue audiences for hours, spreading hatred and propaganda, whether it is nationalistic, religious, Fascist, or Communist.

During World War II, Churchill's and Roosevelt's integrity were never in doubt. Stalin's and Hitler's were. Churchill and Roosevelt encouraged and galvanized millions when the hours were darkest: during bombings, sinkings, defeats, and losses by the Allies. On the other hand, in dictatorships, fear still keeps their peoples nervous as conscious victims of ignorance and oppression .

In modern times, most of the great speakers of our country made clear, interesting, and effective presentations. The ideas had substance and made sense to the audience. The material was selected with care and arranged in an organized manner. The words used were simple, vivid, and pregnant with impact. The delivery was inspired and forceful. The audience felt strongly that the speaker sincerely believed what he expressed. These characteristics were especially true of Churchill, Roosevelt, and Kennedy.

When we respond as if we want a speaker to come back and address us again, that person must have been unassuming, yet inspired; entertaining, yet not comical; informative without boring; and, enlightened without disturbing our sensibilities. He was able to absorb our attention to its fullest. Whether he was a salesman, preacher, politician, athlete, or teacher, we hoped he could go on.

How does one achieve such spellbinding attraction? It's not looks or promises of a fortune. Rather, it's a form of charisma, characterized by ideas that make sense, a delivery with candor, an arrangement that rises in interest as it moves along, and a few stories or illustrations that entertain as they emphasize a point. It's creative communication that enthralls the listeners in a rewarding experience.

ANALYSIS OF AUDIENCE

You've been asked to make a speech and you accept. The situation now calls for an analysis of the audience you expect to address. This is an opportunity to present something of value and enjoyment to a large group. What you have to say should be entertaining, informative, enlightening, persuasive, or a combination of these characteristics. The nature and the needs of the audience come first. The response you seek from this audience relates to the subject and purpose, both of which must be recognizable.

In the process of establishing the subject and purpose, one asks questions and conducts research about the potential listeners. Within the time frame before the day of the speech and resources available, you collect as much information as possible about your potential audience. *A Guide to Preparation and Presentation* can start you off. However, you'll need more specific information, as applicable and significant for the speech or occasion. Try to get as much information about the audience under the 12 headings listed:

1)	Age	7)	Education
2)	Sex	8)	Prejudices
3)	Professions	9)	Interests
4)	Religion	10)	Concerns
5)	Ethnic Group	11)	Political Persuasion
6)	Economic Level	12)	Specific Subjects

SPEECHES

A GUIDE TO PREPARATION AND PRESENTATION

PREPARATION

AUDIENCE	RESEARCH	CONTENT	STYLE
Occasion	Experience	Subject/Purpose	Clear
Composition	Books	Stories/Jokes	Simple
Organization	Magazines	Arguments	Accurate
Size	Journals/Papers	Quotations	Brief
Background	Readers' Guide	Explanations	Unified
Attitudes	Microfilm Indexes	Comparisons/Contrasts	Original
Beliefs	Interviews	Figures of Speech	Vital
Mood	Surveys	Definitions	Varied
Expectations	Catalogs	Wit/Humor	Candid
Speaker's Impact	Organizations	Logic/Persuasion	Urbane

PRESENTATION

SETTING	VISUALS	PSYCHOLOGICAL	DELIVERY
Day/Time	Integration	Rapport	Voice
Location	Props	Empathy	Dynamics
Facility	Charts	Emotions	Articulation
Dinner/Seating	Maps	Associations	Pronunciations
Acoustics	Slides	Motivation	Pauses
Microphone	Projections	Conflicts	Gestures
Platform	Film	Continuity	Eye Contact
Lectern/Podium	Graphs	Intellect	Rate/Rhythm
Lighting	Models	Values	Breathing
Security	Drawings (Easel)	Complexes	Tone Quality

Important questions one can ask include:

A) What are attitudes of audience toward speaker, occasion, and anticipated subject?

B) How flexible and open is the audience about certain subjects and what responses can be predicted?

C) Is the audience a homogeneous group with common interests or a mixture of classes, political persuasions, and ethnic groups?

D) How important are age, sex, and income level of audience with respect to speaker, purpose, and anticipated subject?

As you gather data about the audience, you may want to change your subject and/or purpose. For example, you can't discuss subjects about which members of the audience are better informed. If you're a stranger to the audience, you may decide to satisfy their curiosity with an entertaining treatment of a government policy decision. In the process you can insert a few personal details to help the audience know what kind of a personality you represent. If the audience knows much about you, you may have to talk about a side of you that's removed from the established image.

You can't underestimate the audience, especially by going over familiar stories and ideas. You must try to provide something special for those who have come to listen to you. If you do a good job of analyzing the prospective audience, you'll select a realistic purpose, that suggests an interesting subject, presented in an appropriate style for the occasion. This is a tall order, but that's what it means to analyze an audience.

You'll have a challenging exercise juggling subjects, purposes, and treatments—all for the benefit of the audience and for the possible positive response you'll earn. The audience pays in time (sometimes including money) for the privilege you have of providing entertainment, enlightenment, information, a persuasive message, or a combination of all. The listeners and observers of your presentation deserve their time and money's worth. Addressing a large audience is a privilege and often an exciting honor.

SUBJECT AND PURPOSE

The best subject to talk about is the one with which you're most familiar and in which the audience is expected to have keen interest. Churchill, a well-traveled correspondent, a member of the British Parliament, a master of the English language, and a seasoned writer, could speak on many subjects with authority. Before assuming the Presidency, Lincoln had been a lawyer, an experienced debater, a Congressman, and a raconteur. Although he was surrounded by strife, hate, and the heavy responsibilities of conducting a war of attrition, while President to save the Union, his problems did not diminish his skills as an excellent writer and effective speaker.

Writing and speaking do not necessarily go hand in hand. At the same time, a good writer has an advantage when exercising efforts to become a good speaker. Public speaking is tough: a dynamic, challenging, and creative communication skill. Not only is the speaker on the spot, but boredom must be overcome as one's eyes scan the multitude of eyes focused on the speaker. As you get started and move along to deliver your speech, you must shake off fear, respond to reactions of audience, and take advantage of feedback. These may suggest adjustments in your presentation and treatment of material you have prepared for the occasion.

Even if you're an authority on the subject you or your host selected, you still conduct some research on the subject and purpose. This consists of tapping your brain for ideas, collecting facts, reading books and magazines, and conducting interviews. For a 15-minute talk, about eight hours of research and preparation are recommended. You can count on another three hours to write and revise; and, an hour or two to rehearse. This brings the time for preparation to at least 12 hours. If you have spoken on the subject before, you still have preparation time of six to eight hours.

In selecting a subject, consider topics in which you have a strong interest and with which you feel comfortable. At the same time, take into account the concerns of the audience and subjects of interest that reflect something new or original. The selection process may develop into an exercise of listing and eliminating. If the subject appears to interest you and you feel confident of making a meaningful contribution to others, get to work on it at once.

During research, continue putting the subject to tests of suitability to the audience and occasion; practical in purpose. There's nothing wrong with abandoning ideas and material with which you may have reservations. It's like a suit. If it doesn't fit and you're not comfortable with it for any reason, such as style, color, or size, drop it. It may cause more troubles later, and perhaps at the critical stage: during delivery. When you feel comfortable about the audience, subject, and purpose, you'll probably do a good job of preparation and practice.

Take your time to investigate a subject thoroughly and to anticipate its implications for the audience. Selecting a subject is an important decision and the process must not be arbitrary or impulsive. Also, there are instances, when developments in events and changes in situations suggest dropping the subject and working on an alterative. Being prepared means having a plan for contingencies up through final rehearsal or a few hours before delivery—when late changes can be made.

We are all unique individuals in the sense that our heredity, upbringing, education, and experiences contribute to our differences. From that standpoint, we can be interesting to others, provided we know how to talk about ourselves: what to say and how to say it. On the other hand, we may bore the audience if we talk too much about ourselves, even though we know the subject well. When we talk about ourselves, the more lightly and the more humorous, the better.

The speech should not be a mystery story or a menu with a variety of dishes served to the audience. As soon as possible, the audience wants to know what the speech is about. If you cover too many topics, you won't be able to go into depth on any one. If you're comfortable with the subject, based on what you know of the audience and what is expected of you, go ahead. You can think of a speech as entertainment with redeeming values or a message packaged for the benefit and enjoyment of the audience.

Nobody ever settled a controversial subject, like abortion, integration, unions, gun control, etc. There's nothing wrong with being social minded, if you have ideas that can alert your audience to possibilities and approaches to current problems. During the Presidential campaign in the fall of 1932, Franklin D. Roosevelt addressed a large crowd in Detroit on the social philosophy of the New Deal. Even though the ideas were revolutionary at the time, he was able to gain considerable moral support for his views. Like Roosevelt, if you're inspired, the combination of ammunition in the form of cogent arguments and forceful delivery can elicit favorable response from the audience.

If you want to talk about patriotism, the Communist threat, or women's rights, you should have something new or different to present. If your stories or arguments have been heard before, you're inviting negative reaction or disinterest. Controversy, if handled expertly, can galvanize an audience and win over many converts or admirers to your side. Regardless of subject, it's good practice to clear your speech with your host to avoid shock, surprise, or the barrier of insulation from the people who invited you to speak.

COLLECTING MATERIALS

Your audience, subject, and purpose will suggest directions to take in gathering materials. To influence or inform an audience, you may have to concentrate on statistics, supporting facts, authoritative sources, and arguments. To entertain, you may include anecdotes and stories of human interest as they relate to the subject. Most speeches have a cohesive blend of humor, wit, personal experience, facts, and compelling logic.

A reliable approach to materials is to collect more than you need and record your ideas on cards or sheets identified by subject, source, author, date, and page, as applicable. If it's a conversation or a personal experience, label it accordingly. A well-organized file of information for speeches can be used as a storehouse for future reference.

Newspapers, magazine articles, and books are major sources of information. Unless you speak often or operate out of a speakers bureau, there's no need to maintain a file of clippings. Large general public or college libraries are good sources for access to speech material. You'll also find abstracts, indexes, and documents stored on microfilm with facilities for obtaining copies. As a general list of sources for gathering material for speeches, the following are suggested:

1) Personal experiences

2) Inquiries of friends and acquaintances

3) Newspaper indexes of speeches, articles, and news events

4) New books from bookstores and libraries

5) Magazines, reviews, and digests

6) Abstracts, references, and special libraries

7) Interviews and surveys

8) Legal, medical, and scientific journals.

During your research to gather materials, check your sources for bias or one-sided views. As you read and select, start planning your speech. It should reflect views with which you agree or feel comfortable. Your approach should uncover nuggets of information, quotations, statistics, and illustrations you can fit into your outline. You may find it convenient to identify all material and then key each item to use in a separate column of the outline which can resemble a worksheet.

As you arrive at some conclusion or conviction, make notes in outline form to insert in the summary. Then, relate the material for the main points to the outline in the body. If you have gathered sufficient material for your speech, you'll have little difficulty outlining the body of your speech. You can reduce work on the introduction by preparing it after you have completed the body and conclusion of the speech.

OUTLINING THE SPEECH

In preparing an outline for the speech, the *Guide for Outlining Speeches is* recommended, since all speeches must have an introduction, body, and conclusion. As a matter of practice,

GUIDE FOR OUTLINING SPEECHES

Structure	Approaches	Techniques
INTRODUCTION (Opening and Central Idea)		
1. Opening	An illustration or anecdote	Interest factor
	A quotation	Emphasize point
2. Main topic or purpose	A challenging statement	Capture attention
	A personal reference	Human relationship
	A question	Underline subject
3. Transition to body	A statement of purpose	Define goal
	A response to introducer	Personal continuity
BODY (Development)		
I Superior head	Definition	Exposition
	Functional breakdown	Narration
A. 1st main point	Chronological order	Description
—Support	Order of support	Dialogue
	Order of climax	Dramatization
B. 2nd main point	Comparison and contrast	Argumentation
—Support	Cause/effect relationships	Persuasion
	Geographical/spatial breakdown	Visualization
C. 3rd main point	Analysis	Sense perception
—Support	Amplification	Illustration
II Superior head	Integration	Abstraction
A. 1st main point	Logic	Figures of speech
—Support		
B. 2nd main point	Arguments	Quotations
—Support		
CONCLUSION (Summary)		
I Recapitulate purpose	A quotation	Summary statement
	Resolution of main point	Emotional appeal
A. 1st point	Illustration or anecdote	Motivating goal
B. 2nd point	A question or reference	Call for action
II Appropriate end	An appeal	Supporting conclusion

outlining should not be done until the analysis of the audience has been completed with the subject, purpose, and occasion in mind. In addition, we should gather enough materials for a speech prepared for extemporaneous delivery.

Review the materials selected to prepare the outline. Trust your memory to recall the topics and general content of what you've read or perused. Before outlining, try to organize the speech in your mind, arranging the most effective points in the latter part of the body. The introduction will make a statement and even suggest a promise—what you're going to talk about. You're not going to resort to dramatic suspense or surprise. State your purpose and introduce the central idea in an approach that attracts attention.

You may use humor, a quotation, an anecdote, or a rhetorical question. Your material and your feelings about the subject, purpose, and audience will determine the content, approach, and techniques or patterns of organization to use. Try to end up with an arrangement of ideas which best support your purpose and cover the subject in a manner that will encourage response; or better, involvement by the audience.

If possible, enlist the help of experienced people around you, taking advantage of their contributions and criticism. During outlining, it is important to determine the best pattern of organization. The following patterns are suggested:

1) Order of support
2) Order of climax
3) Topical order
4) Chronological order
5) Functional order
6) Space order
7) Problem—solution
8) Causal relationships (cause-effect; effect-cause)
9) Logical (induction or deduction)
10) Elimination process

Organize the structure in outline form by inserting heads, main points, and supports. Depending on the main point made under a superior head, select the most effective pattern of organization and key the material reference in another column of your outline sheet. At first your outline looks like a page of disorganized notes. After revisions, retype the outline, occasionally checking the material each topic represents. A fresh and clean outline then becomes the basis for preparing the text.

Before you start writing the speech, test the outline for effectiveness and sufficiency. You may even try rehearsing the speech in outline form; i.e., using the outline as notes. Recheck the conclusions, the headings, supporting material, and the introduction. Make changes in the outline, as needed, to clarify, emphasize, and strengthen the proposed speech as a whole. Eliminate redundancy, unless you want to repeat important points for emphasis.

Look for variety in supporting material, knowing that too many statistics or too many quotations from authorities will lose effectiveness through sameness. If there are emotional appeals or persuasive points to motivate the audience, ask yourself if they sound credible or genuine. If everything appears adequate for the speech and in effective order, you can start writing.

WRITING THE SPEECH

Much of the writing of a speech consists of recording what you formulate in your mind, as suggested by the outline, and what you select from the material collected. In your efforts to be original, it is better to express your own ideas where possible, than rephrase what you've read in the material. The words used to make your points should be clear in usage and the language should be appropriate to the subject and occasion. Appropriate language is essential, because it helps in the selection process of material for content and style.

As you write, think of the words as spoken. You know the result will not be an article to be read, but the preparation of the substance of a one-way conversation. Concentrate on words, expressions, and figurative language appropriate to the subject, purpose, and audience.

When using a quotation from an authority or public figure, you want to be certain the source or person is familiar to the audience. If you tell them a story that hasn't been heard before, you know they'll pay attention. Try to be original with material that makes a point. Instead of listing some qualities of a great person, for example, tell a story that emphasizes or illustrates an important quality of that person. If it's based on a personal experience no one else knows about, so much the better.

When persuading an audience, write down the major points and support them with facts, figures, and examples. If you have been convinced by a statement, assume the audience will be convinced, providing you have backed up the statements with evidence, proof, or supporting details. Stories, illustrations, and examples generally convince audiences better than logic or rationale. Stories are easy to follow and the audience can identify with experiences of other individuals. Members of the audience can put themselves in similar situations.

Writing the speech is equivalent to doing your homework as a speaker. If you're entertaining the audience, as you impart significant information or personal philosophy, include your stories, illustrations, and humor. How do they sound to you as you put them down on paper? As you write, you enlarge your resources of expression and test how appropriate your language sounds for the audience and occasion. The language should be simple enough for every listener to know what you're talking about.

People can change what they think you said, but cannot alter what you actually expressed. Naturally, how you say something can suggest meaning in context. Consequently, as you write or revise, read the sentences aloud for exact meaning as you hear them. You know the listeners must grasp the meanings of words and statements at once, as you move along in your speech. Unless you feel the meaning is unclear, you're not going to stop and rephrase or repeat something. Consequently, you plan for transitions between points through repetition and summary. You bridge gaps you think you need for reinforcement.

You also help the slow listeners keep up with the rest of the audience. As in music, the transition picks up the end of one theme, summarizing in the process, and ties it with (or builds a bridge across) the new idea or the next theme. Since you're writing an extemporaneous speech, you may decide what to use for transitions, based on the feedback you receive from the audience.

Let's examine some appropriate language, as used in speeches by Churchill, Kennedy, and Lincoln. During Britain's darkest hours of World War II, Churchill could have said, "The time has come to make sacrifices. We shall not waiver or lose. We shall defeat the Nazis on land, on sea, and in the air...We owe so much to our soldiers, sailors, and airmen." This is what he actually said. "We shall not flag or fail. We shall go on to the end...We shall defend our island whatever the cost may be; we shall fight on the beaches, landing grounds, in streets, and in the hills...Never in the field of human conflict was so much owed by so many to so few."

During his inaugural speech, John Kennedy could have said, "Don't ask what the Government will do for you, but what you can do for Government, democracy, and freedom." He actually said. "My fellow citizens of the world: ask not what America will do for you—ask what you can do for your country...ask not what America will do for you, but what together we can do for the freedom of man."

Lincoln's Gettysburg address could have begun, "In 1776, the statesmen representing the Continental Congress of our thirteen colonies declared their independence to establish the United States of America, a new republic dedicated to liberty and equality." The solemn occasion suggested a funeral oration with a poetic cadence and sonorous effects. Try to hear the sounds of: "Fourscore and seven years ago, our fathers brought forth on this continent a new nation, conceived in liberty and dedicated to the proposition that all men are created equal."

Take your time writing by thinking in short positive sentences. State your ideas in the active voice rather than the passive one. Specific and concrete words should generally prevail over general and abstract ones. Useless words may be tolerated in a conversation, but have no place in a speech. The tighter the sentences, the more effective the meaning. Your punctuation marks in writing will be translated into pauses and emphases; in rising and falling inflections, the invisible punctuation of speech.

Nouns and verbs are the body and soul of ideas, whereas adjectives and adverbs are the muscle and nerves. Relate pronouns to their antecedents by positioning them as close as possible to each other. Write as you would speak, in a natural and relaxed style, reserving force to emphasize a point and occasional humor to lubricate the wheels of interest. The figurative language and imagery you use should evoke identification and meaning in relation to the ideas expressed, rather than distract the audience.

You can't go astray if you say something simply and clearly to make a point. The discipline you impose on yourself can reflect an attitude to make a positive contribution with candor, humility, and originality. You are unique and you can prove it if you work hard enough in any effort in creative communication, such as public speaking.

Figurative language, like metaphors, similes, and hyperboles, must be appropriate and not overused. It's more important to be effective than call attention to unnecessary alliteration. "Nattering nabobs of negativism" has little meaning that's useful and does more to call attention to the speaker than apparently making a point. Although figurative language seems more suited to poetry and fiction, knowing how to use them appropriately and usefully in a speech can reap dividends.

An artist would know what alazarin crimson looked like, but an audience would not, unless it consisted of a group of experts in landscape or portrait painting. "The rich color of a red cherry" is a more effective sense impression enhanced by the image of the cherry evoked in the imaginations of the listeners.

As a speaker you can resort to imagery and sense impressions like storytellers. You can stimulate the audience's imagination, stir the emotions, and make appeals to evoke responses. "When she slapped my face, I was embarrassed by the clap heard around the room. All eyes were turned on me like double-barreled shotguns. I was too shocked to talk, even though I had the attention E. F. Hutton would have envied."

You have written, revised, and polished your speech. The time has come to test it by reading it aloud, taping it, then listening to it as you play it back. If you can use a videotape recording with the benefit of a video camera and cassette recorder, you'll have an excellent tool for rehearsal and evaluation. Put yourself in the position of a critic or evaluator of the content of the speech and check for the following:

1) Treatment of subject for the audience

2) Structure of speech: recognizable

3) Variety of approach and content

4) Achievement of purpose for audience

5) Appropriate language for subject and audience

6) Value of speech to audience

We have arrived at what is considered the most challenging communication skill of all: speech delivery.

Speech Rehearsal
and Delivery

Most everything comes easy after one has rehearsed a performance, whether it is acting a part, playing an instrument, or delivering a speech. In fact, practice in delivery and rehearsal add to the confidence of the performer and the quality of the performance. Those who depend on luck or miracles ask for trouble or possible failure. Even telling a simple joke or anecdote takes practice, ensuring minimal problems in delivery, memory, or timing.

Practice in rehearsing a speech, whether it is taped or before a live group, pays off in two types of dividends: those that relate to the content and those that indicate how effectively the speech was presented. There is nothing wrong with reading speeches of others aloud just to get the feel of the emphases, the pauses, and the dynamics of delivery.

In real situations, such as Toastmasters, the speaker can obtain criticism that is normally not received in other formal or informal situations. Self-criticism is not easy, but should be a part of the speaker's agenda; generally with the use of a tape recorder. Ideally, criticism should be sought from professionals, if possible. Many experienced speakers look for friends and acquaintances as sounding boards to test a speech or get reactions about the delivery. Like everything else, practice delivery by using a full-length mirror, a tape player, or if you can afford it, go as far as delivery before a television camera for playback on a VCR and monitor.

Opportunities to speak in public are open to most people who have a desire, especially for those who develop their skills in speaking to large audiences. If you follow Lincoln's precept that every occasion is an important one, you'll take advantage of every opportunity to address a group. The opportunities range from conversations, interviews, and sales talks to meetings. Taking active part in local politics, joining organizations like Toastmasters, and getting involved in charitable activities also offer many opportunities. Much depends on the time you're willing to invest and effort to improve your skills.

Motivation to learn, practice, and participate is an essential factor in one's development as an effective speaker. Perfection in speech as a goal can deliver unexpected rewards. Dorothy Sarnoff stated it aptly by the title of her excellent book, "Speech Can Change Your Life." The abridged passage from "Kennedy" by Theodore C. Sorensen offers a valuable insight of the principles the late John F. Kennedy applied in preparing texts for speeches, his style, and del.ivery.

Kennedy's development and growth as a speaker was evident in his televised debates with former President Nixon. Even though Nixon had a large staff of writers, it appears Kennedy was more in tune with his smaller staff. Also, Kennedy took public speaking and statesmanship more seriously; involved himself more in self-improvement, whereas Nixon never did reach his potential. His "ah's" sound more memorable than the substance of his speeches.

MANNERISMS

As soon as possible, one has to rid oneself of mannerisms, which can be distractions of habit heard too often. As mannerisms, they are often too characteristic of conversations and speeches. Mannerisms can range from unnecessary physical movements to "ah's," "and ah's." "you know's" and "I'm going to tell you something." Like habits, the speaker often has little control and may even be unaware of these distractions. The "ah's" are convenient and superfluous pauses for considering or formulating statements. Their presence is often overlooked, but their absence can surely be appreciated.

Self-control and respect for the audience is evident when mannerisms are not present during a speech. Practices, such as swaying, gripping the sides of a lectern, adjusting articles of wear, or overuse of fingers, hands, and arms should be avoided. The audience will often pay more attention to what you're doing than to what you're saying. The net result is a cancellation of positive efforts. Sometimes it's a case of nerves conjuring up jitters that speakers display in a variety of forms.

The key word is *control*— of the voice, speech, and manner. Here's a list of items to consider before speaking in public:

1) Dress for the occasion: neatly;

2) Prepare for the occasion: thoroughly;

3) Stand up straight: confidently;

4) Stay in one spot, unless necessary to move for a gesture;

5) Stand poised: avoid rocking or swaying;

6) Use fingers, hands, and arms for useful gestures;

7) Practice continuity between statements, avoiding "ah's";

8) Look at persons being addressed in the eyes, not up and down.

REHEARSING SPEECH

You have completed the jobs of researching, outlining, and writing the speech. The time has come to test your text. Like an actor, use rehearsals to prepare for your live performance. Not only does rehearsing provide a chance to check out the speech, but it also enables you to practice delivery. Using a tape recorder will be of great value during rehearsal. Read aloud a double or triple-spaced copy of the speech from a simulated lectern. Read the speech several times for evaluation, revisions, and practice in delivery.

A) Check ideas as they relate to each other for continuity and the sense they make for the listener. Edit it as necessary.

B) Mark up speech for emphasis by underlying key words and statements that may be reinforced with gestures. Allow for pauses at appropriate intervals so that the meanings can be grasped. You may know what the speech is about, but if you race through words and phrases, the audience may not be able to interpret your ideas as the sounds of words flow through space.

C) After your editing, read the speech for a tape recording. Play it back and listen to the speech as if you are the audience. Make notes of weak areas in voice, diction, intended meanings, and general effectiveness.

D) Prepare an outline of headings, subheads, stories, statistics, etc., on cue cards, which you will eventually use during actual delivery.

E) Rehearse speech this time from the cards and use the tape recorder again. During playback, check for language, pace, and emphases making necessary changes on cards.

F) Using a final version of the cards with outlined notes, deliver speech as a "dress rehearsal," and record it again or have someone listen for a final evaluation. If you anticipate applause, be prepared to stop briefly. Listen to the playback of your final version and make appropriate notes, or accept criticism from listener. Make the changes you feel are necessary before delivery.

Some of the items that can be checked during rehearsal are:

Voice	Volume	Articulation	Pitch
Tempo	Rhythm	Manner	Appearance
Pauses	Variety	Effect	Identity
Involvement	Gestures	Eye Contact	Diction
Emphasis	Mannerisms	Slurring	Inflections

VOICE AND DICTION

If you taped your speech during rehearsal, you had opportunities to listen to your voice and check your diction. The quality of your voice and the manner in which you use it make impressions on the audience. How you speak, how you sound, and the confidence with which you express yourself are as important as what you have to say. Your voice can convey conviction, sincerity, and a sense of importance about your message. If you say something in a light vein or with indifference, your audience will sense it immediately and interpret it accordingly. Even though you may use simple words in a conversational manner, you must be prepared to make the best possible presentation of your message.

Most difficulties with a voice can be overcome through training and exercises. Many speakers go so far as to take up singing or voice lessons and acting to improve voice quality, breathing, projection, and articulation. Reading aloud, and in some cases, speech therapy may be in order for problems in articulation. Your voice, in concert with your speech organs, must produce words in a stream intelligible to the audience.

Diction refers to the selection and use of words in expressing yourself orally. Decisions for these should be made from the audience's point of view. Enunciation is distinct pronunciation, which must conform to standards and be free of mistakes. Articulation involves the clear natural sounds that make the speech intelligible to the audience, and it comes with practice.

Good voice production, like most skills, takes effort for goals to achieve *ease* of expression, clear speech, and attractive tone quality. Recent discoveries indicate that the mind and body are much more closely knit than previously considered. The body is also involved with the voice and speech organs. Consequently, speech delivery is more effective when your body is in good condition and synchronized with speech activity.

Breathing can be a problem when the speaker doesn't have enough air to complete a statement. Relax and breathe fully, smoothly, and slowly to get enough air. You can run out of air if you use too much force at the beginning of a statement. It's good practice to read poetry, speeches, and drama, while trying to adhere to the punctuation and the intended sense of passages, such as pausing, emphasizing, etc.

Your rate of speech depends on how long you sustain sounds and pause at various intervals. if the articulation is clear, the rate can be increased. Much depends on the subject, the words used, and fluency. Variety for interest and control for emphasis are matters of practice and listening to yourself on a playback of a tape recording. Timing yourself at various rates, between 100 and 200 words a minute will help establish a comfortable rate. Important points can be uttered at a slower rate for the benefit of the audience, the ultimate judge of a speech.

There should be no doubt about the pronunciation of each word. When preparation has been adequate for the speech and the occasion, your self-confidence and control of the situation are translated into an effective presentation.

When you look up the pronunciation of a word in a dictionary, check its spelling, derivation, and shades of meaning that can depend on context. Enunciate the word slowly several times and use it in a sentence where the meaning is defined by its context. Look up words to avoid mispronunciation or slurring. This consists of adding sounds that a word does not contain or omitting sounds they do contain. As you speak, you want no distracting influences for the audiences you face. You want them to concentrate on what you have to say.

On the other hand, if you are too precise in the pronunciation of certain words, especially when certain sounds in a word are combined in a process known as assimilation, (nature; soldier) are not literally pronounced as spelled. If you talk too slowly and distinctly, the assimilation disappears. If you talk too fast, assimilation shows up. (I gotcha vs. I got you.)

Another element related to the voice is intonation, the use of pitch and its variation to stress various words in a sentence. Intonation can be considered as a pattern of inflections: level, rising, and falling. For example, questions are usually asked with rising inflection. (Are you *going?*) Inflection can have a rising-falling-rising pattern. *(What* do you *want?)* An example of falling inflection: *this is* the last time. Level inflection can obviously be dull, like a solemn speech or biblical passage. When listening, during a conversation, note the average pitch of a voice; how it rises and falls; and, ends rising on an important word or when a point is emphasized.

EYE CONTACT AND GESTURES

Eye contact with the audience is very important. No one likes to listen to a person who looks at the ceiling or the floor when talking. When the speaker looks at the audience, each listener can feel as if he or she was being addressed personally. A person appears to mean what he says when looking at the audience or a person directly as he makes a point. Individual members like to feel that they have been singled out for personal attention that only eyes can reflect, except when a person's name is called out.

Experienced speakers, notably effective preachers, like Dr. Robert Schuller of Garden Grove, California, and Dr. Richard Jackson of Phoenix, Arizona, combine effective gestures with eye contact. In the process, they reinforce their inspiring messages as they captivate large audiences before their pulpits in sanctuaries and on television.

Some speakers get carried away with gestures. They think they must move across the podium, emphasize points with arm movements, heads, and fists. When gestures are overdone, the audience can get the impression that the speaker has been carried away with body signals (and emotions) without the appreciation that the audience understands English.

Gestures should be coordinated with the words and statements as reinforcements of ideas, beliefs, and emotions. Uncoordinated or artificial gestures have a self-defeating effect. They can confuse the audience and give the impression of a weak point. The use of effective gestures takes practice and the speaker must feel comfortable with them. Gestures should be practiced and should only be used when they appear natural and necessary. Unless the audience is very large or the acoustics (lack of microphone) are limited, gestures should be reduced in number and magnitude, depending on the type of speech.

During delivery, you'll be concentrating on what you say to the audience and how you express your ideas as you look into their eyes. Your gestures and speech dynamics can reinforce the meanings intended through your powers of speech. To improve and control body movements, as well as coordinated gestures, acting lessons can be of great help. The dynamics of speaking, moving naturally, and the ability to use your eyes, face, and other parts of your body will be enhanced.

DELIVERING THE MESSAGE

The moment of truth is near. Your turn to speak is coming up. The host or emcee is making the introduction. You are ready because you wrote the speech, take pride in it, and rehearsed it from the text and notes. You're about to deliver the message. It's time to control your feelings. You think and feel enthusiasm. You smile with self-confidence. You have something important to say. If you're not prepared for the occasion, the audience will sense it, especially if you take this opportunity too lightly. You must get the audience on your side at once—get their wholehearted attention, like a hero we're rooting for in an exciting drama. You don't want a sea of eyes staring for a surprise or disappointment; smug or disinterested.

Before a salesman can sell his product or service, he sells himself. He starts by establishing rapport. You can do this as you approach the lectern with a genuine smile of confidence. When you exhibit confidence based on self-respect, self-control, and deliberate movements, you'll get immediate attention and respect. As soon as you begin, make your eye contact. Scan or pan the audience like a camera. Include everybody present, even those on the stage or platform.

Open your speech with excitement. You can start off with an anecdote, a challenge, or a dramatic idea. If you're intimate and affectionate, the audience will respond similarly. The most important sentence in your speech is your first. Make it establish contact and rapport between you and the people who are watching and listening. Do it without referring to notes.

Brighten your beginning with humor, a cordial greeting, a tribute, an expression of gratitude, or humorous story. If possible, tell the story on yourself. A humorous story should not just be told for a laugh, but to illustrate a point, a universal truth, something revealing. Will Rogers related his topic for ten days to everyone he met, before he uttered his thought on stage as spontaneous.

When reason and evidence are well dressed, the arguments are organized effectively. Having prepared a case and a cause well backed with evidence, the speaker can exert a strong persuasive force. Minds can be swayed when truths are presented in logical fashion. Be sensitive to your audience, but take command in your own way. Whenever necessary or effective:

a) Pause dramatically;

b) Do the unexpected;

c) Raise your voice suddenly;

d) Lower your voice to a whisper;

e) Meet the situation with humor;

f) Use handy props;

g) Turn an interruption into an asset;

h) Pick out one member of the audience and speak to him;

i) Take the audience into your confidence to show, describe, reveal, share, ask rhetorically, and recognize. (Never scold or tear down an audience.)

j) The audience is a thermometer measuring your temperature. Provide positive stimuli to which the audience can respond with warmth and enthusiasm. Use feedback for positive purposes.

End confidently. When you have said what you were prepared to express, stop. Have your last sentence ready and speak with all the conviction you have or can put into it. The last important sentence can be ringing in the ears of the audience as you leave the lectern. Use significant words that signal and summarize ideas, the climax of your thinking and appeal. As you use those words which stir the emotions with extra effect, you should be moved by your own last sentence. Say your last sentence with force and leave quietly. Leave the podium with dignity and return to your chair.

When you know what you're talking about and have something to say, stimulated by an intense desire to tell it to others, you'll make a good speech. Here are a few suggestions that summarize the subject of speech preparation and delivery.

OPENING   Start with a clear and dramatic statement that arouses the interest of the audience. If you're afraid you'll leave something important out, memorize the opening remarks.

PURPOSE   Tell the audience why you brought up the subject and how it concerns them. Use illustrations for clarity and emphasis.

BODY   Put across points; back them with facts; and, put life into your speech with examples, stories, and rhetorical devices. Dramatize with quotations.

CONCLUSION   Recapitulate major points to underline what you've tried to put across, and why. Close by evoking an emotional and memorable response from the audience.

Be prepared: with facts you can share with the audience.

Be brief: as possible to communicate your message.

Be confident: by memorizing essentials, especially the opening and close.

Be specific: about something you know best — original ideas and unique experiences.

Be clear: using words your audience can understand; strive for simplicity.

Be interesting: from the audience's viewpoint; talk about things that concern most of them.

Be lively: wake them up.

Be funny: Make them laugh and help them lose their tensions.

Be positive: make them feel good.

Be short: so that time, which is of the essence, won't run out.

Innovation and Problem Solving

Innovation and problem solving are treated together because of their interrelationship in similarity of approach. As expressed in writing, inventing, composing, or painting, innovation or creativity is a form of problem solving. The artist or inventor has a goal, concept, or purpose, and tries to achieve it. The phrase, creative solutions to problems, is often misused in political areas. However, the situations in which problems are actually solved creatively are many. Generally involved in both creativity and problem solving are analyses, ideas, research, testing, hunches, motivation, logic, etc.

G. Polya's "How To Solve It," emphasized the mathematical method. His approaches and suggestions can be applied to many problems that affect our lives. Solving scientific and mathematical problems may not concern us as much as important tasks of communication and survival in our society. Of more concern, on the one hand, are those problems of our own creation; on the other, social, economic, political, environmental, and transportation types.

One of the basic approaches to solve something is to think about it rather than ignore it or consider it insurmountable. Doing something about a situation, rather than putting it off, can make it easier to solve. Too many people think that problems left alone, like a dirty backyard, will go away. Often each situation will suggest a policy, an approach, an action, a decision, or a possible solution.

Surprisingly, some people don't want to solve problems, whether it's out of habit, laziness, selfishness, or hate. Peace, for example, is not difficult to attain. All one needs is a sincere desire and an unselfish attitude on both sides of issues. Much of the talk (or rhetoric) about peace is deliberate propaganda to stall, discourage, brainwash, and defeat prospects for a world without tensions.

The fact that we don't put our problems down on paper doesn't mean we don't want to solve them. Much of what our brains do, with their memories and processors, so fast and often taken for granted, escapes us. We don't realize the intermediate steps involved in solving or creating. Problems can appear from many sources and group themselves into several categories. They can be artificial learning (to solve for exercises), physical (to repair or fix something), emotional (psychological disturbances), political, medical, defense, financial, etc.

Before we can move ahead and recognize these challenging areas, we should get familiar with some of the important terms used. Those in the business of creativity, problem solving, and thought processes know the meanings and uses of the following:

Association	state of being joined or related in the mind by time, place, meaning, or situation
Cognition	whatever comes to be known through perception; to get to know; learning
Heuristic	serving to discover; guiding or furthering investigation; encouraging to learn independently through own discovery
Serendipity	faculty of making fortunate and unexpected discoveries by accident

It takes more than ideas to be creative or inventive. The necessary factors include knowledge of the subject or process, where to find pertinent information, the ability to recall and retain facts, the capacity for judgment, and imagination. The creative process results from manipulating symbols, ideas, facts, and structures to form new combinations. Reduced to stages, the creative process involves:

1) Orientation: selecting and defining the problem;

2) Preparation: collecting, analyzing, and organizing data;

3) Production: generating ideas as alternatives or approaches;

4) Development: selecting, adding, and reprocessing by combining, manipulating, comparing, and modifying ideas;

5) Illumination or Insight: birth of clarifying idea or tentative solution;

6) Verification: evaluation or testing resultant ideas or tentative solution; and,

7) Adoption: deciding to implement the idea or solution.

According to Dr. Albert Einstein, "The formulation of a problem is far more often essential than its solution, which may be merely a mathematical or experimental skill." He also stated, "Imagination is more important than knowledge." According to Alex F. Osborn, "In ideative effort, quantity breeds quality." Facts are essential, but obsession with fact-finding and the neglect of ideas cannot guarantee solutions or innovations.

Creativity implies the ability to judge ideas as they develop, but there must be a competitive spirit and the practical motivating forces of money, fame, and inspiring leadership. Individual and group brainstorming sessions can provide many ideas in a short time span. Sensitivity to problems, exhibited by an awareness of their existence and the ability to state them verbally, is one important characteristic of the creative personality. Fluency in intellectual processes, as exemplified by broad experience and a wealth of ideas, is another.

The flexible personality can adapt himself or herself to a situation and recognize the interrelationships as they exist in a problem. Originality is another mark of the creative personality, exemplified by the restructuring of ideas to turn up something completely different, or apply principles of one field to another in a unique approach.

Creativity and innovation, like speculative investments, require a gambling spirit and a willingness to work hard, because there's no guarantee of winning. The person who wants to be creative, whether solutions to problems are sought, or an invention developed, can consider four basic approaches:

1) **Question:**   a phenomenon or a condition. A daring spirit
                       of inquiry or an insatiable curiosity can start
                       the creative process. Put the operational
                       question into words and/or symbols. Look
                       for answers to why, what if, and how.

2) **Observe:**   to collect data, but be careful of influences
                       exerted by your past experience. Avoid
                       preconceptions and prejudices absorbed by
                       exposure. Observe the broader aspects and
                       look out for the unexpected.

3) **Associate:**   information from the past to provide
                       alternative solutions for the present situation.
                       Good questions and keen observations lead
                       to productive associations.

4) **Predict:**   A solution. This is done when you make a
                       decision, but it must be verified with reliable
                       tests before presenting it for final acceptance.

THE CREATIVE PROCESS

Observations of creative action reveal a person achieving
increased unity or order in a situation. The creative person works
with relations, selects and organizes them; and in the process,
discovers one or more of their essential aspects. Apparent is the
urge to simplify and abstract or express the essence of the
situation. Observation leads to a hypothesis, which is tested to
discover some order within a framework which appears chaotic.
This is how most scientific ideas or theories are produced.

There appears to be a psychological process with a purpose, and
it leads to a new way of thinking about things that are going on.
The inventor can think about a new way of brewing coffee or
cooking potatoes. If one looks at operations of fast food
restaurants, everything seems to be pre-cut, pre-packaged, or
prepared to achieve the "fast" service. Many people take for
granted the innovations that have made these restaurants
profitable, and yet acceptable to the consumer.

One does not have to be a scientist or a genius to get acquainted with events and interpret facts through observation. It's a matter of concentrating; combining curiosity with desire and effort. It doesn't come to the person who watches the clock as a time to go home, but to one who is so absorbed in the idea or apparent problem in mind, that nothing matters more, even when there are interruptions.

In the learning process, we open our minds to acquire new information, methods of dealing with it for further use, and to test the ways of manipulating the information. When we learn about a subject, we find out what was done with it in the past and generalize on its potential or implications. We may store this information in our brain for future application in a problem or discovery.

Although there are a few exceptions, the learning of mathematics provides a reliable basis for intellectual development. Physical operations are reduced to images, which in turn are translated into symbols for manipulation in a convenient manner. Eventually the learner can grasp the abstract properties of the materials involved. The collection of images built helps in the act of discovery and in learning how to solve problems. Various disciplines, such as physics, chemistry, biology, and psychology help develop various ways of thinking.

Remembering is often like problem solving. We need clues, associative links, and often a relaxed state to recall or retrieve information stored in the memory. If we are organized during the storing process, we can use various types of mediators, words or ideas which will join with what we are trying to remember.

Like associations, the mediators can be word groups in terms of function, subject, or some physical relationship, such as "metal-structure-steel," or "the high-rise was framed with structural steel girders," or "the steel girders were attached with steel bolts." People tend to develop or use their own mediators, depending on their education, experience, practice, or development. Whatever works to make the material in question more accessible for retrieval, especially when the material is organized in terms of the person's interests, is acceptable.

On the one hand, we have the cognitive structures developed in the brain, pathways of intellectual activity used to store information. On the other, we have motivation, attitudes, and activities involved in acquiring information. Using mediation techniques, among others, the material stored becomes more readily accessible during recall. Like problem solving, we learn how to place material in memory, so that we have no difficulty getting to it on demand.

Nobody has a monopoly over achievements of the mind. It may be more difficult for some people to develop their intellectual faculties. However, most people are in a position to train themselves and attain mental skills for achievements. Discovery is a matter of arranging, rearranging, or transforming proven facts in such a manner that new insights are developed. It takes organized persistence, rather than random stabs or an attitude that nothing can be found (without real proof).

Practice in discovering for oneself does not make perfect, but it does lead to putting information acquired for better uses, improved learning skills; and, helps make the information alive for creativity and problem solving. It supports the adage about the busy person finding time to do many things, whereas the one who has nothing pressing on schedule suffers from inertia.

The study of logic, mathematics, statistics, and the sciences, as well as the arts, are important to skill in inquiry. In addition, one can develop attitudes and activities to support inquiry so that the process or heuristics will better serve the individual. How to go about learning; how to approach a problem; and, how to transform the different types of forms in various discoveries, such as models, appear helpful in solving problems.

Whether it is in problem solving or the actual efforts involved, the practices help develop the process of discovery. Like exercise, what one learns in mental gymnastics as a result of inquiry and attempts to solve can be applied to almost any type of task. As Jerome S. Bruner wrote in "Act of Discovery," "Of only one thing I am convinced: I have never seen anybody improve the art and technique of inquiry by any means other than engaging in inquiry."

John W. Gardner, in his excellent book about the individual and innovative society, "Self Renewal," offered some excellent ideas about creative traits in his chapter on innovation. He listed four, followed by a discussion of "The Revolutionary."

1) **Openness**—This is receptivity to sights, sounds, events, and ideas that impinge on the individual. He suggests one keep a freshness of perception, an unspoiled awareness. The creative person has fewer internal barriers or watertight compartments of experience. He is self-understanding and self-accepting. A writer, for example, has access to the full richness of one man's emotional, spiritual, and intellectual experience.

2) **Independence**—Gifted in seeing the gap between what is and what could be, a person has achieved a certain measure of detachment from what is. We build on others —independent, but not adrift, with social support, stimulation and communication. The person reserves independence in the area in which his or her creative activities occur.

3) **Flexibility**—The creative person will toy with the idea, look at it from a dozen different angles, test it, argue with himself or herself that it is true, and then argue that it's untrue. Directions can be changed and strategies shifted. One can give up the initial perception of a problem and redefine it. One has the capacity to maintain a certain detachment from the conventional categories and abstractions that people use; hold a similar detachment from the routines and fixed customs of those around him.

One even manages to exercise a reasonable detachment from one's own past attitudes and habits of mind. (We tend to forget the limitations imposed by one's own compulsions, neuroticisms, habits, and fixed ideas.) The creative person also has the capacity to tolerate internal conflict and a willingness to suspend judgment. There is no indication of discomfort in the presence of unanswered questions or unresolved differences. This person does not find it difficult to give expression to opposite sides of his or her nature at the same time; e.g., conscious and unconscious mind, reason and passion, aesthetic and scientific impulses.

4) **Capacity of find order in experience**—The creative person has an extraordinary capacity to *impose* order on experience; find order out of chaos; connect things that previously did not seem related; sketch a more embracing framework; and, move toward larger and more inclusive understandings.

The person has a remarkable zeal or drive—is wholly absorbed in his work; willing to work hard and for long hours; and, appears to have sustained energy over years of application. You're aware of the confidence, assertiveness, and sense of destiny. He has faith in his capacity to do things he wants and must do them in the area of his chosen work.

5) **The Revolutionary**—This is the creative person of another sort and has the tendency to shatter rigidities of tradition. With good reason, this person finds a better way in opposition to the familiar cliche, "We've always done it this way."

Shakespeare, the creative genius of Elizabethan drama, was open, honest, free in nature, and open to criticism and change. He dramatized stories with consummate skill to entertain, enlighten, and excite his contemporaries.

Too many ideas are never developed, primarily because the working knowledge in the field of creativity is lacking. The world is full of composers, writers, and inventors who claim to have wonderful ideas, but nothing to show for the world to see, and often inadequate skills to develop anything significant.

The sciences and the arts are cumulative disciplines on which the creative person can build with a strong background or heavy working knowledge. Science presents more fields for discovery, but the restrictions or possibilities for new discoveries are more limited. Artists, on the other hand, do not have to master the techniques of the great painters to develop original ideas and execute with professional skills.

HOW CREATIVE PRODUCTS EMERGE

There are many directions from which creative products can emerge; i. e., achieve results from various approaches, such as:

A) **Transfer**—The application of a solution from one field to another. The person who recognizes analogies or similarities is in a position to see an answer from a personal, symbolic, or direct application.

B) **Recurrence or routine reduction**—One can develop a table, a formula, a graph, or a program that reduces the complex and recurring problem to a routine. Data processing shows many examples in which complex scientific and business problems have been reduced to libraries of routines.

C) **Elaboration**—The electronic chip is an outgrowth of the integrated circuit, and the handheld calculator is a development of data processors rather than the old electro-mechanical calculators and adding machines.

D) **Innovation**—The deliberate invention is often the result of a desire or the urgency to fill a need. The atomic bomb is the outgrowth and development of a need sponsored by the Federal Government and identified as the Manhattan Project.

E) **Catalytic action**—This is called the development of a new theory or process which owes its existence to a device. The electronic microscope has made possible many advances in biology, metallurgy, and physics.

F) **Replacement**—Often there is a situation in which another solution is necessary to check or test the existing solution to a problem. There are many situations in which people apply other approaches to come up with the same result.

G) **Troubleshooting**—This is another name for the process of recognizing errors, isolating problems, finding things wrong and making constructive changes to existing operations.

SOLVING PROBLEMS

In our complex society, problems appear to be a substantial part of our existence. Is there a person, a region, or a country without problems? Problems affect the wealthy and poor alike. Different people can worry about: rent, food, property, investments, illness, weight, jobs, security, etc. Money is often at the root of many problems, rather than of evil. With some problems imaginary, but most real, our lives are filled with a recurring series of them: confronted by familiar ones and occasionally imposed by new ones.

Health, longevity, and on occasion our survival, depends on our ability to solve recurring and unusual problems. As an integral part of many conversations, problems reflect our concerns in general and specific terms. One who is hit by problems from all sides finds little comfort in being concerned about those of others; much less those on a national scale we often hear about.

There are many problems over which we have control and which involve our personal lives. When we hear about problems of others, we can be sympathetic. However, not many realize that how many of their problems are of their own creation through ignorance and neglect. Control of our drives or restraint in some of our excesses can help eliminate conditions, such as overweight, alcoholism, addiction to drugs, and compulsive gambling.

Unsolved problems, like debts, have a propensity for getting bigger or more serious. Many persons get uneasy and depressed when problems are staring at them, figuratively, in the face. Some people say, "The hell with it," and then proceed to get drunk. They have developed an artificial formula that has the effect of immunity against worry, but no control over the problem. The attitude is all right if one recognizes or identifies the imaginary ones and does something in time about the real ones.

Sometimes we get free advice, but human nature often seems to enjoy paying for it, treating the unpaid advice as some illegitimate brainchild. Like babies, problems need attention—a desire or habit of trying to solve them. It helps if you've had experience solving problems similar in nature. Auto mechanics are paid well for helping one out of car troubles. For solving problems over which we have some control, four requirements are outlined:

First, we must be aware of its existence. There is a segment of society which simply doesn't realize there's a problem or a situation about which something's got to be done.

Second, one must care sufficiently to do something about the problem identified. This implies understanding the consequences of letting things continue; i.e., doing nothing about it.

Third, one should have some knowledge and experience to handle the problem with the right approach; be willing to spend the time and/or money necessary to solve it.

Fourth, one must follow through the solution to completely resolve it, like getting an acknowledgement or receipt, or testing a repaired item.

Who are the principal problem solvers in our society? Mostly, they are attorneys, physicians, engineers, scientists, mechanics, consultants, and leaders in management. The list could be longer, but it's important to realize that we pay well to have our problems solved for us. Courts of law, for example, and law enforcement are expensive adjuncts of our free society. We must pay for litigation and protection.

Since no one knows your problems better than yourself, why not solve your own? If you can be objective, get the facts and organize them. Restate the problem based on the real issue. What's holding back the solution? It is money? If so, one can concentrate on making more or finding ways to raise it. However, it's foolish to fall into the trap of the bank robber who confessed, when caught, that he was exercising his brand of free enterprise.

One must operate from a legitimate premise or an approach that won't backfire. For example, if you can't change the neighborhood, it may be time to move out. One must seek alternatives to a situation. Is there another way out? If you receive too many traffic citations, hating highway patrol won't help. It may be time to turn yourself around by checking driving habits and attitude behind the wheel. A change of attitude is much cheaper, and probably easier, than the high price of time in traffic courts, the cost in fines, or even incarceration. If nobody loves you, it's more than a hint that your personality needs some overhaul.

Can one change a point of view or reference to see a problem as others may see it? Asking questions is a low-cost method of finding out. One can invite trouble with insistence on seeing things from one's own narrow perspective. One can mix individual experiences with emotions, and even develop complexes. Some people run away from everything that needs attention, whether it's a dirty ash tray or a flat tire.

Do you avoid mathematics? You may later regret not exerting that extra effort it took to learn algebra or calculus. There are homes where the television set is on and nobody is watching it, or the stereo blasts away to drown out the ringing telephone. In some places, there are living symbols of waste: faucets leaking or air conditioning on all day. Some mothers wait for the baby to cry before changing its diapers. No wonder why problems of some pile up like stacks of rubbish.

Among other things, solving problems includes the ability to assemble facts for specific purposes. Whether the situation is based on a challenge or necessity, one must have a strong desire to solve specific problems as they confront one. The rewards can come in terms of well-being, money, or freedom from worry. The will to do something about problems under one's control enables one to survive and thrive.

THE PRACTICAL APPROACH

The human being adapts well to the physical environment. In cold weather we wrap ourselves or warm up the area in which we are sheltered. We have the means and intelligence to protect ourselves from the elements. We have the equipment, the senses, and the brains to apply as situations develop. Education and experience are a big help. However, more is often needed to actually solve certain types of problems.

The practical approach consists of looking at problems with a purpose, examining the facts involved, and establishing a point of view. For most problems, a series of questions are suggested. Answers to these, in ten areas, should help one concentrate, manipulate, and evaluate. These ten areas are directed towards coming up with answers to real and challenging problems.

1) **PURPOSE**—Does one have a purpose? Does one really want to solve the problem? Is it accepted as a challenge for a specific purpose? Is the goal worth reaching in terms of time and costs? Can it be handled objectively even though one may be emotionally involved in the problem?

2) **DEFINITION**—Can the actual problem be defined? Can it be stated in terms of where one is and where one wants to go? In other words, what is the present situation and where does one want to go? Are there any milestones or check points on the way to solving the problem? Are there any minor goals on the way to the major goal?

3) **FACTS**—Does one have enough facts to bridge the gap between the problem and the goal? Are the right questions being asked? (Shorter? Cheaper? Faster? Simpler?) Are the questions relevant to become organized into a system or something with meaning? Do the facts have anything to do with the problem or purpose? Are any relevant facts being ignored? Are the fact-finding questions meaningful? How are the questions being phrased?

4) **EXAMINATION**—How are the facts being treated? Is one rushing into inferences and conclusions? Are any false assumptions being made? Is anything being taken for granted? Is one responding to facts; reacting emotionally; or, out of habit? Has one's mind been made up in advance, or is there an open mind for significant facts? Can one take a fresh look at the facts? Can the facts be viewed from different directions? How do others see the facts? Is it possible to see the facts through another person's eyes?

How do the facts relate to other facts? Can one see any relationship beyond the details? Do some facts suggest related facts or open new doors? Can one make inferences from one fact to another? Do additional facts corroborate the inference made? Has one asked: who, what, why, when, where, and how, as applicable? If cost is a factor, has it been adequately taken into account? One can get statistical or check probability. Are sizes, numbers, and quantities involved? Does one take into account measurements, such as degrees; or, consider percentages?

5) **VIEWPOINT**—Has one considered the situation and facts from various viewpoints? Will additional information change one's perspective and definition of the problem? What is the specific frame of reference based on facts? (Frame of reference, like context, can greatly influence the facts and meanings derived from them.) Are there any gaps in the organization of facts based on one's viewpoint? Will the addition of missing links lead to a solution? Does one need all the facts to reach a solution? Is there a recognizable pattern? (Instead of asking, "How can we sell more copiers?" Why not ask, "How can we fit or fill the copy needs of customers who don't use our product?") Is the problem being viewed from a man or woman's angle?

6) **RELATIONSHIPS**—Do the facts establish some significant relationships from which one can make an applicable statement? (If one's car battery keeps losing its charge, can one conclude that there is either a defective battery, an alternator not charging, or a short that drains the battery when the car is not driven?) Can one generalize? Can the situation be tied to a general principle? (Short messages get more attention than long ones.) (When sex is involved, a female attracts more attention.)

Can one come up with a concept based on observations? Can one take a series of facts and select abstract ideas? Is the generalization correct? What is it that unifies the facts? What is the best

way to organize and relate the facts as a pattern? Can one penetrate what is not immediately visible? Can one abstract; i.e.,
emphasize characteristics out of a group of facts? Has one
identified and classified facts to develop an abstraction? Are there
any relationships among the abstractions? Has one rearranged the
facts, abstractions, and relationships?

7) **VISUALIZATION**—Can one see the abstraction or the
relationships as physical images? Can one see in one's
own mind what is described? How can the generalizations
and situations they represent be visualized? As John
Dewey suggested, can one "promote the flow of
suggestions into your mind?" Can an analogy be
applied—a partial similarity? Can the visualization be
pinned down for testing? Can the generalization be
visualized?

8) **SYMBOLS**—Can the generalizations be reduced to
symbols with relationships? Is the problem complicated
enough to require the use of symbols. Can the simple
symbol stand for complicated objects for easy
manipulation? Can one put the problem into words?—
explicitly in writing? Have the symbols for the real thing
been separated from reality itself? (If a symbol stands for
something, then we must not confuse it with reality.) (The
seal of the office of the President of the United States
stands for the office, not for the President who happens to
be there at the time.) Can the symbol be treated as a
focusing point for associations?

Can the problem be broken down into elements, each with a
symbolic value? Can one relax and think about the problem by
letting one's mind wander? Can one reduce symbolic
relationships to visual representations, such as maps, charts,
diagrams, or models? Can the problem be visualized in its
simplest terms?

9) **TEST**—Does one have alternatives to select and study the consequences of each? Can one identify the critical factor that created the problem? Does one need an innovative solution because the problem is unique? Can the problem be classified? Can the solution be adapted from another problem? Can one try or test the solution to prove its correctness? Has the real problem been identified to arrive at the logical or correct solution?

What stated the problem? Can one get at the root? (Can one apply Franklin's logic: "for the want of a nail, the shoe was lost; for the want of a shoe, the horse was lost; for the want of a horse, the rider was lost?") (The accidental explosion may have been caused by a small leak.) Can cause and effect be transposed? (Because something happened, this could be the reason. Can we check it out?) How is the solution like something else that was tested? How is it different?

10) **IMPLEMENT OR ADOPT**—This is the moment of glory, achieved because one asked whether one was able to stay motivated, with periods for rest and relaxation. Dedicated and singleminded people solve problems. They rarely give up, get tough, and stay that way, some without displaying their determination. They know problems won't solve or correct themselves. The problem solvers and innovators stay on top of problems or projects until success shines through.

Appendixes

The appendixes provide an assortment of ideas and suggestions designed to help improve various skills and practices. The materials can be used to stimulate and develop ideas as products of communication disciplines. As cues, reminders, and techniques, they are tools to put to work. Applying the suggestions depends on the individual needs and desires. Progress and achievements in positive or productive directions grow naturally out of effort.

There is no particular pattern or order in terms of priorities. In some cases, an appendix summarizes a section in a convenient form. In others, like Appendix CC, they serve to suggest approaches to achieve specific goals. In addition, there are guidelines and notes for executives and supervisors to help get things done efficiently, such as interviews (App. HH) and making decisions (App. E).

Under various subjects and titles that relate to daily activities involving communication, this general approach can serve the user as he or she sees fit. The material can be used by an executive, as well as a student; the office manager, as well as the sales person; and the needs of most businesses, as well as those of individuals engaged in almost any kind of endeavor.

If some of the problems of society and government reflect incompetence and/or neglect, one hopes that some of these suggestions are taken seriously enough to help raise our living standards Much can be done by cutting costs and reducing the wastes of time. No country, including democracies with politicians in positions to exercise leadership, can survive if its problems continue to mount and its citizens continue to deteriorate. It may come down to matters of morality and integrity over legality and expediency to raise standards of living and a higher quality of life.

A. REMINDERS—TO STAY ON TOP

1. Not to Forget _____
_____
_____

2. People to See _____
_____
_____

3. Work to Do _____
_____
_____

4. Persons to Call _____
_____
_____

5. Material to Read _____
_____
_____

6. Meetings to Attend _____
_____
_____

7. Problems to Solve _____
_____
_____

8. Plans to Make _____
_____
_____

9. Speech to Prepare _____
_____
_____

10. Places to Go _____
_____
_____

11. Things to Buy _____
_____
_____

12. Appointments to Keep ____
_____
_____

13. Errands to Run _____
_____
_____

14. Appointments to Make ____
_____
_____

15. Writing to Perform _____
_____
_____

16. Fun to Arrange _____
_____
_____

17. Goals to Set _____
_____
_____

18. Visits to Make _____
_____
_____

19. Exercise to Get _____
_____
_____

20. Interviews to Conduct ____
_____
_____

B. KEEPING YOURSELF INFORMED
What Is Going On Of Concern?

We often find ourselves in situations where we must make decisions, occasionally in a variety of ways, depending on our work, responsibilities, and authority. Some mistakes can be costly and what makes it difficult is dealing with specialized knowledge or unfamiliar territory. In this age of heavy paper work (paper tape), and diverse sources of information, including electronic media, how does one keep informed? How much time does one have? How much detail is necessary? What is the ideal plan or program for keeping informed?

First, let's deal with approaches:

1) Contact specialists to discuss new problems and news of concern to the individual or company.
2) Conduct regular and impromptu questionings of key personnel.
3) Review selected media that report current and significant developments.
4) Assign staff members to study areas where change is occurring.
5) Maintain an active curiosity.

Consult documented sources for a regular reading program, using selectivity and scheduling to avoid the possibility of material getting stale, such as:

1) Books (check with libraries and book stores)
2) Technical papers
3) Newspapers
4) Magazines and Journals
5) Briefs
6) Memoranda
7) Reports
8) Proposals and Presentations

Consult personal sources, such as:

a. Plant visits, field contacts, branches
b. Meetings, conferences, and seminars
c. Trade shows and conventions
d. Key personnel and briefings by specialists

C. MAXIMIZING TIME

1. **Organize Activities**—Examine self objectively for possible improvement. Analyze job for changes and growth.

2. **Delegate Tasks**—Turn over some responsibilities or projects to associates and subordinates. Hire new or temporary help for added tasks and peak workloads.

3. **Plan and Schedule**—In terms of next year, month, week, day. Plan ahead for long range periods. Plan next day at end of previous.

4. **Keep Open-minded Attitude**—About new and better ways of handling responsibilities. Use services of personnel and facilities to help get jobs done.

5. **Control and Screen Essentials**—Be concerned about the major tasks and costlier projects. Remove distractions instigated by small jobs and routine matters.

6. **Seek Results and Accomplishments**—Over budgeting time and resources.

7. **Cut Down Routines**—In preference for major programs and commitments.

8. **Take Breaks and Set Favorable Climate**—Promote relaxed and motivated environment for personnel treated like professionals.

9. **Manage Stress**—Limit worry and concentrate on things you can do something about, overlooking things for which you have limited or no control.

10. **Set Goals and Monitor**—Think of quality within framework of accomplishments and within a reasonable schedule.

D. GETTING THINGS DONE

A. **Remove Chaff and Simplify**—Eliminate bottlenecks and buffers that stifle or block communication channels. Clear the air of emotions and rivalries to promote movement.

B. **Examine Self-Image**—Fearful dedication to routines or fearless programmer after results. Stuck with routines and paperwork or person who gets things done and helps others to do likewise.

C. **Maintain Control**—Over self, over the big bucks, the big purchases, the big costs, and large contracts. Don't let the big one get away.

D. **Update and Improve Files**—**Clean** out old and useless data that occupy expensive space, making it difficult to store and locate important documents.

E. **Eliminate Obsolescence**—Don't hang on to old typewriters, computers, and obsolete systems. Get rid of old papers and files that occupy valuable space.

F. **Keep Priorities Flexible**—Do some things yourself and juggle priorities. Time seems to change importance of some priorities. Review problems and projects with subordinates.

G. **Check Deadlines**—Anticipate problems of meeting dates, completing tasks, and integrating elements. Extend deadlines in the interest of avoiding mistakes and sacrificing quality.

H. **Put In Writing As Necessary**—Determine if documenting and signing are required. Use writing as a follow-up to coordination and approval.

I. **Limit Meetings**—They take time to prepare, to hold, and to report progress of committees associated with meetings.

J. **Analyze and Review**—Break problems down into parts or details and question each for improvements in quality, performance, and fewer operations (efficiency).

E. MAKING DECISIONS

1. Are you authorized to make and enforce or implement the decision?

2. Can the problem or situation be defined clearly7

3. Do you have all the available facts to make a decision?

4. Can you list all the alternatives or choices7

5. Are you aware of the impacts of each choice?

6. Are there any precedents or similar situations that arose?

7. Is it possible to consult others with similar experience?

8. Are there trade-offs among the alternatives?

9. Is there any possibility of a confrontation or revenge?

10. Does the decision open the door to future problems?

11. Can the decision be tested or implemented on a temporary basis?

12. Trust your judgment, make your decision, and go over it later to confirm the accuracy or correctness of what you decided.

    NOTE: Some problems cannot be decided.

    Some problems may have to wait for additional data.

    Some decisions cannot be enforced.

    Some decisions should be made by others.

    Some decisions should never be put off, like limiting losses, eliminating waste, arresting ignorance, and removing neglect.

F. CREATIVE PROCESS

Science and arts have flourished together. Science needs artist's sense that details of nature are significant. Intuition is useless unless it is followed into the details of nature.

There is always an infinite set of alternatives among which we must choose. Theories are proposed by imaginative choices which outstrip the facts. Every intuition is a speculation and it guesses at a unity which the facts present but do not imply.

A theory is inevitable only to a scientist; a choice among alternatives open to everyone. Simplicity is a principle of choice which cannot be mechanized. An esthetic sense of unity—a theory that is simple and beautiful.

Creativity is finding likenesses—Create what *will* become acceptable. Creative minds look for unexpected likenesses. Arts and sciences have value in originality. Both are preoccupied less with facts and numbers than with arrangement. We are now concerned with relation, structure, and shape—logical structure—meaningful form.

Inductive reasoning is the essence of the creative process. Basic element in process is intuition of a special kind. Intuitive creation of new theories thru subconscious appraisal of facts, followed by a conscious objective analysis.

Informed intuition for ideas—appropriate to problems. Creative mind is always open to inspiration. Ideas—hopefully new and fresh and desirably different. Creative people probe beyond the rules—technique left open to idea. Creative people prove validity and then sell. Create—Test—Promote. Intuitive process of science and arts are precisely the same.

Intuition—meeting of old and new—quick and unexpected harmony—a feeling for the order Iying beyond the appearances. In art the significant is compressed and intensified. The arts embrace substance and form. Good ideas must be really different. Intuition involves a stringent application of judgment values— analysis of creative and judgment functions—conflicts between inner vision (intuition) and outer vision (objective judgment). Self-discipline and judgment are inherent in the creative process. There must be standards and criteria in judgment for criticism. Creative judge must have insight, discrimination, and consuming interest to further develop natural sensitivity—a unifying phase. Creative ideas are linked to initiative—fun from work.

Creative expression conceived in inspiration and boldness. An idea developed must end up doing a sales job. Cut through nonessentials to heart of problem. Go from facts and intuitive judgment to decision. Define goals—what are we aiming at? Simplify issues. Technologies, attitudes, emphases, and requirements shift. Creative persons must be ready to go beyond requirements.

Creative people tend to think in pictures...ability to pick meaning out of a mass of detail. Key elements: judgment, responsibility, and capacity for choice. You cannot have ideas without exploration. Express something with a breadth of vision. Build future with some reference to past.

G. OBSERVING AROUND US

The ability to observe relates to developing an awareness of an environment and a sharpening of perceptual skills. Improving the ability to observe is primarily a matter of training in the visual arts, such as painting, sculpture, and design. Visual composition consists of manipulating and arranging various forms, colors, textures, and lines into some abstract concept. A basic discipline in learning how to paint relates to the study of anatomy and drawing of various forms, especially human figures. Perceptual skills involve a complex integration of visual senses, including the eyes and the brain.

The dynamic human environment includes gestures, movements, and action. This suggests the value of training in acting, which covers such elements that enable the student to be more aware of a scene and to observe static and dynamic environments. The ability to observe suggests more objectivity on the part of the observer. It is easy to see more or less in a situation than actually exists. It is not difficult to project our prejudices from our experiences in similar situations. In addition, things or faces that are not familiar do not arouse as warm or friendly responses as those we've seen before. It's a matter of fear, comfort, suspicion, or uneasiness.

Before we can arrive at conclusions about persons, places, or things, we can double check; i.e., take a second or third look at the object of our observation; similar in principle to seeking a second or third opinion before deciding on a significant surgery. If we are aware of the fact that this earth of ours inhabits billions of beings with different faces and unique backgrounds, and that a smile on any face can make a difference in our subconscious assessment or acceptance, we are much closer to making more accurate and objective observations.

In art, the elements of color with its infinite hues, shades, and textures; the variety in lines, forms, and textures, most of which can be simplified or reduced to symbols, provide unequalled opportunities to train our perceptual skills and observe the environment with more competence. The study of gestures that display various emotions and those that react to various stimuli, represent advantages that training in acting offers.

H. THE PRACTICE TREE

ENGLISH

Read—(newspapers, magazines, books (variety)

Write—(prose, fiction, and drama)—technical & edit

Vocabulary—Usage—words in context, meanings, grammar, punctuation, spelling

MATH

Logic—Boolean Algebra

Numbers, sets, uses of calculations and computers

Probability & Statistics

MUSIC

Practice with professional guidance

Listen

Compose

SPEECHES

Write—Your own—what you would for others

Read—Old and current—Pronunciation

Rehearse & deliver

ART

Photography

Drawing and Sketching

Painting and Design

Motion Pictures (Video Camera)

In all these disciplines, get professional guidance. Think of the golfer who picked up a golf club, swung it like a baseball bat, developed new muscles, and taught himself all kinds of errors. When he decided to take lessons ten years later, he gave his golf teacher one hell of a challenge. There's nothing wrong with starting from the beginning, right from the basics, and practicing regularly to overcome the bad old habits by replacing them with good new ones.

I. LISTENING PRACTICES

1. Try to concentrate on what another is saying.

2. Be patient until the speaker is through.

3. Avoid roadblocks, such as daydreaming, criticizing, prejudging, or interrupting.

4. Try not to think about what you're going to say until the speaker is finished.

5. Listen objectively even though you may have conflicts or problems.

6. Sense differences in tones and sounds with eyes closed and open.

7. Sense body positions, eye contact, and gestures while others speak.

8. Notice differences in listening habits between men and women.

9. Stay neutral on issues or give responses that make it easier for others to communicate.

10. Accept complaints of others without personal involvement.

11. Increase awareness of listening habits in all spoken communications.

12. Try to share or exchange ideas and feelings when communicating with others.

13. Concentrate on what the other person is saying by being attentive and maintaining eye contact.

14. Listen for ideas, feelings, emotional content, and real meaning.

15. Accept the rights of others to speak; try to understand, even empathize.

16. Accept some risks and the unpleasant possibility of seeing oneself as others see one; avoid emotional blindness and refusal to accept facts as presented by others.

17. Reduce length of speeches and avoid fake listening.

18. Avoid escalating a conversation to an argument, raising the voice, or overreacting in emotional situations.

19. Give no advice unless requested, nor remain silent to avoid involvement or through fear of disapproval.

20. Willing to listen even when ego is involved and when taking a defensive posture during criticism.

J. TELEPHONE USE AND LISTENING HABITS

1. The less you talk, the more you can listen and learn. (It's difficult to do both creatively at the same time.)

2. Concentrate on what the caller is saying. (It may be necessary to cut off distractions.)

3. Ask questions about things that you miss or are not clear. (Avoid embarrassing explanations or need for call back.)

4. Listen for ideas, focusing on the main issue. (Think as you listen and take notes for future reference.)

5. Avoid interruptions and wait for a question or a sign of ending. (A pause may not signal completion.)

6. Respond or acknowledge with a "yes" or "I understand." (You are letting your caller know you're still on the line.)

7. Listen for emotional overtones that may come across. (How the caller says things and feelings about an issue may be important to know.)

8. Try not to prompt the caller or anticipate what will be said. (You may be making assumptions or saying things that were not intended.)

9. If you can't be helpful, be tactful. (Promise a call back or ask the caller to contact a specific person who can answer the question.)

10. If you ask the caller to hold, reduce the hang time. (Periodically call back for reassurance if the caller chooses to stay on the line.)

REMEMBER: So much business is conducted by telephone, it is of paramount importance to be responsive, prepared, courteous, clear, sincere, friendly, and show warmth with a smile in your voice from the time you identify yourself at the first ring to the end of a pleasant conversation.

K. READING SUGGESTIONS

Although reading has been identified as a passive skill, its importance and relationship to the memory and thought processes cannot be overestimated. Reading stimulates thinking, triggers associations, arouses emotional responses, and most importantly, adds to our reservoir of information. Unfortunately, it is not easy to remember most of what we read because we go through so much material in a brief span. Often we remember the gist of the material or make a mental note of the decision we've made about what we've read. Another essential feature of reading relates to its use as a tool for learning, primarily in the educational environment. In addition, there are many situations in which we must read so that we can respond or perform responsibilities. These may include letters, reports, documents and various other sources of printed information.

Suggestions for improving reading skills:

1) Take a qualified course in speed reading and faithfully practice the exercises required.

2) Plan a reading schedule of material that includes books, magazines, and newspapers.

3) Select some reading material for enjoyment, such as fiction and drama.

4) Select new reading material in the category of nonfiction.

5) When reading, take notes and look up words for meanings in and out of context.

Variety is not only the spice of life, but also the spice of reading and other productive activities.

L. PRACTICING WRITING

How does one practice writing? Like other sophisticated skills, one learns how to write by writing after receiving formal instruction or training. Even after learning the essentials of writing, the services of a coach or professional consultant are often worth using. When learning how to write, practicing under the watchful eye of an instructor helps ensure the discipline necessary to avoid mistakes and to promote development. It's the seasoned writer who can claim that the product of one's imagination comes forth without an outline or a plan and extensive research. Whether experienced or not, writing for most can be effective or evoke response when the purpose, the material, and the approach have been determined with the help of an outline and consideration for the readers' needs.

Since writing is unidirectional, how does one put down words in sequences that help make the message unmistakable? Much of learning how to write consists of imitating established authors and writing about subjects with which one is familiar. As in painting, learning the styles of others through imitation serves to increase awareness and facility. Eventually, one develops a unique style of one's own. One of the best approaches to the practice of writing consists of selecting a subject of interest, collecting information from various sources, including personal contact, and preparing an outline. There's nothing wrong with changing the structure after the actual writing has begun. One should do everything necessary to sustain reader interest and improve the impact of the message. This can include the help of an editor and rewriting as part of the process of revising.

In addition to practicing writing, one can develop proficiency in written expression by analyzing the writings of established authors of fiction and nonfiction. You can make an outline of the material presented, define the purpose as interpreted from the writing, evaluate the approach, check the language, continuity, and style. What was the author's purpose and how well did he or she achieve it?

M.   HIGH PERFORMANCE CHARACTERISTICS

1. Self-Esteem (Self-respect)

2. Sense of Responsibility (Accept)

3. Sense of Optimism (Results)

4. Goal Directed (Motivated Sets)

5. Sense of Imagination (Visualizes and Pictures for Others)

6. Awareness (Perceives)

7. Creative (Associates ideas—Solves—Fills needs)

8. Communicative (Deliberate)

9. Positive Response to Pressure (Challenge)

10. Growth Oriented (Seeks)

11. Sense of Nowness (ASAP)

12. Enthusiasm (Enjoys—Adjusts)

13. Persistence (Dependable—Flexible)

14. Dedication (Application)

15. Healthy—Active (Exercise—Diet)

16. Constructive Imagination (Builds pictures)

17. Empathy (Point of view of others)

18. Confidence (Based on Knowledge)

19. Leadership (Teamwork)

20. Likes People (Persuasive)

21. Listens (Rapport)

22. Asks (Positive)

23. Plans and Organizes (Works)

24. Relaxes (Sense of Humor)

25. Agrees (Stimulates)

IMPACT ON OTHERS

Rate your influence on others in terms of:

a. Courtesy b. Empathy c. Kindness d. Manners e. Humility
f. Expectance g. Constructiveness h. Cultural responsibility
i. Growth j. Spirituality

N. CREATIVE SUPERSTAR

1. Expert at something—concentration

2. Joy of accomplishment—zest for challenge

3. Motivated through envy and desire

4. Knows when to make a move—has a sense of timing

5. Desire for money

6. Satisfied with nothing but the best—dedication

7. Organized and regimented, but flexible and relaxed

8. Healthy and active—love what you're doing

9. Sense yourself in your bones

10. Feel like somebody special—ego

11. Have a natural talent and sense of environment

12. Exceptional individual—have something unique that sets you apart

13. Run things in your mind, which is always under control

14. Use emotions for energy and accomplishment of something productive

15. Better than anyone else—better each time—try to do best always

16. Pressures are off the late bloomer—relaxed

17. Go through a slump with grace

18. Sense electricity in air

19. Effervescent amiability

20. Become a legend as a competitive nice guy

21. Physical condition helps mental attitude

22. No fear of mistakes, but take losing seriously

23. Rapport between superachiever and audience or witnesses

24. Drive for success with confidence and positive mental attitude

25. Hard work—drive against time—put in hours with joy of accomplishment

O. KEY ELEMENTS TO THINK ABOUT

PRODUCTIVITY—The best use of time—without sacrificing quality or priorities

VALUES—They can be relative and absolute—consider them

STANDARDS—They've got to be set and with consistency

PERSPECTIVE—Try to look at things in proper relationships

SHAPE—Keep your body, mind, and emotions in shape

PROPORTION—Relative importance, properly measured—in balance

EQUANIMITY—Means calm and even tempered—nothing too much

REALITY vs RHETORIC—Reality is more important; lose verbal battle, but win the real prize—something tangible or at least good will.

VARIETY—The spice of creative communication, in interests, in skills, and in life style.

GROWTH—Take up new skills, mental and physical

PROGRAM—Activity, effort, rest, and fun

TIME—Race against it by putting it to work, eliminating waste, and staying on top of things—will involve errands and solution of problems. (Want of a nail, etc.)

P. CREATIVE COMMUNICATIONS CREED

A. CONTACT people, places, and things for useful purposes by maintaining an *awareness* of the environment in human terms.

B. CONTROL thoughts, emotions, actions, and movements.

C. Develop COMPETENCE by concentrating on communication skills and practicing to improve them.

D. Generate CREATIVE response to ideas, when possible, for productive results.

E. Stay in CONDITION through exercise, nutrition, rest, and practice of communication skills on a practical and flexible schedule.

F. Avoid and manage STRESS so that the messages received in the real world are understood and those sent are clear, free of emotional overtones.

G. THINK objectively and logically with emphases on facts, trying to eliminate preconceptions or prejudices.

H. READ regularly a variety of books and material, including newspapers, magazines, and useful literature.

I. LISTEN attentively and patiently to others for meaning and purpose.

J. OBSERVE carefully with attention to details and general effect.

K. SPEAK with precision, economy, and a purpose for mutual interests.

L. WRITE clearly and unmistakably for the benefit of reader(s).

M. SENSE to identify with empathy and understanding.

N. ACT with deliberation, having made a decision based on facts.

O. Maintain a professional and positive ATTITUDE towards work, tasks, and service.

P. Set short and long-term GOALS for work and achievement of communication skills, as the QUALITY OF LIFE is enhanced.

Q. CREATIVE TYPES, CHARACTERISTICS, AND SKILLS

It takes a person with self-confidence, a constructive attitude, and ability to generate products of creativity. It helps if that person practices skills towards the ability to perform under pressure. It's like programming your own processor, with the ability to concentrate on various tasks and routines; and, coordinate activities.

The brain contains 100 billion cells, many of which we put to work instinctively and subconsciously—many of which we can control, operate, and develop for creative pursuits, one of the most important—communication.

TYPES	CHARACTERISTICS	SKILLS & PROCESSES
Actors	Assured	Abstraction
Analysts	Aware	Analogy
Artists	Challengers	Analysis
Composers	Creative Attitude	Arrangement
Craftsmen	Curious	Association
Designers	Fearless	Composition
Dramatists	Flexible	Comprehension
Engineers	Fluent	Contrast/ Comparison
Entrepreneurs	Individual	Elaboration
Innovators	Inquisitive	Enlarge/Diminish
Inventors	Knowledgeable	Experiment
Novelists	Motivated	Extrapolation
Painters	Open-Minded	Logic
Philosophers	Original	Metaphors
Poets	Perceptive	Orientation
Programmers	Productive	Similes
Scientists	Responsive	Synthesis

R. ELEMENTS OF PERSUASION

AUDIENCE ELEMENTS

a. Research (Information about audience)

b. Rapport (Common ground with audience)

c. Attitude and Beliefs (Reinforce or support)

d. Receptivity (Agreement with views)

e. Needs (Satisfy)

f. Wants (Gratify)

g. Acceptance of Change (Overcome resistance)

MESSAGE ELEMENTS

1. Credible (Confidence in speaker)

2. Appeal (Rewards inherent)

3. Opinions (Authoritative—Testimonial)

4. Alternative (Two-sided presentation)

5. Clear (Unmistakable meaning)

6. Objections (Overcome—Discount)

7. Action (Attainment of rewards—Achievement of goals)

MENTAL, EMOTIONAL, AND PHYSICAL INFLUENCES

MENTAL (Mind)	EMOTIONAL (Feelings)	PHYSICAL (Body)
Ideas	Fear	Music
Promises	Sex	Rhythm
Threats	Love	Pain
Goals	Spirit	Incarceration
Blackmail	Death	Starvation
Conditioning	Happiness	Alcohol
Catechism	Authority	Drugs
Logic	Recognition	Water
Arguments	Ostracism	Air
Statistics	Herd	Food

S. NONVERBAL COMMUNICATION SIGNALS

We tend to believe what our eyes tell us since our perceptions and memory of what we have seen before reinforces the resulting image. The interpretation of signals, as well as what we generate nonverbally, represent significant types of communication. The pupil size of our eyes, for example, increases when the interest in the objects of our vision increases. This, in turn, increases the widening of the pupils of the opposite party, as if the person was "turned on." The basic emotions, such as fear, surprise, love, hate, approval, disgust, sadness, happiness, and anger show themselves as a composite expression or nonverbal gestures, communicating more effectively than words. The left and right sides of the face express emotions differently, and characteristically, each side is controlled by the opposite hemispheres of the brain. Nonverbal signals can be sent or received by everybody.

When words are used, their effect can be reinforced by tone, inflection, pitch, attitude, volume, and/or gestures. For the listener and observer, it's a matter of detection by summing and correlating the verbal and nonverbal elements. Interpretation of nonverbal signals may suggest a contradiction of what was said, whether it's assent, denial, confrontation, acknowledgement, disinterest, or opposition. It may even be a complex situation to which our awareness and attitude responds. The resulting interpretation is based on a collective impression as processed by the brain.

TYPES OF SIGNALS:

Physical	Emotional	Intellectual
Sexual	Sartorial	Territorial
Cultural	Racial	Religious
Status	Age	Gender
Head	Face	Hair
Clothing	Makeup	Jewelry
Gestures	Expressions	Postures
Mouth	Lips	Pupils
Hands	Fingers	Legs
Smiles	Grins	Laughs
Scents	Touching	Behavior
Carriage	Walk	Feet

What is the image of our perception and how does it differ from what we actually see in our vision and interpretation of what we hear? How can we communicate creatively by reinforcing verbal messages with effective nonverbal signals?

T. INFLUENCES ON CREATIVE COMMUNICATION

There are several factors that influence creative communication. These factors, positive and negative, have a major bearing on the efforts, as well as, results. For creative communication to thrive, it needs an environment and a climate conducive to initiate efforts, which are generally borne of confidence. An important factor is attitude, that can affect an environment or be affected by it. If the climate is conducive, and if the attitude or interest leads to motivation, then positive results are the consequence. Ideas can develop, through concentration, into useful results. If, through discrimination, fear, or restrictions, the environment effectively chokes off attitude, then one can ignore it or seek change.

Lack of incentives or motivation can also stifle interest, effectively imprisoning self-expression or freedom to use imagination. Other enemies of positive results are distractions, physical and psychological. These distractions can be deliberate or accidental. There are many instances that against odds and a host of distractions, creative persons have been able to generate new theories, works of art, and revolutionary inventions. Concentration means the ability to focus on a concept or idea with some kind of driving force and sustained effort to develop something workable and worthwhile.

Roosevelt said it best, "The greatest thing we have to fear is fear itself." Whether it is fear of failure or fear of reprisal, find out what that fear and its impact is, and overcome it. If the odds are stacked against you, try to change the climate. If that's not possible, you can wage a battle or opt for a strategic retreat. Life in slavery or hell on earth can be no worse than death. The worse alternative can be the acceptance of misery, a lingering illness as demonstrated by a loss of freedom of expression. The dark room of paralysis through fear should not be tolerated.

Facts to consider in fostering creativity:

1. Ideas originate in individual minds.

2. If two partners are compatible, teamwork can accomplish or produce more than individuals or committees.

3. Encouragement and regards for suggestions.

4. Rejection of discouraging responses and encouragement of interest.

5. Marshalling of resources to go all out and focus on goals.

6. Using brainstorming sessions, headed by a leader who outlines the problem and explains the ground rules.

7. Brainstorming sessions are more creative and productive if;

   a. They deal with specifics.

   b. Criticism of ideas is suspended.

   c. The emphasis is on quantity.

   d. No restrictions are placed on wild ideas.

   e. Ideas can be combined or used to turn up other ideas.

   f. Sessions are informal.

   g. All essential facts and requirements are collected.

   h. Sequences are rearranged to form working combinations.

U. CREATIVE COMMUNICATION

1. A living process of *sharing* ideas and feelings

2. Messages that are *accurate, purposeful,* and *responsive*

3. Ability to *think* clearly and process *facts*

4. *Readines to perceive* with all senses *objectively*

5. *Observing* situations alertly and with attention

6. *Listening* with consideration and thoughtful interest

7. *Reading* enjoyably, usefully, and rapidly

8. Deliberate *action* after knowledge and evaluation of facts

9. Efficient *learning* through education, training, and practice

10. *Speaking* with adequate *preparation* and effective *delivery*

11. *Writing clearly* and *concisely* on subjects that interest readers

12. *Ideas* for constructive and satisfying *results*

Management helps maintain an environment to motivate, standards to communicate, and opportunities for creativity. Individual responsibility and the free flow of ideas which are dedicated to company goals can help all who work here to prosper.

V. SUMMARY OF STEPS AND SKILLS
FOR CREATIVE COMMUNICATION

A. Steps in the Development:
   1. Awareness
   2. Understanding
   3. Approach
   4. Practice
   5. Efficiency
   6. Mastery
B. Skills Developed and Sharpened:
   1. THINKING (Process—Memory—Decisions)
   2. LISTENING (Deliberate—Patient—Analytical)
   3. SENSING (Intuition—Sensitivity—Reliance)
   4. OBSERVING (Perception—Re-creation—Imagination)
   5. READING (Knowledge—Comprehension (words and contexts)—Speed)
   6. WRITING (Organization—Practice—Usage)
   7. SPEAKING (Formulation/Preparation—Rehearsal—Delivery)
   8. ACTION (Movements—Gestures—Interpretations)
C. Tendencies, Habits, and practices to Watch (and correct):
   1. Snap Judgements (decisions and tendencies without facts)
   2. Dispositions (Feelings for or leanings towards without bases)
   3. Partialities (Feelings through familiarity, ethnic, religious)
   4. Priorities (Confused sequences, expenditures, arbitrary)
   5. Behavior Pattern (A —Fast, impatient) (B —Slow, no demands)
   6. Stress (Responses to and diminishing productivity)
   7. Conflicts (Causing minor incidents to be related to crises)
   8. Inactivity (Mental, physical, and lack of play)
   9. Workload (Burdens, no exercise, relaxation, or change)
   10. Health (Drugs, alcohol, tobacco, excessive caffeine or food)
D. Skills and Achievements Through Relaxation Response:
   1. Matter of mind over body
   2. Meditation program of relaxation
   3. Resolution of problems and tasks
   4. Elimination of worries and abstractions

W. EXPERIENCE AND EXPOSURE

We tend to remember the significant things that we see, hear, and read. The other day I happened to sight read a few numbers from an album of songs, called a fake book. Since only the melody and lyrics are displayed, the accompaniment left out is 'faked' or improvised by the player. One song must have subconsciously turned me on, because half an hour later, as I got out of my car and walked to my office, one of the three numbers I played rang in my aural memory.

As I listened to the melody literally play in the inner recesses of my ear, I concluded that throughout our lives, things of significance that happen leave their trail indelibly—to provide a storehouse for future recall as experience, material for response, or for creativity. By engaging in significant experience and exposure, we prepare for potentially exciting enrichment, with material for future use and invention. Experience and exposure can be considered an extension of learning available at any time, but not necessarily exactly when we want to tap it.

Our brains are so unique and highly developed, not only do we have short term and long term memories, but also different types that are associated with our senses. We even have different categories of memories within the various types, forming a tremendous data bank for processing and retrieval.

The childlike curiosity of artists and scientists can be considered a learning attitude about the world with which we come in contact. It may appear simple or instinctive, but there is nothing wrong with being curious, exploring the environment, taking risks, and engaging in creative pursuits to solve nagging problems or to fill needs that are starving for attention. Specifically, what does it take in terms of developing skills or applying tools we don't use properly or to their maximum capabilities?

1. Self-discipline to fuel desire and sustain a sense of commitment.

2. Unconventional thinking by departing from the norm and searching in different directions.

3. Concentrate or collect thoughts and various disciplines on a problem or a need.

4. Accept and meet challenges that appear to defy solution, so that a problem is no longer neglected or accepted as impossible.

5. Try to open mind to understand arts, sciences, and cultures.

6. Self-confidence based on knowledge and a self-respecting image.

7. Try to enjoy tasks, the difficult, occasionally routine, especially something original.

8. Analyze and constructively evaluate your output, as well as those of others; balanced criticism of people, places, and things.

9. Aware of one's self, one's environment, interested in what is going on, and extrapolating the future for some positive good.

10. Develop ability to turn people on with attention, respect, and humor, so that the response creates an atmosphere of mutual love, consideration, and understanding.

X. STIMULATING THINKING THROUGH PHYSICAL ACTIVITY

Whether we are young or old, all of us need stimulation to preserve function—use it or lose it is the biologist's expression. Physical activity benefits the brain. During physical activity, chemicals are turned loose in the body, and the hormones, have a stimulating effect on the brain. The best known ones are adrenaline and its close relative noradrenaline. The more you keep up the physical activity, the higher and more prolonged are their resultant effects or elevations. These get-up-and-go hormones are survival signals to body tissues for fight or flight, however, their stimulations can be channeled into positive and productive directions. During any period of exercise, adrenaline soaks all tissues of the body—including the brain—to speed up its processes.

In the absence of exercise, such a flood of stimuli has the effect of provoking sensations of fear or panic, but during exercise and several hours later, it produces a sense of increased energy, alertness, and the reassurance of being ready or poised for performance. The hesitation and delays that are characteristic of older people or uncertainty are cast aside. Rather, it is a state of affairs that builds confidence. As children reach puberty and start asserting their identities, the parents appear a neglected species. No extra survival behavior is programmed into our habits after we pass the milestone of our reproductive capacities. After 35 or 40, we are essentially on our own. If we've had children at relatively older ages, we may have to make adjustments.

As we grow older, we'll have to think about concentrating on our bodies in terms of physical activity and programmed exercise. As a useful start in this direction, there's nothing wrong with generating a mild or heavy sweat, depending on our age, using dancing, brisk walks, or mild jogging. The synergistic effect of physical activity or exercise is the reduction of tensions in the stimulation of brain functions.

One of the most common and popular ways many people relieve stress and get their brains on the right, relaxed, and positive track is to take a brisk walk. This is preferably done in a serene, parklike, and smog-free setting. If you can't change your local environment or neighborhood, get into your car and drive to a place where conditions promote health with fresh air in a relaxed atmosphere. The combination of clean air and a brisk walk will help you feel younger, fitter, and mentally alert.

Some people find apparent comfort or security from boredom by listening to music as they go about their private activities, exercise, or jogging. There is nothing wrong with low key music that comes in a variety of styles and balanced with sage advice from the ancient Greeks: nothing too much. On the other hand, loud, stressful, primitive, and rhythmic beats, treated as music by many addicted adolescents, can do more to stimulate excitement and sex —less to stimulate the memory and the precious thinking functions of the brain.

Y. THE ABILITY TO CONCENTRATE

Whenever we concentrate on a task or a person, we consciously focus our attention with sensitivity and psychological selectivity. In the process we adjust our bodies and sense organs, mainly our eyes and ears. We try to see things clearly and vividly as we get set for some potential form of action. Shifting from one stimulus to another often depends on how important we think the new data is. At the same time, we put a damper on information coming from other senses to reduce the distraction. Inadequate lighting can be a distraction by reducing our ability to concentrate. Noise also affects this ability. On the other hand, there are instances in which we do such a good job of concentrating, we overlook important things that are going on around us.

Television has become such a powerful medium of attention capture, that the viewer is often oblivious of what is going on and apparently disinterested in persons trying to get his or her attention. Similarly, if we try to take part in or just listen to two different conversations at the same time, typically we fail. In spite of the collective power of the mind, the eyes, the ears, and the body to function effectively in a concentrated effort, a minor distraction can literally defeat a purpose. Comedy routines often exploit sex, like a bathing beauty interrupting a serious contest. It proves how easy it is to distract the mind or the ability to concentrate.

Fatigue, stress, and various types of noise are common forms of distraction in the ability to concentrate. Attention span weakens, the mind-body entity's ability to function weakens, and the ability to focus on an object or issue wanes. In some environments, people must perform while burdens are placed on the ability to concentrate. When you can't concentrate, you can feel frustrated or inadequate. Whether it's listening, working, reading, playing an instrument or correcting a problem, you must find a way of removing the distraction, one way or another. Otherwise, you lose time and ability to perform. Here are a few tips to promote the ability to concentrate:

1. Whenever possible, reduce or eliminate noise and interruptions.

2. Try not to compete with sounds, noises, or music.

3. Take a break for a few minutes from what you're doing to help regenerate the faculties and reduce the effects of pressure.

4. Change activity from one form to another; from reading to writing; talking to listening; walking and running; playing and resting; and, sleeping or napping.

5. Occasional exercise to promote a healthy body and mind, as well as freedom from the damaging effects of tobacco and alcohol, enable the mind and senses to concentrate better.

6. Change the environment or setting. Occasionally, music helps.

7. Deal with anything that puts a burden on concentration.

8. Try to see the whole picture; otherwise, break task down into pieces or logical parts.

Z. HOW TO REMEMBER

Memory is the mental faculty to store and recall information of various types, such as verbal, visual, musical, symbolic, and sensory. Psychologists tell us that sensory information entering our brain through our eyes, ears, and other senses, passes into our short-term memory in the form of electrical impulses. If the information has physical or emotional impact at the time it enters, or if it is studied and repeated (memorized), that information is stored in long-term memory. You can remember a phone number long enough to use it right after you hear it, but unless you use it often or make a written record of it, the number will be forgotten.

Most stored information is retrieved through the interaction of recognition and recall. Both depend on the brain's ability to make associations. These associations, must have some meaning and be supported with visual images and/or aural support, such as rhymes. Songs, music, the smell of flowers, or a visual scene can be a stimulus to promote association and recall. Most persons with good memories have developed systems for associating one fact with another.

The brain's capacity of over 100 billion nerve cells, or neurons, involves a chain of electrical, chemical, and physical changes. Electrical impulses, converted from the stimuli of incoming sensory information, are transmitted from one neuron to another. Like transmitters and receivers, axons and dendrites transmit the information they carry across synapses, or junctions between the nerve cells. To facilitate the passage of these impulses, chemicals called neurotransmitters are produced at neuron junctions. The number of neurotransmitters and synapses increase in the process of training the memory. However, if the neuron circuits are not reinforced by repetition or rehearsal, they tend to disappear or deteriorate.

We train our memories at all ages, and like physical exercise, the exercise and improvement of memory is essential for thought processes and the ability to communicate. Public speakers, actors, musicians, lawyers, educators, and politicians rely heavily on their abilities to remember massive amounts of information and don't hesitate to train themselves in mnemonics. In addition to simple repetition, a few methods of exercising your memory include:

1. Make up rhymes. (I before E, except after C—to spell receive)

2. Set words to music. (This is the symphony that Schubert wrote and never finished.)

3. Break up a number. (941-6623 can be treated as exchange 941, route 66 and 23rd Psalm.)

4. Convert a name into a relationship. (Bill Johnson—John's son, Bill—or John's son paid his bill.)

5. Repeat the name with various associations. (Don Stovall— Don is short for Donald, but not the duck, because it's Stovall, which rhymes with wall behind the stove.)

6. Remember the lines and spaces for notes in a music staff. (Lines: E, G, B, D, F = Every Good Boy Deserves Fun; Spaces: F.A.C.E.)

If names, rules, or facts are important, concentrate and make a game of storing them for later retrieval and use. A practical approach is to relate the information to something else by what it sounds like, a logical relationship, or some useful association. Then use it by rehearsing or repeating it. Consider association as a system of cross-indexing, such as similarities, contrasts, and mnemonic devices, such as acronyms or abbreviations.

AA. INTUITION

The ability to use intuition, a sense of something not evident, depends largely on how we sharpen our mental skills. We can verbalize the pros and cons of an issue or give positive ideas a boost; conjure images or mental pictures; and, even sense our awareness in an environment through our bodies. Like a daydream, our minds can wander about a potential disaster or a stunning achievement.

You may not be 100% certain, but that should not stop you from acting on your intuition when the emotionally charged evidence in your mind tells you to make a decision and act. Because you cannot force intuition, and yet face the possibilities of losing an idea of a product of intuition, why not take notes? Use a notebook or pad near your desk and/or bed. Unfortunately, some ideas are fleeting and to capture or recover them cannot be possible. We can meditate by reaching inward in a quiet and dark setting, moving our concentration from one scenario to another.

A school of psychiatrists who followed Carl Jung, a strong advocate of intuitive thinking, devised a test that concentrates on four facets of personality preference. Known as the Myers-Briggs Type Indicator, or MBTI, the test measures:

Extroversion vs Introversion

Sensing vs Intuition

Thinking vs Feeling

Judging vs Perceiving

Can you rate yourself as to the directions in which you tend to lean?

Actually, one can cultivate the ability to trust our insights, since it boosts our confidence and self esteem. This ability also tends to renew sensitivity and compassion. However, one must train oneself to distinguish between intuition and imagination; between wishful thinking and reality; between creativity and fantasy. Creativity, for example, leads to productive ideas or solutions, whereas fantasy, can represent wild dreams without redeeming values.

The difference in ideas is almost like the person high on alcohol or drugs, versus the confident coordinator of associations that may not generate immediate results, but could lay the foundation for future successes. One can discover what won't work, associate ideas that open new doors of knowledge, or create something through serendipity, the accidental discovery of a productive or useful idea.

BB. HUMAN NATURE

The study of human nature can generally be reduced to the discovery and verification of how people think and act. The sooner we learn the patterns and details about individuals; whether we call it personality, character, or mentality; the more useful, effective, and profitable relationships we can establish. General clues are:

1. What they say about themselves.
2. What they say about others.
3. How they say things.
4. The words used.
5. Whether statements are repeated.
6. Facial expressions during speech.
7. What is said in jest.
8. What is said in anger.
9. Whether statements are original.
10. Do they speak from experience?
11. Do they repeat what others say?
12. Do they know what they are talking about?
13. Any clues about attitudes?
14. Are statements generalizations?
15. Are statements opinions without foundations?
A. What have they done?
B. What do they do?
C. What are their vices?
D. Are they guided by religion?
E. Any patterns of behavior?
F. Relationship of speech to action.
G. Actions during crisis situations.
H. Routine activities.
I. Methods used to reach goals or accomplish tasks.
J. Management and use of money.
K. Response to problems or difficulties.
L. Attitudes towards strangers.
M. Response to censure.
N. Reaction to failure.
O. Conduct under stress.

CC. TO LEAD, MOVE AHEAD, OR ACHIEVE SUCCESSES . . . PROGRAM OR REPROGRAM THE MIND:

1. For self-confidence
2. For a winning self-image
3. For a positive attitude and optimism
4. To attract wealth and prosperity
5. To stop procrastinating
6. To observe and absorb
7. To listen with attention
8. To welcome suggestions and ideas
9. To put a value on time
10. To take notes as you respond and put them to work
11. To set goals and seek ways of reaching them
12. To anticipate achievements and build from them
13. To decide or judge after you understand
14. To organize approaches to challenges and stick to the relevant
15. To ask clear and pointed questions in a courteous manner

START PRACTICING A PRACTICAL PERSONAL PHILOSOPHY

A. Set up a goal or a project.
B. Find a reason to be motivated.
C. Turn others on so that they can turn you on.
D. List things neglected that need solutions.
E. List needs to be satisfied.
F. List wants that should be fulfilled.
G. Investigate enterprises that are potentially profitable.
H. Develop contacts for direct information.
I. Accept advice; don't ignore it because it's free.
J. Avoid litigation; getting even may be costly.
K. Investigate applicants; follow up on resume particulars.
L. Don't overlook hobbies that can turn profitable.
M. Learn how to manage money, including savings as a priority.
N. Expand associations while maintaining a low profile.
O. Avoid excesses and get regular exercise.

DD. SOME KEYS TO CREATIVITY & ACCOMPLISHMENT

1. PLAN—Projects

   —Useful trip

   —Practice sessions (music, sports, speech)

2. ORGANIZE—Files (papers and documents)

   —Personal computer (addresses, lists, accounts)

   —Bills and notes

3. MANAGE—Expenses (cut waste, losses, etc.)

   —Space

   —Priorities

4. CONTROL—Negative thoughts

   —Runaway imagination

   —Stress symptoms

   —Associations (activities, memberships, drinking)

5. REVIEW—Exercise routine

   —Eating habits

   — Nutrition and supplements

6. SEEK—Problems that require solutions

   —Needs that can be fulfilled

   —Opinions and experiences of others

7. COMBINE—Ideas with research as a follow up

   —Contact of people with books and periodicals

   —Radio and television; audio and video tapes

It takes inquiry, organization, and association of ideas which can be mechanized into models for testing...Learning what does not work, from mistakes, failures, and weaknesses. You can be down, but never out. Stay with those who encourage and avoid those who discourage. You can be stimulated, motivated, energized, confident, and satisfied that you're on the right track.

EE. CUES AND HINTS FOR MANAGING OUTCOMES IN KEY AREAS

AREAS	INGREDIENTS & OPERATIONS	OUTCOMES
ACHIEVEMENT	Discipline, Practice, & Progress	OBJECTIVES
APPEARANCE	Dress, Behavior, Smile, & Speech	IMAGE
ATTITUDE	Disposition, Philosophy, & Attention	SUCCESS
CONTROL	Emotions, Stress, & Situation	EQUANIMITY
CRITICISM	Facts, Analyses, Weights, & Ratings	EVALUATION
DECISIONS	Definitions, Facts, & Alternatives	JUDGMENTS
DESIRES	Focus on and Visualize Needs and Wants	GOALS
IDEAS	Abstractions, Patterns, & Analogies	RELATIONSHIPS
IMAGINATION	Control Associations for Productivity	CREATIVITY
LEADERSHIP	Confidence to Turn Others on & Set Example	ACCOMPLISHMENTS
LIFE	Health, Anticipation, Activity, & Love	QUALITY
MARKETING	Contact, Exposure, & Advertising	SALES
MEMORY	Relax, Associate, & Scan	MANIPULATION
MESSAGES	Precise, Directed, & Effective	IMPACT
PEOPLE	Acceptance, Interest, & Understanding	FRIENDS
PERCEPTIONS	Response to Environment & Initiate Good	HARMONY
PERSUASION	Attributes, Benefits, & Logic	ACCEPTANCE
PROBLEMS	Confront, Define, Select Alternative, & Test	SOLUTIONS
QUALITY	Standards, Performance, & Reliability	EXCELLENCE
RESEARCH	Investigate, Design, Develop, & Test	PROGRESS
RHETORIC	Eloquence in Language with Purpose	PERSUASION
SELF-IMAGE	Recognition, Changes, & Reprogramming	POSITIVE
STYLE	Simple, Clear, Vivid, & Sincere	READABILITY
THINKING	Words, Symbols, Images, & Objectivity	PROCESSING
TRUTH	Seek, Learn, & Recognize	PEACE

FF. CONFLICTS

A conflict is a struggle between or among opposing forces. It can be physical, mental, emotional, individual, collective, or any combination of these. Very often one refers to a conflict as a clash between the various tendencies of the mind, often resulting in indecision or procrastination. A conflict may take place in the real world, in the conscious mind, subconscious, or unconsciously. That is why there are times we don't realize a conflict exists even when symptoms point to one.

Conflicts can arise out of differences in age, personality, background, ethnicity, interests, motives, goals, and values. In interpersonal relationships, conflicts are more evident. As we grow older, we become firmer in our beliefs, more resistant to change, and even more difficult to please. We prioritize our values to such an extent, that our relationships become subject to rigid screening.

The two major types of conflicts involve individuals within themselves, such as situations in which we have mixed emotions: (love-hate), mental emotional, evidence vs feelings, close relations vs acquaintances or strangers, and those that concern issues of our lives in opposition to those of the real world with which we are in constant contact.

Conflicts that arise from dealing with others in social, business, and professional activities should be resolved with minimum loss of respect, money, safety, health, or other values. In litigation, attorneys become the winners; in wars, munitions dealers; on freeways, the body shops and hospitals. It is often resistance to change that stifles progress;indecision that weakens positions; and obstinacy or artificial objections to persuasion that turns the clock back on many.

To resolve conflicts with others, one must first establish rapport. Start by asking questions to find some common ground of agreement or similarities. As you move towards the path of resolution of problems, promote discussion and isolate disagreements for weight or relative importance. Come to minor decisions through straight or winding paths of resolution, with the major decision as the goal. Maintain an even level of discussion, with candor, and with a promise of something positive or tangible as rewards for both parties.

All issues must have foundations in fact, rather than hearsay or rumor. Opinions are unnecessary when there is evidence from which intelligent adversaries can draw conclusions. Take time for orientation and clarification. When you can get people to agree on facts and reliable evidence, agreement on conclusions follows. Differences are reduced or eliminated, the atmosphere changes, and conflicts generally evaporate. When all parties can feel as if they are winners, the low-key arbitrator or referee can present genuine compliments to the participants.

GG. SPEECHES

Preparation, Rehearsal, Appearance, and Delivery

a. Audience: Check composition, subject, other speakers, time, place.

b. Framework: Think Opening—Introduction—Body—Conclusion—End.

c. Outline: Ideas from storehouse of memory based on subject and purpose.

d. Research: Source material through surveys, articles, opinions.

e. Write: Rough draft in conversational tone or informal style.

f. Opening: Original with a story, a question, key word, startling fact.

g. Introduction: Clear statement of subject and purpose.

h. Body: Statements of support and proof to persuade and convince audience.

i. Conclusion: Summary of points made, repeating key elements/statements.

j. Ending: Original with a quotation, story, humor, repetition/ variation

REHEARSAL

a. Length: Average is 30 min.; maximum is 45, including question-answer.

b. Time: Each double-spaced typewritten page of 200 words runs a minute.

c. Editing: As you read prepared speech, shorten, revise, and tighten.

d. Taping: Read first clean draft for recording and listen objectively.

e. Rewrite: Edit again and revise or rewrite as a professional listener.

f. Practice: Simulate delivery with pauses, emphases, and gestures.

g. Transcribe: New outline with key words and groups of phrases on cards.

h. Retape: Final version and listen for content; re-edit as required.

i. Record: Polished version and vocalize imagined delivery before audience.

j. Familiarize: Practice at least three times, looking away from cards.

APPEARANCE

a. Physical: Exude a presence of confidence, control, and authority.

b. Animated: Reflect anticipation (expectations), warmth, and ease.

c. Relaxed: Indicate mutual interests, sincerity, and credibility.

d. Enthusiasm: Show positive energy that promotes relaxed attitudes.

e. Dress: Conservative suit, pastel shirts, and black shoes.

DELIVERY

a. Attention: Know what is going on, while you sit waiting to speak.

b. Introduced: Time your rise and stride to lectern.

c. Audience: Pan people in room and make eye contact at lectern.

d. Establish: Rapport and engage attention as you put down notes.

e. Posture: Stand erect and put hands to work as necessary.

f. Gestures: Use for emphasis and meaning, with hands anticipating words.

g. Avoid: Mannerisms and distracting habits (Ah's, and-ah's, you know's)

h. Distractions: Maintain control and keep audience relaxed.

i. Eye Contact: Eyes should be up and looking into eyes of audience at least 80% of the time, embracing audience one by one. Feedback from audience is rewarded by mutual attention from the listeners.

SUMMARY —The greater the preparation, the more rehearsal, the better the appearance, and the finer the delivery, the less tension or nervousness you'll feel as a speaker.

HH. INTERVIEW GUIDELINES AND NOTES

The interview, an important situation for contact and exchange, should be planned and organized for maximum results. Things may not work out as planned, but that is no reason not to put down some ideas on paper and make preparations, depending on the person(s), purpose, and available time. One can even plan for changes. Use the notes as cues or prompts.

1. Person(s) interviewed: _____

2. Purpose of the interview: _____

3. Interview starting time: _____

4. Time available for interview: _____

5. Location of interview: _____

6. Site is available and secured: _____

7. Handling of messages during interview: _____

8. Rescheduling, if cancelled: _____

9. Papers or forms required: _____

10. Questions to ask or information to obtain: _____

    a. _____

    b. _____

    c. _____

    d. _____

    e. _____

    f._____

    g. _____

    h. _____

    i._____

    j._____

NOTES to take during interview:

_____

_____

_____

_____

II. SUCCESS IS NO SECRET WHEN YOU COMMUNICATE CREATIVELY

1. Do you consider yourself a failure and why?

2. Do you know how to learn from a failed attempt?

3. Do you let a failure remind you of other failures and give up?

4. Can you avoid making the same mistake two or three times?

5. Have you asked yourself: what you want—generally and specifically?

6. If something is stopping you, do you know what it is?

7. Have you set down or convinced yourself what your values are?

8. Are you honest with yourself and with others?

9. Can you carry out a determination to accomplish something?

10. Do you visualize what you're after, such as a goal?

11. Can you handle several goals at once and concentrate on the main?

12. Do you set priorities in terms of what things are more important7

13. Do you make plans and look forward to them?

14. Do you try to have fun to break the routine of work and chores?

15. Do you have time for friends, acquaintances, and relatives?

16. When you succeed, do you ask yourself; what did I do right?

17. Do you meditate or pray with regularity?

18. Do you have a schedule for reading a variety of useful literature?

19. Do you make yourself available to respond to questions?

20. Do you seek help from others or support others in need?

21. Do you know what is going on in your fields of endeavor?

22. Do you get involved in environmental, political, and social activities?

23. Do you exercise regularly and seek nutrition for health?

24. Do you get carried away and turn wasteful with success?

25. Do you try to make the best of every day?

Index